ASTON MARTIN
AND
LAGONDA

Other Titles in the Crowood AutoClassics Series

Aston Martin and Lagonda
The V-Engined Cars

DAVID G. STYLES

Crowood AutoClassics

First published in 1994 by
The Crowood Press Ltd
Ramsbury, Marlborough
Wiltshire SN8 2HR

British Library Cataloguing-in-Publication Data

A catalogue record for this book is available from the British
Library.

ISBN   1 85223 808 9

Dedication
To my wife, Ann, my daughter, Emma, and my son, Philip, without
whose continuing tolerance and support I could never write books.

Picture credits
Photographs supplied by Aston Martin Lagonda Limited; Roger
Stowers; Jaguar Cars Limited; Lola Cars Limited; RS Williams
Limited; The National Motor Museum, Beaulieu; Paul Chudecki;
and the author.

Typeset by Chippendale Type Ltd, Otley, West Yorkshire.
Printed and bound in Great Britain at The Bath Press.

Contents

Acknowledgements

I could not have even begun to produce this work without the help of several people at Aston Martin Lagonda Limited, beginning with Victor Gauntlett during his tenure of office as Chairman. Further support came from recently retired Chief Executive, Walter Hayes, who allowed me access to information and people to complete my task in the verification of many facts and the collation of a great deal of data.

Then there was Roger Stowers, a name known to anyone associated with an enthusiasm for Aston Martins or modern Lagondas. Roger has been of incalculable help in many ways – from ferreting out photographs and odd facts and figures to finding people with invaluable information. I couldn't have produced this book without his help.

I was also privileged to be at the launch of Derby's new Aston Martin Lagonda dealership, Paramount Aston Martin, and its Sales Director, Ian Tooley, allowed me to clamber all over his precious charges with a camera, some of the results of which are in this book.

Too often, people will either forget or omit to make mention of reference sources, and I'd like to be an exception to that in the spirit of the first sentence of these acknowledgements. I have therefore placed a bibliography of references and further reading at the back of this book. One reference source, which is invaluable and is so often used by authors but then overlooked in their work, is the *Aston Martin Owners' Club Register*. This is a document which does not give one everything, but it does give other source references in abundance and is an immensely useful check point. Anyone who has the vaguest interest in this subject is commended to read it – after joining the Club, of course. Finally, to all Aston Martin Lagonda enthusiasts, if you are reading this, thank you.

Introduction

The purpose of this book is to remind the world of sports car enthusiasts that there is a great British car which has stood for many years, and still stands today, head and shoulders above any of its adversaries as the supreme quality sports car. 'What is a sports car?' you may ask, and the answer can be almost whatever you want it to be. Essentially, though, a real sports car is one that has supreme style, rugged quality, outstanding road manners and high performance. In all those facets, Aston Martin and Lagonda excel.

As with so many things in life, there are always those who will argue that because the business of a watchmaker, gunmaker, silversmith or carmaker has changed hands, nothing is or ever will be what it was, implying that the product's quality and design will suffer at the hands of the new owner. The lie to that statement is embodied in the very existence of Aston Martin Lagonda Limited. Aston Martin and Lagonda, as two separate companies and as one since 1948, have only improved down the years to stay abreast of technology whilst reigning supreme in quality and reliability, right from the days of Wilbur Gunn and Lionel Martin all the way up to Walter Hayes.

When Mr David Brown (as he was then) first thought of buying Aston Martin, he was already an experienced and thoroughly competent engineering manager, equipped with a sense of perception which would be the envy of many an industrialist today. This book would never have had cause to be written if it hadn't been for his acquisition of these two fine companies, borrowing the engine from one to improvise and develop for installation into the other. The result was the Aston Martin DB-2, a model which set in train a sequence of events that brought enormous success to the company, culminating in a Le Mans 24 Hours Win and World Sports Car Championship in 1959.

When Ford Motor Company secured the assets and interests of Aston Martin Lagonda Limited, many people said that this would be the end. Evidence that the suggestion couldn't be farther from the point is the present-day line-up of Aston Martins, including a model which is not embraced in the scope of this book – the DB-7. The company and its cars have benefited from the strength of Ford purchasing power and engineering development technology, resulting in even better vehicles in the process. All this is not to say that there are no quality sports cars made elsewhere, and many come close to Aston Martin Lagonda, but they never quite make it. The sheer luxury and Englishness of an Aston Martin or Lagonda car cannot be equalled.

1 From Two Great Names

The name 'Aston Martin Lagonda' comes originally from two. The two companies that were brought together to make this one name were Lagonda Motors, originally based in Staines, and Aston-Martin Limited, based a few miles away in Feltham, both in Middlesex in southern England.

WILBUR GUNN AND THE LAGONDA ENGINEERING COMPANY

The Lagonda Engineering Company was formed at the end of the nineteenth century by an American named Wilbur Gunn, who came to Britain allegedly to make his name and fortune as an opera singer. When that quest was unsuccessful, he turned his hand to engineering, having been apprenticed to one of the Singer companies in his native land before attempting a musical career. The name 'Lagonda' is a corruption of the French interpretation of the Shawnee Indian name of a place called, in English, 'Buck's Creek': 'La Ough Ohonda', now an industrial suburb of the city of Springfield in Ohio.

Some time after setting himself up as a consulting engineer, specializing in hydraulics, a subject viewed with more favour at that time than electrics, Gunn built a triple-expansion compound steam engine, seemingly to power a boat which, if legend is to be believed, was built in his back garden and raced on the Thames for a bet. The story

continues that he won that bet and so set up a works to manufacture marine engines. Mr Gunn's first foray with the internal combustion engine was yet to come.

Confrontation with the internal combustion engine soon came as the result of riding a bicycle through the mud and muck of late-Victorian streets in the winter. It is therefore hardly surprising to learn that Mr Gunn progressed from steam marine engines to motor bicycles, building his first in 1900 (as far as we can clearly establish). By 1903, Gunn was competing with his

This 1907 advertisement for the V-engined Lagonda 10–12hp tri-car is proud to declare the successes in the 1906 Land's End to John O'Groats and London to Edinburgh trials, having won gold medals in both.

machines to prove, in the manner of the day, their reliability. In August that year, he entered a 2¾hp Lagonda for the ACC 1,000 Miles Trial, securing a second-class award. For a few years Lagonda made tri-cars, and Wilbur Gunn was seen regularly competing against such adversaries as Victor Riley and other pioneers who followed the same route into car making. All were anxious to prove their products in rigorous competition.

The period from 1908 to 1913 is something of a mystery to even the most ardent students of Lagonda history, but it is known that the company went into receivership in the early part of that period. Nonetheless, Gunn built a 10hp car, which seems to have become a 12–14hp by the time it was offered for sale in 1911. This was soon followed by a 14–16hp model and later an 18hp model, an example of which Bert Hammond drove to win the 1909 Brooklands Summer Handicap.

A year later, Wilbur Gunn embarked upon a most daring sporting adventure by entering the St Petersburg Trial in Russia.

There had been a hint that a successful competitor could secure business with the Imperial Russian Court. Unlike many British car makers, Gunn couldn't resist the challenge and entered a car. It finished in Moscow roughly equal with all the other entrants, which included such makes as Benz, de Dietrich and Itala! In typical arbitrary Russian fashion, a further challenge was put to the entrants that the first car to reach St Petersburg from Moscow would be declared the official winner of the event.

Not only was the Lagonda the only car to undertake this further challenge, it actually completed the run in twelve hours and secured a gold medal. The observer of the event was to be the first Russian owner of a Lagonda, so impressed was he with the car's performance. As soon as was expedient after he had received a magnificent certificate for the St Petersburg Trial from the Tsar himself, Wilbur Gunn returned to Staines to start building cars in earnest, for his agent in Russia was selling them in some numbers.

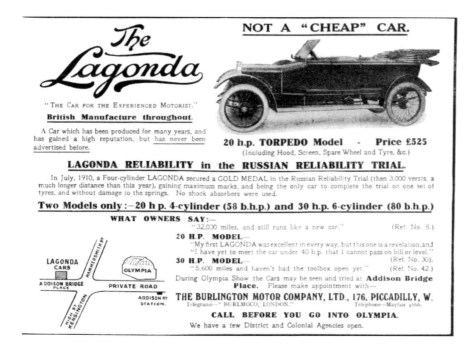

By the 1910 Olympia Motor Show, the Russian reliability trial had taken place and Lagonda had demonstrated its durability by winning the event with a 20hp Torpedo similar to the car advertised here.

The Doctor's Coupé was a common example of coachwork on the 11hp Lagonda before and just after the First World War. This is a 1919 example.

LIONEL MARTIN BRINGS US ASTON-MARTIN

In this same period, a young man named Lionel Walker Birch Martin was showing more than a passing interest in cars. His earliest foray into the motoring world was as a demonstration driver, taking Napiers and de Dions all over the country. As a result of enjoying his work, in 1909 his licence was suspended for two years in penalty for 'habitual speeding' (they were at it even then!). Martin was also a keen cyclist, and it was a result of this activity that he met his ultimate partner, Robert Bamford, with whom he set up a business in 1912 to service and sell Calthorpe, G.W.K. and Singer cars, the business being called Bamford and Martin Limited.

Lionel Martin bought a Singer car off the stand at the 1912 Motor Show, using it to compete at hill-climbs, a favourite being Aston Hill, in Buckinghamshire. Martin tuned the Singer himself and extracted remarkable results. Soon, Bamford and

Martin bought a 1908 Isotta-Fraschini, into which they fitted a Coventry Simplex 1,398cc four-cylinder engine, which is said to have been produced to Bamford and Martin's specification. It was registered as LH7983 and was to be the foundation of Aston-Martin, the name 'Aston' conjured up by Lionel Martin's wife, Katharine, so as to put the firm 'close to the head of any alphabetical list of motoring names'. This car ultimately became known as 'The Hybrid', though it seems that title came after its useful life in the hands of Bamford and Martin.

The first announcement of an 'Aston-Martin' came in a report from *The Light Car and Cyclecar* magazine of 19 October 1914, and a drawing of it appeared in *The Light Car* on 25 November that year. The reports spoke in glowing terms of the specification but, of course, there were other things to deal with in the years 1914–18 which detracted from any interests in sporting cars. Even so, that first Aston-Martin car was built, and whilst it did not carry the

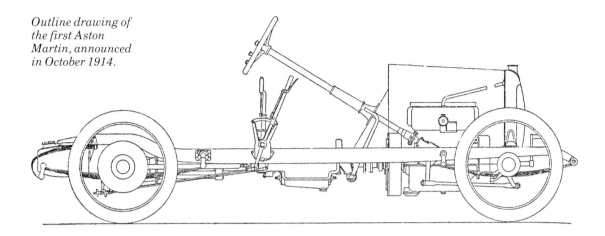

Outline drawing of the first Aston Martin, announced in October 1914.

name on the radiator, 'Coal Scuttle' (so named because of the shape of the body-work) is universally accepted as the first Aston-Martin car. It was registered in Wilt-shire as AM4656.

'Coal Scuttle's' maiden outing was in the 1919 London–to–Edinburgh Trial in which it won a gold medal. By December 1920, the first Aston-Martin car to carry the maker's badge (a letter 'A' superimposed over a letter 'M' contained within a circle) was completed – an open three-seater registered in Wilt-shire (to secure the prized 'AM' registration letters) as AM270. Immediately in its wake was listed another Aston-Martin car, this time a three-seat saloon, which was regis-tered as AM273, though the truth of its existence is a mystery, for the number AM273 appeared in 1921 on a most famous early Aston-Martin – 'Bunny'.

INTO THE FRAY – SERIOUS MOTORING

Aston-Martin's first foray into serious motor racing under its own banner was in 1921, when Lionel Martin drove a three-seat clover-leaf bodied car to victory in the Essex Short Handicap at Brooklands at a speed of 69.75mph (112.24kph) in May that year.

This car's performance paved the way for Aston-Martin to take its place in history among the great names of motoring.

After a debut in the 1921 Grand Prix des Voiturettes at Le Mans, one of the most famous Aston-Martins ever, 'Bunny', a car rebuilt onto the chassis of the first clover-leaf bodied prototype, did battle at Brook-lands in the Junior Car Club's 200-Mile Race in October, where four Aston-Martins were entered – the only four so far built! 'Bunny' was driven by B.S. Marshall, 'Coal Scuttle' by the Hon. Victor Bruce. There were two brand new cars: a side-valve and a car with a new 16-valve overhead-cam engine designed by H.V. Robb. This last car was driven by Count Louis Zborowski (of *Chitty-Chitty-Bang-Bang* fame).

Lionel Martin was disappointed with the 200-Mile Race, having expected better than ninth and tenth places. The ohc engined car should have outperformed 'Bunny', and when it did not, Lionel Martin retained Marcel Gremillon to design a new cylinder head. The rest of the engine's reliability was not in question, so the cost of a redesign was saved.

In that same race were two Lagondas, driven by Bert Hammond and Captain W.H. Oates to eleventh and thirteenth places. Later, Captain Oates took an 11hp single-seat Lagonda to Brooklands to secure five

AM270, the Cloverleaf three-seater Aston Martin, taking part in the 1921 Land's End Trial.

light car records, including the Flying-Start Mile at 86.91mph (139.86kph) and the One Hour Speed Record at 79.17mph (127.4kph), which included a stop for a wheel change. However, Oates' records were short-lived, for five days later 'Bertie' Kensington Moir drove his 'J.C.C. 200' Aston-Martin to take all but the Flying-Start Mile records to a new One Hour Record of 86.21mph (138.73kph).

'Bunny' posed with Clive Gallop at the wheel in 1922.

THE RISE AND FALL OF BAMFORD AND MARTIN

By 1924, production Aston-Martins were a fact of life, some twenty-six cars leaving Abingdon Road works that year. Whilst saloons were not listed in the product range, two such cars were certainly built in 1924. G.L. Francis became the London agent that year and quickly gained for the firm a high reputation. Mr P.R. Callard, of the Callard and Bowser confectionery firm, recorded that 'nothing is too much trouble'.

However, the high cost of competition over the preceding four years, the price of the product and the delay in its reaching the public had all cost Lionel Martin dearly. At the end of 1924, he was owed over £31,000 by the company and it is said that his total investment in the company rose to somewhere between £100,000 and £150,000, all in the cause of bringing his dream to fruition. He had to look for outside support. This came from Lady Charnwood, mother of a young designer who had recently joined the company to produce a new twin ohc version of the Robb engine.

The year 1925 saw Aston-Martins in fine racing form, both on the track and on water, as several speedboats competing in the Duke of York's Trophy Race in June were powered by Aston-Martin engines. Then the Olympia Motor Show saw Aston-Martin exhibits on display for the first time, with a boat-decked three/four-seater, a Standard Tourer and John Benson's 8-valve twin ohc engine, polished and mounted on a special stand. However, 1925 was also to deliver the final blow to the fortunes of Lionel Martin and his fellow directors. The elation of the Motor Show was short-lived, as a receiver was appointed on 11 November – Armistice Day. Martin's services were dispensed with, and he left the Abingdon Road factory two days later for the last time.

LAGONDA AND ASTON-MARTIN RISE AGAIN

1925 was a year of realization for Lagonda too, for it had a model which was too long in the tooth to sell in viable numbers any more, so Arthur Davidson was recruited to design a new engine, a 2-litre to be called the 14/60. The four-cylinder twin cam engine of 1,954cc was coupled to a four-speed gearbox and fitted into a chassis of 120in (3,048mm) wheelbase. This ultimately led to the model known as the 2-litre, a popular car in its sector of the market and one which bore more than a passing resemblance to the

This is the Benson 8-valve twin-cam engined 1925 Grand Prix Aston Martin with Humphrey Cook at the wheel. (Cook was later to finance Raymond Mays and the immensely successful ERA.)

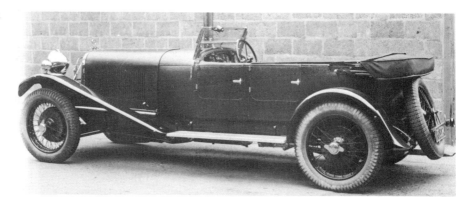

The 3-litre Lagonda in Tourer form in 1929

Bentley 3-litre. By 1929, a supercharged version of the Lagonda 2-litre was catalogued, with a 10mph (16kph) higher speed, though a significant increase in fuel consumption. This, in turn, led to the six-cylinder 16/65 pushrod-engined model which, because of its disappointing performance, was enlarged to 2,692cc and later to 2,931cc to become the 3-litre.

Whilst Lagonda moved towards greater success, Aston-Martin floundered out of receivership for a new lease of life and a chain of events that brought it greater fame and acceptability. This began with a visit by the Charnwoods to a small firm in Birmingham, named Renwick and Bertelli, to meet with one of its partners, Augustus Cesare Bertelli. 'R. & B.' was a small engineering firm which had been closely involved in development work for Enfield-Allday motor cars. The Charnwoods approached the firm, knowing Bertelli's reputation and that his aim had been to make and sell engines to the car industry, but he had found no takers. He was also a competent racing driver and had achieved much success with his own Enfield-Allday special.

After a series of careful negotiations Renwick and Bertelli paid £4,000 for the name and goodwill of Aston-Martin and, with the Charnwoods, set up a new company, registered on 12 October 1926 and named Aston-Martin Motors Limited. John Benson went with the deal, and the whole company moved to the former premises of the Whitehead Aircraft Company in Feltham near London.

A.C. Bertelli took the engine he and Renwick had designed in the hope that Enfield-Allday would be interested and which had been tested in Bertelli's own Enfield-Allday-based car named 'Buzzbox', to Feltham for ultimate installation in the new Aston Martin. Within a year, they had designed the engine, gearbox, back axle and a whole new car, to be called the 'T' Type.

This new car was announced to the world at the Olympia Motor Show of 1927. It was a fine machine, but during its development John Benson and W.S. Renwick discovered they didn't get along together. Before long both departed, leaving A.C. Bertelli alone to run a company he didn't have enough money to support, at a time when the market place was in the early stages of decline. What was more, the new car, like its predecessor, was expensive at prices between £550 and £675.

LAGONDA HITS HARD TIMES

Like many manufacturers of its time, Lagonda took the view that it needed a wide

'Bert' Bertelli's 'Buzzbox', the Enfield-Alldays-based special, which carried the engine that was to be developed into the Aston Martin power unit after Renwick and Bertelli rescued the company and moved into the Feltham factory.

range of models to satisfy a wide range of tastes and so had in its portfolio of products a very wide range of models. Furthermore, it had embarked upon the development and production of a small 10hp car, known as the Rapier. Many have said that this was the straw that broke the camel's back, for the production of Rapiers must have taken some of the space and skills employed in producing the larger cars.

The larger cars now included the 3½-litre and the M45 4½-litre cars, as well as the last of the 16/80 2-litre six-cylinder engined car which had succeeded the 2-litre model.

The Lagonda 16/80, with its six-cylinder Crossley engine, succeeded the four-cylinder engined 2-litre model in 1932.

W.O. Bentley

Walter Owen Bentley, 'W.O.' to all who knew him, was born in 1888 and, after enjoying a childhood interest in steam, served an apprenticeship in a locomotive works. Bentley then decided railways were not the career for him and joined the National Motor Cab Company. Later, he invested £2,000 in an agency for three French makes of cars – Buchet, DFP (Doriot, Flandrin et Parat) and La Licorne. In 1912, Bentley and Bentley was formed with W.O.'s brother H.M. Bentley, out of which was born Bentley Motors. So began a legend of British motoring.

The Great War of 1914–18 saw the now-famous Bentley rotary aero engines come to significance, the BR1 powering thousands of Sopwith Camels, the BR2 – among other aircraft – the Sopwith Snipe. As the war ended, so W.O. returned to the world of motor cars and of course the famous company which won the Le Mans 24 Hours Race no fewer than five times.

By 1931, the Bentley motor company was sold to arch-rivals Rolls-Royce. The name 'Bentley' was retained and the world's first badge-engineering took place with the 3½-litre and 4½-litre. Because of the nature of his contract with Rolls-Royce Motors Limited, he was unable to set up in business again on his own account, so he finally joined L.G. Motors Limited at the invitation of Alan Good, then chief executive of that company, the makers of Lagonda.

It was W.O. Bentley who gave Lagonda the V-12 engine and so he who sowed the seeds of V engines for Aston Martin Lagonda Limited, W.G. Watson's V-12 design for DP115 (the 1954 Lagonda prepared for that year's Le Mans) being the first extension of that original thinking, the direct connection being that Watson worked under W.O. on the original design.

There were Tourers, Saloons and Chassis offered. The Rapier was being produced at a rate faster than that of the bigger models, and whilst it was only being assembled at Staines, from components bought in from hand-picked suppliers, it took time and attention away from the larger cars. That the Rapier did not sell in the numbers expected also meant that whatever individuals thought, it was a drain on the resources of the company. Finally, Lagonda Motors Limited went into receivership in 1935.

The appointment of a receiver in May could not have been less opportune in many ways, for Le Mans was just a month away, and Lagondas had been expected to do reasonably well, though no one could express genuine surprise, for Arthur Fox, owner of the entering team, had been very wary of carrying out any major development work on BPK202, originally the sole car entered. However, he decided to buy a second car for the race, BPK203, the entry for which was accepted as a reserve.

The new company, headed by Alan Good, brought in one of the most famous names of British motoring as Technical Director, a man who had brought his cars to victory at Le Mans no fewer than five times. That man was Walter Owen Bentley, whose aero engines had been at the forefront of British victory in the skies during the Great War and whose Cricklewood-built cars had been a legend of power and luxury. Bentley had been committed to Rolls-Royce after they had bought Bentley Motors, but his contract with them had now expired, so he was free to move to the newly formed L.G. Motors, as Lagonda had become.

TEMPORARY REPRIEVES

L.G. Motors went to work on developing the

An interesting view of a 1934 Rapier, showing just how different these little cars were from the conventional view of a 1930s Lagonda.

famous 4½-litre Meadows-engined cars in 1936, whilst 'W.O.' (Bentley) sat at his drawing board and conceived a magnificent new 4½-litre V-12 power unit which, in his view, would be the ultimate extension of thinking from his earlier Bentley cars, now (as far as he was concerned) badge-engineered Rolls-Royces. However, the V-12 was some way off yet, for Bentley had to supervise the improvement of the M45 series of cars into the LG45s, with minor 'tweakings' here and there in styling to update them, quite apart from putting the Bentley 'stamp' on them.

The LG45 was produced as a chassis for coachbuilders to produce their own variants, also as a Tourer, a Saloon, a Coupé and a Sedan de Ville, not forgetting the very sporty Rapide. By 1937, it had evolved into the LG6 – still a 4½-litre – now with independent front suspension among its many

A typical 4.5-litre Lagonda of the mid-thirties period, big and Bentley-like, the epitome of the British Grand Tourer.

W.G. Watson

W.G. ('Willie') Watson joined Lagonda in the 1930s, following his old employer, W.O. Bentley, having had a spell with Invicta. With Lagonda, he worked on some of the drawings for the V-12, but his major achievement was the design of the 2.6-litre LB6 engine for the planned post-war car which, of course, David Brown used for the Aston Martin DB2.

Watson joined Aston Martin in 1952 to work under Professor Robert Eberan von Eberhorst as a senior design engineer. That von Eberhorst was as capable of bringing out the worst in an individual as of bringing out the best seems to have been demonstrated in this relationship, for when Watson designed the chassis for the DB3S, he took his ideas to John Wyer, not Eberan von Eberhorst. Willie Watson was also a loner, developing ideas in isolation until he was satisfied that they could be shown.

Taking the lines of the now-Aston Martin six-cylinder engine, Willie Watson went to work on the task of designing a new V-12, the engine to power DP115, a racing Lagonda for 1954. David Brown had made it clear that he wanted a Ferrari-beater and concluded that the only way to achieve this was with a V-12, so 'matching fire with fire'. Watson was actually recruited for this task, but had been side-tracked by the need for a new racing chassis to succeed the DB3, which he created as the DB3S.

It had always been David Brown's intention to have two engine sizes from the V-12 design, so Willie Watson's design provided for an increase in the bore to allow a 5-litre unit as well as a 4½. However, the risks were thought to be too great to take, because everyone felt the bottom end of the engine would not take the strain of the greater power and higher torque anticipated.

Nonetheless, the contribution that Willie Watson made to V-engine design ideas at Aston Martin Lagonda (AML) left its mark, as the very first V-format engine to be built under the AML banner.

attributes and offered in all the same variations. The year 1936 was magical for Lagonda in terms of making its market sit up and take note, for that was the year in which the magnificent V-12 hit the headlines.

The V-12 Lagonda engine in a state of partial assembly. Much of the design work for this engine was actually carried out by W.G. 'Willie' Watson, who later came to the post-war V-12 engine for DP115/DP166.

This beautiful 60°-V engine really was a work of art, and the chassis into which it was installed was pretty advanced for its time too, with the possible exception that it didn't have hydraulic brakes (but when you consider the average reliability of hydraulic brakes of the day, perhaps there was some wisdom in that!). The 4½-litre engine produced a phenomenal 180bhp in road trim. This was the car that was to bring about the change of fortunes for L.G. Motors – and it was a version of this car that was to take Lagonda near to victory at Le Mans in 1939.

In this same period, Aston-Martin had been going through troubled times again, too. Remembering that 'Bert' Bertelli had lost his partner and was struggling on to turn his company's fortunes through a recession, it was not an easy time. Fortunately, he found H.J. Aldington of Frazer-Nash fame was sympathetic to his problems and bailed the company out for a period with a guarantee to the bank and a sales promotion agreement, but it was Sir Arthur Munroe Sutherland, via his son R. Gordon Sutherland (who became Bertelli's partner in the business), who finally stepped in and provided Aston-Martin with a haven, for it was he who provided the finances for the company to continue in business when other resources finally ran out.

Thus, Aston-Martin was on the road to recovery, and the 1935 Le Mans gave great encouragement to all because an Aston-Martin finished in third place, driven by Charlie Martin and Charles Brackenbury (who were to finish third again four years later, driving a V-12 Lagonda, deprived of a win by exhaust valve and oil feed troubles). That car also won for Aston-Martin the Rudge-Whitworth Biennial Cup for the Index of Performance for the second time. The Mark II Series arrived and – with the performance of the Ulster racing two-seater – gave a boost to flagging fortunes, but the cars were still expensive and heavy. Then, in 1936, came the 2-litre 15/98 models, offered in a range of Two/Four Seater, Tourer, Saloon, Drophead Coupé and Speed Model.

PROBLEMS AND SOLUTIONS

In 1937, 'Bert' Bertelli left Aston-Martin over, it seems, a disagreement which resulted in a reduction of the number of Saloon model cars to be bodied by his brother 'Harry's' firm. This left the company in something of a quandary, but work had to continue, and, whilst his departure was a great loss, cars continued to leave the Feltham works, though not in such large numbers (not that they ever left the works in *large* numbers). Not all was gloom and doom in 1937 though, for that was also the year in which Aston-Martin won its third Rudge-Whitworth Biennial Cup at Le Mans.

The Aston Martin Ulster was one of the most successful models in pre-war competition. This example is the pale-blue car, which had a chrome radiator (instead of the more usual painted one), supplied to Prince Bira of Siam and raced by him in the 1935 Ulster Tourist Trophy Race.

By 1938, however, car production at Feltham was brought to a deliberate halt by Gordon Sutherland because the factory was amassing a large stock of unsold cars. This bold decision was seen by some as the beginning of the end for Aston-Martin, but Sutherland saw it rather as the start of a new beginning. Rearmament of Great Britain followed the Munich Crisis of 1938 and demanded the kinds of skills possessed by the work force at Feltham, so that was the direction that the company took. The manufacture of aircraft components brought greatly increased security measures to the factory, but it kept the work force together and provided the revenue essential to keeping the company going 'until better times'.

In that same period, the motoring reputation of Aston-Martin was upheld by a young man named 'Jock' St John Horsfall. He entered the Leinster Trophy Race with a 2-litre Speed Model, which had been prepared by the Works, and shot to instant fame by winning. Then, he entered the 1938 RAC Tourist Trophy Race at Donington Park (a terrible accident two years earlier had caused the Ulster authorities to ban further racing there). Against all the predicted odds, Horsfall finished second only to a 3-litre Delage, driven by a very professional driver, none other than Louis Gerard.

The Munich Crisis had scared off many of Lagonda's prospective customers, for it produced large uneconomical cars, so by the end of 1938, it too was looking for other work to take up manufacturing capacity. Fortunately, back in 1936, Alan Good had supported the formation of a new company called F. Wyndham Hewitt Limited, which was formed to make cooling gills for radial aero engines on behalf of the Bristol Aeroplane Company's engines division. The decision to form the new company was based on the need to provide more work for the oversized Lagonda machine shop and, as its work expanded after Munich, so more floor space

The thermostatically controlled cooling gills on the rear of the engine cowling of this Bristol Beaufighter were made by Lagonda, like thousands more that helped to cool Bristol's Hercules and other radial aero engines.

was taken up by Wyndham Hewitt, and members of the Lagonda work force were also transferred at the same time.

Early 1939 was a black period for car manufacture at Staines, the Lagonda V-12 Le Mans project being almost the only car work in the factory, apart from the odd few V-12s returning from coachbuilders for finishing before delivery. However, at that time, Alan Good was concentrating on the expansion of the small industrial diesel engine market through another company of which he was chairman – Petters – now world famous for their small diesels and refrigeration equipment. That same company was later to occupy the Staines premises as its main manufacturing base.

Few drophead coupés of the period before the Second World War were pleasing to look at with the hood raised, but the graceful lines of this James Young version on the V-12 Lagonda proved it could be done.

THROUGH WAR TO COMMON DESTINY

As the Second World War unfolded, so L.G. Motors gave over its entire production capacity to the manufacture of aero engine cooling gills, aircraft fuel tanks and fire-fighting equipment, giving the odd hour of leisure time here and there to illicit thoughts of motor cars. At Feltham, too, the efforts of the work force were directed to the defence of the nation, as the entire Aston Martin facility was put by Gordon Sutherland at the disposal of Vickers-Armstrongs Limited, makers of the Spitfire fighter and the Wellington bomber. The 'C' Type Aston Martin had been developed and was now shelved, whilst the 'Atom' had been created in an attempt to produce a less expensive car. It was all suspended in the cause of victory.

After the war, both Aston Martin and Lagonda began to look towards a future making cars again, but both had to ask on what resources. Lagonda had used odd moments to devise a new car and a new engine, which was now to be announced as the LB6. It was the original intention to call this car a Lagonda-Bentley, but Rolls-Royce Motors insisted that 'Bentley' was its trade

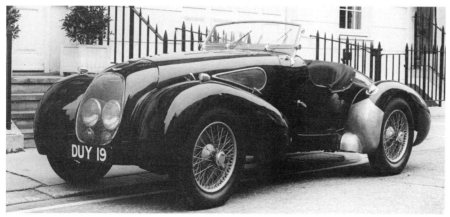

Aerodynamics as applied to the C-Type Aston Martin.

21

Aston Martin and Lagonda

If you thought the C-Type was a little ungainly of line, then what would you make of the 'Atom', Claude Hill's development vehicle for the intended next phase of Aston Martins?

mark, and the name had to be dropped in favour of LB6 (Lagonda-Bentley six-cylinder).

Aston Martin, in the meantime, had continued work on a pushrod engine, designed by Chief Engineer Claude Hill and now developed a 2-litre Sports in Saloon and Drophead versions, as well as the Spa Special, all of which were finally on display at the 1948 Earls Court Motor Show. However, money was tight, and investors were actively being sought to reconstitute the company.

As the result of an advertisement in *The Times* newspaper, the interest of a Huddersfield-based engineering entre-preneur named David Brown was aroused. He met Gordon Sutherland and drove a hard bargain to purchase Aston-Martin and all its assets for just £20,500 in 1947. In the meantime, L.G. Motors Limited was also looking for a buyer, having hoped to interest Briggs Motor Bodies Limited in a supply deal which could have put the company back on its feet but which failed for lack of assurances of continuity to Briggs.

The LB6 Lagonda was a fine example of elegance combined with economy – economy in terms of coming down from a 4.5-litre car to what was visualized as its post-war successor.

The post-war 2-litre Sports Aston Martin on test at Silverstone in 1948. This was the last model designed before David Brown took over the company and is often now incorrectly referred to as the DB1.

A casual telephone call, it seems, alerted the interested David Brown to this opportunity, and when he examined the situation, he decided it was worth buying the name 'Lagonda', all its stock, engineering drawings and the rights to use them. The deal complete, he allowed both firms their heads for a while, developing the LB6 Lagonda and the 2-litre Sports Model Aston Martin.

Before long, however, he saw that there was merit in adapting the Lagonda twin-cam 2.6-litre engine for use in the Aston Martin chassis. He then proceeded to have the engineering team commence work, so the Aston Martin DB2 came into being with its 2.6-litre engine, and much manufacturing work transferred to Huddersfield.

The first 'DB' car was the DB2, one of the famous prototypes of which is seen here in late stages of build.

Sir David Brown, KBE

David Brown was born in 1904, the son of a Huddersfield pattern maker turned gear manufacturer. His grandfather's business was established in 1860, and his father moved it to Huddersfield in 1903, concentrating on gear making at the expense of less profitable pattern making.

Educated at Rossall, young 'D.B.' went on to Huddersfield Technical College and, at seventeen, began an apprenticeship with David Brown and Sons (Huddersfield) Limited. Working his way up the ladder, just as anyone else would, he was appointed foreman of the Worm Gear Department in 1926, then assistant works manager a year later. In 1928, he was made manager of the Keighley Gear Company (Huddersfield) Limited. After an overseas trip to study manufacturing methods in the United States, South Africa and Europe, he became a director in 1929, then joint managing director of David Brown and Sons in 1932.

Sir David Brown, KBE

Early in 1933, his co-managing director died and D.B. became sole chief executive of the family group.

Active in motor sport in the late 1920s, David Brown was delighted when the family firm was asked to make a supercharger for Raymond Mays' Vauxhall Villiers, then the blowers for the 1929 Le Mans-winning 4½-litre Bentleys. In 1934, his attention was diverted to tractors in a venture with Harry Ferguson, followed by the formation of David Brown Tractors in 1939 – stars of that year's Royal Agricultural Show.

War production between 1939 and 1945 included gears for anything that moved in the war effort – from battle tanks to aero engines. Then, in 1947, he acquired Aston Martin Limited, followed a year later by Lagonda. Knighted in 1969, Sir David died in 1993 at the age of 89.

2 The Foray into V Engines

As long ago as 1951, a David Brown Lagonda V engine was put into the development programme at Feltham, and Willie Watson was recruited in 1952, having worked on the pre-war Bentley Lagonda V-12, to take charge of Development Project 115, as it was known, and bring the engine to reality.

A NEW LAGONDA V-12 FOR LE MANS

This new engine was to be different from its pre-war counterpart in several ways, the most obvious being that it was to be a quad-cam, two per cylinder bank, instead of a single cam per bank. As the engine took shape, it showed a deliberately visible resemblance to the existing LB6 in-line unit. This new power plant was to be David Brown's Ferrari-beater, an engine to compete with the 4.1-litre 340 Mexico and the 4.5-litre 375MM.

The crankcase was to be of barrel-type, with its seven main bearings retained in alloy diaphragms. This brought a warning from Feltham's bearing supplier, the Glacier Bearing Company, that there would be an inherent weakness in a design incorporating crankcase and bearing diaphragms of the same material. The LB6 had a cast-iron crankcase, but to use cast-iron for the V-12 would have taken the weight well beyond acceptable design limits. The decision was made to take the risk and live with the known weakness which would, it had to be accepted, limit the ultimate engine speed and perhaps even the development of the engine itself.

Of all the consequences this design weakness placed on Willie Watson's shoulders, the worst was to wonder whether the engine would even hold up under high-speed running, because of the problem of expansion coefficients. In an engine with a cast-iron crankcase and alloy bearing diaphragms, the alloy diaphragms expand in hot running to a greater extent than does the crankcase, with the benefit that the whole bottom end of the engine tightens up under high-speed hot running conditions. However, when an alloy crankcase is employed, it expands at approximately the same rate as the bearing diaphragms, conferring no tightening benefit and, in fact, possibly even expanding away from the bearings, so loosening up the bottom end! In the interests of weight-saving, it was a risk he had to take.

With a bore and stroke of 82.55mm × 69.85mm, the capacity of the Lagonda engine was to be 4,484cc. It was a dry-sump unit, with the cylinder banks inclined at 60°, like the pre-war Bentley design. Two Scintilla magnetos sparked twenty-four plugs and combined with three four-choke Weber carburettors placed between the cylinder banks, to make the engine a fearsomely complicated-looking device. The power output has been quoted at various figures, but the aim at the outset was 350bhp, to compare favourably with the Ferraris against

*The barrel-type
crankcase of DP115,
the new quad-cam
Lagonda engine,
which was to be
David Brown's
'Ferrari-beater', but
which was destined
not to achieve the
hoped-for success
because of the
bearing diaphragm
design.*

which it was aimed. In fact, the two most commonly quoted outputs lie between 312bhp and 305bhp at 6,000rpm. Since the late John Wyer went into print to say that the most ever achieved was 312, it is reasonable to believe the former is more accurate.

*The chassis into
which the V-12 was
to sit was an
extension of the
DB3S design, beefed
up to look like this.*

DP115 with the engine in place shows a neat chassis installation.

Having assembled this gargantuan machine, it was installed into an 100in (2,540mm) wheelbase development of the Aston Martin DB3S chassis, equipped with trailing link front suspension and a de Dion rear end, with transverse torsion bars and telescopic dampers. The gearbox was a David Brown Type S532 5-speed, whereas the DB3S used only a 4-speed, and the drum brakes were of the same diameter as those used on the DB3S, but three-quarters of an inch wider at the front and a quarter of an inch wider at the rear to cope with the 2,513lb (1,130kg) weight of the car.

THE LAGONDA GOES TO WORK

As history relates, the V-12's performance was not all that was expected, or even hoped for, though it wasn't all down to the engine. Even so, because of the limitations placed on the engine at the outset, its development was very limited. It had, for example, been designed at drawing board stage to be of wet liner type, so that larger cylinder liners could be fitted to increase the bore to 87mm, so increasing the capacity to 4,983cc to enable the engine to hold its own against the 4.9-litre engines Ferrari was known to have in his racing arsenal and which had appeared in the Type 375 Plus. Because of the fear of taking the engine too far beyond its limits, the larger liners were never used, and the engine was never taken to 5 litres.

Four Lagonda V-12 cars were built, first as Project 115 and then, in 1955, as lessons were learned, it became DP166. It had always been intended to field two cars wherever possible at racing events, though only one appeared at the Lagonda's Début at Silverstone in May 1954. The year 1954 was probably Aston Martin Lagonda's worst year in competition. It had performed outstandingly well in 1953 and, on paper, 1954

Very shortly after completion, this picture was taken of 'DB' sitting in DP115 as it was ready to go for testing.

could and should have been at least as good or better. However, both Aston Martin and Lagonda team cars were run in the major events, with the same number of people in the team; there was the Lagonda development programme to cope with as well as the existing DB3S race cars; and – as if that was not enough for an already over-stretched team – it was trying to develop a supercharged version of the six-cylinder engine as well! Put simply, the company took on too much for the number of people available with the result that, in John Wyer's own words: 'We had lost all the advantage we had gained in the latter half of 1953 and our position, relative to the competition, was worse than it had been at the end of 1952'.

With only one Lagonda of the intended two assembled – and that in a hurry, so that the normal 'de-bugging' process was virtually denied it – the team went off to Silverstone on 15 May 1954. This was to be the Lagonda's first outing and, driven by Reg Parnell, it finished fifth. This was certainly

no disgrace for a car's first race, but more had been expected, and it was clear to all concerned that insufficient preparation was behind the car's inability to do better.

Le Mans was next on the calendar, and this was the event which, in John Wyer's words, was the 'team's undoing'. It had been intended to take two Lagondas, two DB3S Coupés and the supercharged DB3S. Because the second Lagonda was still not ready, and because an initial entry of five cars had been made, he succumbed to the persuasion of making space for a DB3S that Carroll Shelby wanted to drive with Paul Frère, in substitution for the incomplete V-12. The Shelby/Frère car was a 1953 specification car and was not expected to do well but was in fact the last Aston Martin running before it expired with a stub-axle failure.

For the Aston Martin Lagonda team, the rest of the Le Mans 24 Hours Race was a total débâcle. It began with Eric Thompson putting the Lagonda out of the race in the

The V-12 at Le Mans, parked by Eric Thompson after spinning early in the 1954 Race.

4½-Litre Lagonda V12 Sports Racing Car (DP/115 – 1954, DP/166 – 1955)

Vehicle construction
Tubular chassis with aluminium bodywork (DP115)
Space frame with central spine (DP116)

Engine

Crankcase/cylinder block material	Aluminium alloy
Cylinder head material	Aluminium alloy, twin-plug
Number of cylinders	12 in 60° V-formation, wet liners
Cooling system	Water – pump and thermostat
Bore and stroke	82.55mm × 69.85mm
Engine capacity	4,484cc
Number of main bearings	Seven
Valve gear and operation	Two chain-driven overhead camshafts per cylinder bank; two valves per cylinder
Fuel supply method and type	High-pressure pump and three Weber Type 401FC4C carburettors
Quoted maximum power output	312bhp @ 6,000rpm
Quoted maximum torque output	Not quoted

Transmission

Clutch type and operation	Single dry plate, hydraulic operation
Gearbox ratios	9.99, 6.40, 5.90, 3.70, 3.05:1
Final drive ratio	3.70:1

Suspension and steering

Front suspension	Trailing link and transverse torsion bars
Rear suspension	De Dion tube with transverse torsion bars and telescopic dampers
Steering type	Rack and pinion
Wheel type and size	5½J × 16in
Tyre size and rating	7.00 × 16 racing
Brakes: type and actuation	13in × 2½in Alfin drum front and 12in × 2¼in Alfin drum rear, hydraulic actuation

Vehicle Dimensions

Wheelbase	8ft 4in (2,540mm)
Track (front and rear)	4ft 1in (1,245mm)
Overall height	3ft 6in (1,067mm) (over screen)

second hour, by crashing at the Esses. A sheared steering arm key was found during the 'post-mortem', and it was supposed that this may have been the cause of the car's demise. Later, both of the DB3S Coupés crashed in the same place, but at different times, just over the hump at the White House. The first out was the Whitehead/Stewart car at 65 laps, followed at 138 laps by the Collins/Bira car. The supercharged DB3S ran for eight hours, at the hands of Reg Parnell and Roy Salvadori, during which time it proved itself faster than the Lagonda or any of the non-supercharged Aston Martins, before retiring with a cylinder head gasket failure.

Silverstone was the venue for the Lagonda's third outing, still only one car being ready to race. It was David Brown himself who made the decision to race this time, his reasoning being that it was better to go back to a race and prove the team capable than to creep away and lick its wounds. When John Wyer protested that he had no cars with which to race, the response came: 'That's your problem, but I insist we get back to racing rather than just retire hurt!' Thus, more midnight oil was burned, and four cars were readied for the start-line.

The event was the sports car race held in support of the British Grand Prix, and again the driver was Reg Parnell, this time in company with three Aston Martin DB3Ss, these driven by Peter Collins, Roy Salvadori and Carroll Shelby. This time, all the glory of 1953 returned to the Feltham team, with a first, second, third and fourth result. Collins led Shelby and Salvadori to an Aston Martin first three places, whilst Reg Parnell brought up the rear, disappointed that the Lagonda – with its bigger engine – didn't do better but pleased that the four cars had vindicated the Le Mans experience.

ECLIPSE OF THE V-12

The V-12 Lagonda didn't appear again in competition until 1955, now in the guise of a new development prototype number – DP166. This was not simply a renumbering exercise, however, for DP166 really was a new chassis. In fact, it was Feltham's first attempt at a true space-frame chassis. Driver and passenger seats were placed outside the central 'spine' of the mainframe, and this new car had disc brakes for the wider wheels. Engine and gearbox were much the same as in the previous year.

Le Mans was once again the target of all this development work (some called it stubbornness, with the view that the car was never competitive) on the Lagonda, and so, along with three Aston Martin DB3Ss, it went to the Sarthe Circuit. Of the Aston Martins, the Salvadori/Walker car retired with a broken crankshaft after 106 laps, whilst the Brooks/Riseley-Pritchard car went out with a flat battery after the dynamo had failed. Nevertheless, Peter Collins and Paul Frère finished second that day, behind Mike Hawthorn and Ivor Bueb with their 'D' Type Jaguar.

The Lagonda, in the meantime, driven once again by Reg Parnell, accompanied by Dennis Poore, managed 93 laps before its

Now known as DP166, the V-12 at Le Mans in 1955, driven this time by Reg Parnell and Dennis Poore.

leaking fuel filler caused its retirement. In most of its races (this second Le Mans was the last of its career), the V-12 Lagonda had failed to perform for reasons other than its engine's inability to produce the power, though it had been a disappointing exercise, for it had never produced the power output expected, nor had it been much – if at times any – quicker than the Aston Martins. Without further ceremony, the first post-war exercise at Aston Martin Lagonda Limited with V-form engines was abandoned, and all attention focused for the time being on the in-line six-cylinder, with the DB4 now looming on the horizon.

ENTER TADEK MAREK

A Pole by birth, Tadek Marek joined Aston Martin Lagonda Limited in 1954, with the initial task of undertaking a modification programme on the DB Mark III Saloon. Whilst Aston Martin had considered the prospect of developing a V-8 engine as long before as 1953, and whilst Marek had produced a design for the manufacture of a V-8 from existing components for the Austin Motor Company, his first new engine design task for Aston Martin Lagonda Limited was the daunting job of creating a new six-cylinder in-line engine for the DB4 model, which was to succeed the Mark III.

Marek's entry to the Aston Martin design team might be viewed as a little odd, in that he had no personal experience of aluminium alloy crankcase design, only cast-iron. He also had no experience of racing engine design – which should come as no surprise for an engineer whose career experience had been spent in other areas, not least designing battle tanks during the Second World War, though he had spent two years with Austin at Longbridge before returning to military vehicle engineering.

The original design parameters given to

Tadek Marek

Tadek Marek was born in the Polish city of Cracow in 1908. To become a Technical Engineer (Dipl. Ing.) in Germany, where he chose to study, he had to attend studies at a technical institute for seven years – the duration of engineering apprenticeships in Britain in those days. Marek acquired his technical education at the Charlottenburg Technical Institute in Berlin, during which time he developed a keen interest in motor racing, driving in club events at the famous Avusrennenring on many occasions. His racing career, however, was brought to an abrupt end in 1928, after a serious accident in which he lost a kidney.

After graduation, young Marek returned to his homeland and went to work with the Polish division of Fiat, then moved on to the General Motors subsidiary. As war engulfed eastern Europe, including Poland, Marek left his home country, and by a tortuous route which took him almost three years to cover he found his way to Britain, where many of his compatriots had already sought refuge. He joined the Polish army, but his skills found their way to a drawing board, designing battle tanks, including work on the famous Centurion. After Hitler's war was brought to its close, Tadek Marek joined the United Nations Relief and Rehabilitation Organization, returning to Germany to help the reconstruction of that country's industrial base.

Marek found himself back in Britain in 1949, when he went to work with the Austin Motor Company. There, he was responsible for creating a V-8 engine built from A40 components. From Austin, he joined Aston Martin Lagonda in 1954, developing first the 3.7-litre, then the 4-litre six-cylinder engines and later the V-8, first used in the Lola-Aston Martin racing car and then the DBS-V8 – the basis of the engine still used in today's Aston Martins.

Tadek Marek for the DB4 engine were that it had to be of an ideal 3-litre capacity but be capable of being stretched to nearly 4-litres for use in any Lagonda range of cars, which by their nature and position in the market would almost certainly have either an automatic transmission as standard or at least as a strongly preferred option. Typical of the man, he designed an engine which had a bottom end that would have been a credit to a 5-litre, let alone a 3-litre! Combined with the fact that casting suppliers were unable to provide iron castings in anything like the time-frame required, so forcing Marek's hand and making an alloy crankcase the only option, the consequence was that the ultimate capacity of the DB4 became 3.7 litres (Lagonda-sized) with a bore and stroke of 92mm × 92mm. Thus, John Wyer's promise of allowing Tadek Marek to design an iron engine went out of the window – and of course this new engine would be raced, though there was consultation about that, with the first car to carry it being the DBR2,

a combination of Marek's new engine and the chassis from Project DP166, the abandoned V-12 Lagonda.

NEXT LINK IN THE CHAIN – DP215

If Aston Martin Lagonda Limited had a fixation, it was about winning at Le Mans. Twenty-four years had separated Lagonda's superb win in 1935 from Aston Martin's magnificent victory in 1959, but AML has, whenever it has re-entered the competitive arena, pursued a burning ambition to win the 24 Hour Race again.

In the early 1960s, that ambition was worked towards with development of the DB4, starting with the prototype DB4GT, DP/199/1, the lone team car of 1959. Work continued with the 1962 Team car, DP212. Then, via the two DP214s of the same year, came the DP215 – announced in mid-1963 and visualized as the ultimate winner.

DP215, the car that took Aston Martin back to Le Mans in 1963 should have received the prototype V-8 engine. This picture was taken at the Museum of British Road Transport's magnificent display of Aston Martins at Coventry in January 1994.

DP215 was intended, right from drawing board stage, to be one of three and 'the new Aston Martin'. DP215/1 was in fact the only car of its type built. Whilst fitted initially with a six-cylinder 4-litre engine, it was designed to accept a new power unit which was on Tadek Marek's drawing board – a 90° V-8 of similar capacity, but intended to have a worthwhile power increase, a marked increase in torque and great reliability.

This new car was to be the fastest front-engined Aston Martin so far built. With its 186mph (300kph) run down Mulsanne Straight, it was to achieve that part of its manufacturer's ambition at the 1963 Le Mans. It looked invincible as it put up such a magnificent performance, and Ferrari was beginning to worry about this supercar driven by Phil Hill and Lucien Bianchi. However, a transmission failure took it out after barely two and a quarter hours, on lap 29, taking with it the challenge to Ferrari, but not before it had made its mark.

The withdrawal of Aston Martin Lagonda Limited from racing at the end of that year brought with it the end of further development on DP215, so it never did receive its intended V-8 engine. In fact, it slowed down the project to the extent that it would not now appear for two more years, then in the guise of a renumbered project – DP218. This would be the forerunner of the next generation of Aston Martin and Lagonda car engines, with its ultimate successor being in production some thirty years later.

PROJECT DP218 – THE 5-LITRE V-8

Tadek Marek's six-cylinder engine had been ultimately developed and stretched until it became a 4.2-litre unit, though it was from the 4-litre DB5 that he took his guide lines in drafting the design objectives for his new V-8 engine, a concept which had been shelved at Feltham in the 1950s. The power output of the new engine was finally deemed to require a 32 per cent increase over the existing 4-litre of the DB5, so 300–350bhp would be sought. The frontal area of a car destined to house this new engine was calculated, as well as an optimum increase in overall weight.

The outcome of all this pre-calculation was a design specification which now called for an optimum capacity of 5.3 litres, the power output already mentioned and a low weight achieved by use of an alloy crankcase/cylinder block. Playing typically safe, Marek went for an initial capacity of 4,806cc, using a bore of 96mm, the same as that used in the 4-litre six cylinder engine, and a stroke of 83mm. Clearly, the stroke could be increased as development trials decreed the reliability of the unit.

DP218 became a reality at the end of July 1965, after two years' intensive design work. On the day the prototype engine was finally assembled, it was put on to the test bench and run. The compression ratio of this first engine was a relatively modest 8.36:1, and fuel was supplied by means of four Weber Type 46IDA carburettors. Fuel injection was not yet a chosen route because sorting the basic running of the engine was first on the priority list, so keeping things simple was the rule of the day.

On its first measured run, the engine was recorded as producing 275bhp at 5,750rpm. With a bit of 'tweaking' this was soon raised to 285bhp at 6,000rpm but it was still not enough, the original objective being 300–350bhp, though 5.3 litres had also been the calculated optimum capacity, so there was some latitude to be taken up there. With modifications to the induction passages and an increase in compression ratio, the engine was finally run up to 329bhp at 6,200rpm. After some work on an oil feed problem, it was decided to do some road testing, using the car model around which the initial

These two drawings were the first indication to the world that Aston Martin Lagonda Limited was building a V-8 engine – and once again for racing – now for use in the Lola T70.

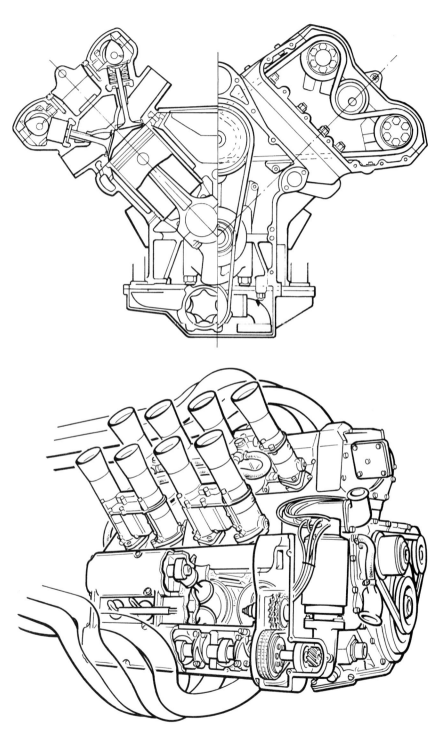

development ideas were calculated – a DB5.

The really punishing test for the V-8 was to come with its installation in a racing machine. Once again, Tadek Marek had found himself producing an engine which, whilst not intended for racing at the outset, was destined for that role anyway. John Surtees, former Grand Prix World Champion Racing Driver, wanted to know if Aston Martin would be interested in providing an engine for use in his Lola T70 in his 1967 attack on the World Sports Car Championship. He had already won it in 1966 with a Lola, but that had used a Chevrolet engine. Now, Surtees wanted to use a British engine with, as he saw it, a true potential for success.

TEAM SURTEES AND THE LOLA-ASTON

Tadek Marek was, of course, opposed to racing his new engine before it had a chance of being 'de-bugged' on the road to his satisfaction. However, at the hands of Mr Surtees, it

was about to go through a very thorough shake-down, something far more 'testing' than the DB5 chassis would give it. As a result of the company's agreement to co-operate with Team Surtees, the engine went under the microscope. First, the bore was increased to 97.5mm, to give a capacity of 4,983cc. Next, the compression ratio went up to 9:1, whilst four Weber 45DCOE carburettors helped to elevate the power output to 332bhp at 5,500rpm. That was still not enough.

After more midnight oil burning (a commodity seemingly in plenty at Newport Pagnell, for much of it was used over the years!), the camshafts were changed, the carburettors were changed again and a lot of minor 'tweaking' and balancing was done. The result, with high-lift cams and 48IDA downdraught carburettors, was that some 421bhp was squeezed out of the engine, as well as a torque figure which compared remarkably well with that of the alternative Chevrolet engine – some 386lb/ft.

Now came the real testing session. An open version of the Lola T70 Mk III was

Lola's workshop at Slough shows T70s in build.

Lola-Aston Martin T70 Mk III Racing Coupé – 1967

Vehicle construction
Aluminium and steel monocoque with semi-stressed engine and GRP bodywork

Engine

Crankcase/cylinder block material	Aluminium alloy
Cylinder head material	Aluminium alloy, twin-plug
Number of cylinders	8 in 90° V-formation, wet liners
Cooling system	Water – pump and thermostat
Bore and stroke	98.5mm × 83mm
Engine capacity	5,064cc
Number of main bearings	Five
Valve and gear operation	Two chain driven overhead camshafts per cylinder bank; two valves per cylinder
Fuel supply method and type	Bendix high-pressure pump and four Weber Twin-choke carburettors
Quoted maximum power output	450bhp @ 6,000rpm
Quoted maximum torque output	413lb/ft

Transmission

Clutch type and operation	7¼in triple plate, hydraulic operation
Gearbox ratios	Hewland 5-speed, various ratios used
Final drive ratio	Salisbury limited-slip, various ratios used

Suspension and steering

Front suspension	Double wishbones, coil springs, anti-roll bar and Koni shock absorbers
Rear suspension	Lower wishbone to cast upright, upper trailing arm and transverse link, with anti-roll bar, coil springs and Koni shock absorbers
Steering type	Rack and pinion
Wheel type and size	Lola magnesium 15in
Tyre size and rating	Dunlop Racing 15in
Brakes: type and actuation	Kelsey-Hayes 12½in disc with 4-pot hydraulic actuation

Vehicle Dimensions

Overall Length	4,200mm
Overall Width	1,800mm
Wheelbase	2,489mm
Track (front and rear)	1,397mm front and rear
Overall height	1,010mm

---

fitted with the Aston Martin engine, which had gone through yet another bore increase on its way to becoming a racing engine. Now, it had a bore of 98mm, giving an extra 81cc (5,064cc). More development work and more power and torque came. They'd managed to exceed both the bhp and the torque figure of the 5.9-litre Chevrolet now, with an engine still three-quarters of a litre smaller! Now, the power output was up to 450bhp, whilst torque was a massive 413lb/ft. Tightening everything up and making sure nothing was missed were part of the process of determining that this was a fully competitive engine, ready to race. Thus, with the

Lola T70 Mk III announced at the 1967 Racing Car Show, car and engine were ready to go to work.

REALITY AT LAST

We must return now, for a moment, to the views held by Tadek Marek about engines and motor racing. It should be understood that he was not opposed to motor racing, nor to engines being designed specifically for racing. The situation for him was very clear. He had never had any experience of designing or manufacturing racing engines and so

The T70 Racing Car Show car, which shows the spare wheel in the original position and the exhaust pipes before being rerouted.

was always very reticent about his designs being used in that way. When John Wyer first employed him, he explained very plainly that he had no experience of alloy crankcase design, nor of racing engines, but he had been a keen racing enthusiast as a young man and had driven cars 'in anger'.

Imagine how Marek must have felt, then, when he was told that his V-8 engine was to be developed fully and would be used in a production car. No longer would he have to work under the pressures of racing development, where everything was wanted in a hurry, because the team had to win and to do

An overhead view of the Lola T70 on rollout shows what a clean and attractive car it was.

The Le Mans entry engine specification form for T70 SL73/117. Note the engine number (it has been said that V/500/1/R went into SL73/101).

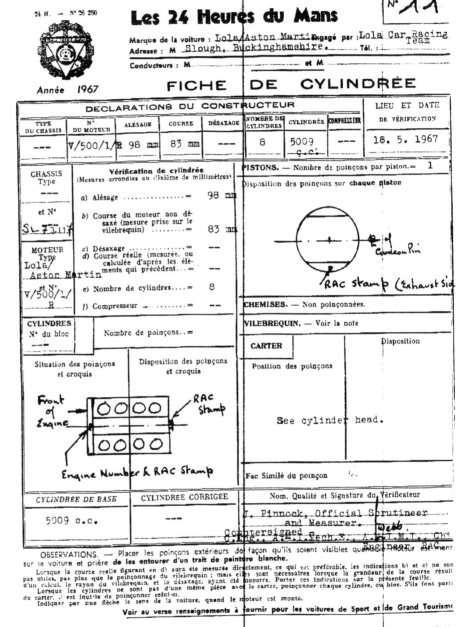

so, it had to stay one step ahead of the competition. Now, he could revert to the process of doing things to plan and, even though a timetable was still involved, he had the time to be as thorough as his German training had taught him to be. The next generation of Aston Martin would carry his engine. That was to be the DBS–V8. Tadek Marek was now, at last, in what he saw as a world of reality – a world of production cars.

3 The DBS V-8 and the Original AM Lagonda Saloon

Having learned that his engine was really to be used for a production car, Tadek Marek was delighted, but which model was the engine to be used in? His answer came with the announcement that two new cars were to be built by Carrozzeria Touring, whose Superleggera designs had been used on earlier DB models. Now, these two chassis (developed under the designation MP226) were six-cylinder engined cars but were to be an indication of things to come.

The Touring cars were strictly two-seaters, in the mould of the DB4GT, but with a de Dion rear end and a striking new un-Aston-Martin-like body devoid of the familiar radiator grille shape. Indeed, they could almost have been mistaken for Ferraris at first glance. It is perhaps this very 'Continental' look that aroused so much interest when they were announced. Labelled 'DBS' these two cars stimulated so much press interest, that it was decided to call the next Aston Martin model the DBS.

However, there was a hitch. It was that the factory at Newport Pagnell had problems finishing the detail design work essential to taking the Touring bodied cars into production, if they had ever been intended

Carrozzeria Touring's DBS, precursor of the V-8, announced at the 1966 Geneva Show. Why 'DBS'? Apart from invoking the spirit of the DB3S, wasn't it also justified as 'DB' for David Brown and 'S' for Superleggera?

for 'production' in a serious way. In addition, Carrozzeria Touring was having serious financial problems and closed its Milan factory down in the autumn of 1966, so that put an end to the Superleggera DBS.

THE TOWNS DBS TO THE RESCUE

William Towns is a name many people associate with Lagonda, rather than with Aston Martin, because of the striking saloon he produced in the 1970s, but he joined the company as a seat designer in 1966, after hearing on the industry grapevine that Aston Martin was looking for a chief body designer as well as the post he filled. Needless to say, his youth and limited experience lost him the job he wanted to Cyril Honey.

Undeterred, Towns looked closely at the DB6, which was now of a lineage rather long in the tooth, and began to doodle with his own ideas of a new car. He had learned that 'D.B.' wanted two-door and four-door cars in the Aston Martin line-up so began to sketch ideas for the longer of the two options first, believing that it was better to shorten to a two-door than to lengthen to a four-door. There are plenty of examples of car designs around to prove how right he was about that, even among cars which were 'stretched' to make 2+2 coupés from two-seater roadsters.

Making sure that his ultimate employer, David Brown himself, was aware of the design ideas he came up with from time to time was part of William Towns' strategy. After all, he was not the chief body designer, so he made sure his seat design work was always up to date and kept 'plugging' his design ideas. Finally, the strategy paid off, for he was instructed to turn his ideas into clay for the two-door car, deferring the four-door version for the time being. This was in late 1966, and the car he designed was the vehicle we all now know as the Aston Martin DBS, forerunner of the V-8 Saloon which immediately preceded the Virage.

This new car was 6in (15.24cm) wider than its immediate forebear, the DB6, 1½in (4.17cm) shorter and 1¼in (3.8cm) lower. It therefore had a somewhat more 'chunky' (some have even used the word 'lumpy', but that's a little unkind) appearance than the preceding model, but then it also had a more 'razor-edged' line than the earlier DB models. Much of the reason for the extra width of the new model was the wider engine and the need to provide the essential clearance for wheel movement in the turning circle of the car, though Sir David Brown is quoted as having once said that the jigs were made too wide, and the mistake was discovered too late to do anything about it! This story is more likely to have been put out because D.B. didn't like the extra width of the new car.

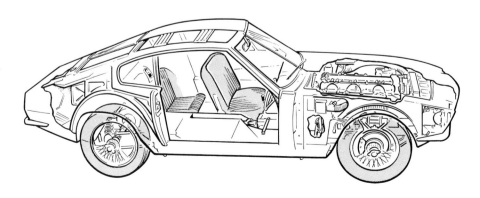

This drawing shows the layout of the original DBS, with its 4-litre, six-cylinder engine. It was another two years before the V-8 engine became available.

Once the definitive lines of the car were resolved, there was the task of making the DBS manufacturable. Fortunately, William Towns was one of those rare stylists who was always aware of the need to make what he had designed, so his design lines took account of what was needed to build the car. His boss, Cyril Honey, decided that instead of using the Superleggera tubular hoop system of sub-structure under the metal skin, he would adopt a series of steel pressings, in the more traditional manner.

A man named Bert Thickpenny, whose experience went back to Salmons coach-builders and Tickford (which company was bought by Aston Martin Lagonda Limited back in the 1950s Lagonda 3-litre days – and whose former premises the company now occupied), was given the task of adapting Towns' lines to press-tool technology. Time was of the essence, so the design work was completed to a tight schedule, but not rushed. The ultimate result was a car which weighed in at 1½ tons, but which was of a striking appearance and seen as a worthy successor to the Mk II DB6.

THE DBS TAKES TO THE ROAD

The prototype six-cylinder DBS was being driven around by the summer of 1967, a remarkably short period of time for any motor manufacturer to bring a car to 'the metal'. For such a small, craftsman-orientated company as Aston Martin Lagonda Limited, it was something of a miracle. A few design modifications were made on the way to 'productionizing' the DBS, but they were really very minor, ranging from using a full-width front bumper instead of a split one to dispensing with body vent 'gills' just behind the rear quarter lights at the side of the car.

After all the detail modifications were

complete, the new DBS was announced to the press and public in the autumn of 1967. However, the V-8 engine was not yet ready for manufacture, as it was still going through extensive development to turn it into a production engine after all the work done with Lola. The Lola experiment had failed in terms of providing a fully competitive racing engine in time for a win in the World Sports Car Championship, but it had succeeded admirably in providing a thorough shake-down for Tadek Marek's masterpiece as a road-going engine.

Why, then, did Aston Martin call this new model the 'DBS' instead of 'DB7'? The answer is really quite simple, though perhaps not entirely logical. The two Touring Superleggera cars shown at the 1966 Motor Show were called 'DBS', the aim being to create a psychological relationship between the new car and the former glories of the DB3S from earlier sports racing days in the process of promoting a new sports two-seater. Alfa Romeo did this kind of thing with considerable success, having gone still farther in using charismatic titles for production cars which had come from racing models – 'Alfetta' to quote just one. The collapse of Carrozzeria Touring and the decision to produce no more than the two prototypes did nothing to deter the charisma achieved by them. Riding on the back of that, the new production car was named 'DBS'.

The six-cylinder-engined DBS (not, as some have described it, DBS-6) was well received by press and public alike, and so – as often as possible – the publicity material reminded the market of the impending arrival of the V-8 version, even to the extent of fitting the wheels destined for the V-8 model and the larger front air dam on a DBS used by Roger Moore in the television series *The Persuaders*. Badging, wheels and tyres and the front air dam were the only immediately obvious differences between the DBS and

The DBS-V8's first recognition feature that identified it from its six-cylinder engined sibling was the slight bulge in the bonnet, fashioned into an air scoop, to accommodate the carburettors.

DBS-V8, although the larger-engined version was not to be offered for another two years, simply because of delays in bringing the engine to production.

V-8 AT LAST

On 27 September 1969, Tadek Marek finally saw his mighty V-8 engine announced to the world at large in the new Aston Martin DBS-V8. It was a proud day for him, for William Towns, whose design had reached its ultimate goal by receiving the power unit destined for it from the drawing board, and for David Brown, Chairman of Aston Martin Lagonda Limited, who announced the fastest production Aston Martin ever, the car being capable of reaching 160mph (258kph), compared with the more sedate 140mph (225kph) of the six-cylinder-engined DBS.

Tadek Marek had already retired before his V-8 finally reached the public eye, though he did know it was coming and had made a significant contribution to the process of its introduction. There had been much debate about the engine before it actually occupied the space made for it under the bonnet of the DBS-V8. Initially, it had been passed down from Huddersfield that an American engine, the Chrysler V-8 which was now powering the Bristol 405 and the Jensen C-V8, should be examined as a production option, in view of the experience with Lola in 1967. That suggestion was, as might be expected, vigorously resisted.

Dudley Gershon, an ex-Riley (Coventry) Limited apprentice who had been involved in quality V-8 engines as long ago as 1935–6 (Riley had developed two V-8 engines in those years), was now Technical Director of Aston Martin Lagonda Limited. His experience, combined with the very strong argument that to employ an engine made by another company – especially an American pushrod unit – would undermine the very reputation of Aston Martin, finally carried the day. Even so, the advantages of 'buying-in' still made the company consider other options, including even the 6.2-litre V-8

The Aston Martin DBS-V8 Saloon and its Adversaries

Car and Model	Engine Type and Size	Gearbox	Max. Speed		Consumption		G.B. Price
			mph	kph	mpg	l/100km	
Aston Martin DBS-V8 Saloon	5,340cc V-8 tohc per bank	5-speed	160	258	11–15	19–26	£7,639 (1970)
Jaguar V-12 E-Type Coupé	5,343cc V-12 tohc per bank	4-speed	150	242	13–16	18–22	£3,387 (1970)
Mercedes-Benz 350SLC	3,449cc V-8 sohc per bank	4-Auto	130	209	12–18	16–24	£5,700 (1970)
Bristol 411 Coupé	6,277cc V-8 pushrod ohv	3-Auto	140	225	14–18	16–20	£7,537 (1970)
Maserati Indy 4.7	4,719cc V-8 tohc per bank	5-speed	160	258	12–15	19–24	£8,852 (1970)
Ferrari 365 GTC4	4,390cc V-12 tohc per bank	5-speed	162	261	10–12	24–28	£9,814 (1970)
Monteverdi 375L GT	7,206cc V-8 pushrod ohv	3-Auto	155	250	11–15	19–26	£9,250 (1970)

from the Rolls-Royce Silver Shadow. However, common sense finally ruled and the Marek-designed quad-cam V-8 finally found its rightful home.

Here, then, was one of the fastest cars in the world for its time, despite the fact that it was defined as a luxury saloon, with plenty of room for four full-sized occupants, an opulent interior and comfort that would have done credit to many a limousine. All these factors combined, of course, to make it a very heavy car, too. It actually weighed in at well over 1½ tons and so, apart from needing a powerful engine to propel it, it needed pretty powerful brakes to stop it!

Stopping the car was no problem, in fact, for the brake discs would have done a heavy truck credit. All the discs were vented, as

The massive vented disc brakes of the DBS-V8 would almost have stopped a 40-ton truck, but then the power output was comparable with only the few most powerful 40-tonners producing over 300bhp.

The DBS-V8 engine was, despite the car being designed to accommodate it, a tight fit.

heavy braking was expected to generate a great deal of heat, and the front ones measured 1¼in (3.2cm) across and 10¾in (27.3cm) in diameter, whilst the rears were 10⅖in (26.4cm) in diameter and of the same thickness as those at the front. Two independent hydraulic circuits provided pressure to front and rear, then the added precaution was taken on the rear discs of providing separate callipers for the handbrake, the lever for which was to the left of the driver and of the fly-off variety in good old-fashioned sporting tradition.

The production V-8 engine had a bore and stroke of 100mm × 85mm, giving a capacity of 5,340cc. Compression ratio was 9:1, and fuel was supplied by means of Bosch fuel injection. The power output was never officially quoted, but press reports gave various figures up to 375bhp, which was highly unlikely, the true power being more likely to be around 345bhp or possibly less on the earlier engines. In any event, it was certainly sufficient to provide a very luxurious, very fast, ride.

Among the 'firsts' for Aston Martin, brought in with the DBS–V8 were, apart

from the vented brake discs already mentioned, the option of a Chrysler Torqueflite 3-speed automatic transmission and specially made alloy road wheels, instead of the traditional wires. Of course, the *big* first was the DBS–V8's performance, beginning with its 160mph (258kph) top speed, which alone was pretty phenomenal for a 1969 production saloon. The top speed was far from all of it though, for according to *Motor* magazine the 0–to–60mph time was an astounding 5.9 seconds, with the continuing 60–to–100mph taking only another 7.9 seconds.

Once the DBS–V8 was established, it and the DBS supplanted the previous model range entirely, and the DB6 was discontinued. Surprisingly though, whilst this new duo looked distinctly different from its predecessors, there were many features which carried over directly from the DB6. The steel floorpan chassis, whilst wider than the DB6, was an extension of the earlier design, which is what allowed the production stage of the DBS to be reached so soon. Of course, the engine and gearbox from the Mk II DB6 were used in the DBS, too, as was the final drive ratio, though the rear suspension was

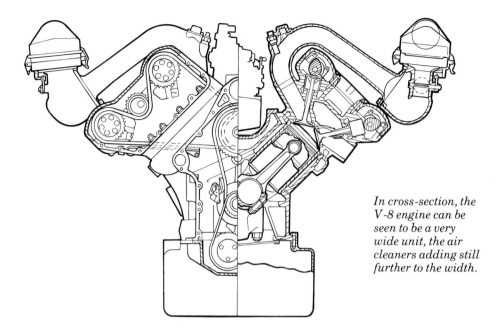

In cross-section, the V-8 engine can be seen to be a very wide unit, the air cleaners adding still further to the width.

clearly different, with the de Dion tube, trailing arms and Watts linkage combining with coil springs and Armstrong 'Selecta-ride' to provide an improved rear-end ride, without detriment to the handling, of course.

INTO PRODUCTION AND THE END OF AN ERA

The first DBS–V8 (DBSV8/10001/R) was completed on 19 September 1969 and was followed by the first true production car on 2 January 1970. The press reaction to the new model was generally ecstatic, though there were a few odd comments about the car being big and bulky. These really were unfounded because it was far from unwieldy. The American magazine *Road and Track* described the DBS–V8 as the result of 'dogged determination', referring to the time it took to develop the V-8 engine, but went on to say of the car: '. . . Sir David Brown's steadfast aim has been to produce a Grand Touring car of highest performance and quality, allied with supreme directional stability and all personal comforts. These requirements have been met . . .'

Motor magazine in Great Britain tested the DBS–V8 to produce the 0–60mph result quoted earlier of 5.9 seconds, whilst *Autocar* came up with the slightly lighter-footed 0–60mph of 6.0 seconds exactly. Either way, it was a pretty sparkling performance, comparable with the then-new Ferrari 365GTC 2+2 Coupé. Of course, the Ferrari used a twelve-cylinder engine of 4.4 litres capacity and was a little faster than the Aston Martin, but the DBS–V8 had the edge on finish, was less fussy and certainly more roomy. It also didn't have quite the price tag.

There really were few direct competitors for the DBS–V8 or its successor the AM–V8 for a long time, because the Ferrari used a smaller-capacity engine, as did the contemporary Maserati. The very elegant Monteverdi was also to use an American V-8, whilst the only British competitor, if it could really be compared directly, was the Jaguar

Aston Martin Lagonda V8 Saloon – 1969

Vehicle construction

Steel box-section chassis with steel superstructure
and aluminium bodywork

Engine

Crankcase/cylinder block material	Aluminium alloy
Cylinder head material	Aluminium alloy, twin-plug
Number of cylinders	8 in 90° V-formation, wet liners
Cooling system	Water – pump, thermostat and viscous-coupling fan
Bore and stroke	100mm × 85mm
Engine capacity	5,340cc
Number of main bearings	Five
Valve gear and operation	Two chain-driven overhead camshafts per cylinder bank; two valves per cylinder
Fuel supply method and type	Twin SU electric pumps and Bosch fuel injection system
Quoted maximum power output	310–320bhp @ 5,000rpm
Quoted maximum torque output	320lb/ft

Transmission

Clutch type and operation	With Chrysler Torqueflite automatic transmission – multi-plate torque convertor
Gearbox ratios	7.52, 4.45, 3.07:1 (reverse 6.75:1)
Final drive ratio	3.07:1

Suspension and steering

Front suspension	Independent – double wishbones, anti-roll bar and Koni shock absorbers
Rear suspension	De Dion, twin radius rods, Watts linkage, coil springs and lever-arm shock absorbers
Steering type	Adwest power-assisted rack and pinion
Wheel type and size	Cast alloy ventilated 7in × 15in
Tyre size and rating	Pirelli GR70VR × 15in
Brakes: type and actuation	Vented discs all round – 10¾in front, 10.38in rear, with split-circuit hydraulic system

Vehicle Dimensions

Overall Length	16ft 2in (4,928mm)
Overall Width	6ft 0in (1,829mm)
Wheelbase	9ft 6¾in (2,915mm)
Track (front and rear)	4ft 11in (1,499mm)
Overall height	4ft 5¼in (1,353mm)

XJ-S, a coupé with a V-12 of similar capacity, which didn't come up to the mark in performance or accommodation. The other British cars which approached the DBS–V8 were the Jensen Interceptor and the Bristol 410, both using the Chrysler V-8 which could have found (but luckily didn't) its way into the Aston Martin, so this car stood alone for some time. Indeed, perhaps it has always stood alone.

Whatever the ultimate judgement, for beauty, it is said, is in the eye of the beholder, some ninety Aston Martin DBS–V8s left the factory in 1970 and by the end of its production run, a total of 405 had been built. Production of the car was interrupted by the disposal of Aston Martin Lagonda Limited to Company Developments Limited in February 1972, though the last DBS–V8 to leave the factory gates was in September of that year.

The David Brown Corporation had, for twenty-five years, been the benevolent parent of Aston Martin Lagonda Limited, but by the end of 1971, Sir David Brown had come to the conclusion that he could no

The car most people saw the DBS-V8 'taking on' was the Ferrari 365GTC 2+2, a 4.4-litre V-12 engined car with less room and a higher price tag.

At home, the nearest thing to the DBS-V8 was the Chrysler-engined Jensen Interceptor, with a price tag £100 below the Aston Martin . . .

. . . But then there was the less expensive E-type Jaguar 4.2 Coupé, which had its own British engine, not quite the performance and was much more cramped. 'Horses for courses'?

47

longer afford to spend the time, money and effort essential to keeping the Newport Pagnell company alive. It had gone through crises during his tenure as Chairman and he had ridden them out, but now the resources were becoming too thinly spread through the rest of his industrial group, for Britain was in another of its difficult economic times, and he had to protect his core businesses. A buyer was sought, and William Willson, Chairman of Company Developments Limited, proved to be that buyer. The deal was settled by the end of February 1972, so ending a long and sound association – and the prefix 'DB' on the model designations of Aston Martin cars.

DIVERSIONS – A SHOOTING BRAKE AND FOUR-DOOR SALOON

Whilst there was never a drophead version of the DBS, nor a hatchback in the fashion of the DB2 and Mk III Aston Martins, the shooting brake concept was considered, though not by the factory. H.R. Owen, one of Aston Martin's leading distributors, decided the company had a customer whose needs were sufficiently worthy of attention to demand the building of a shooting brake version of the car. The project was carefully discussed, and finally the firm of FLM Panelcraft was approached, and it agreed to build the car. The result is that one DBS Shooting Brake exists, on chassis DBS/5370/R. However, the shooting brake story is not for these pages, for it was not a V-8 and the idea, whilst perhaps of great potential (the fastest station-wagon in the world?) was not taken up by Aston Martin Lagonda Limited.

The Lagonda, on the other hand, *is* a part of this story, for this is where the William Towns four-door car comes in. You will remember that David Brown had decided to shelve the four-door in favour of developing

a successor to the DB6 back in 1966, but now, in 1968, he had a personal requirement for a four-door luxury saloon and what else should he have but a car built in his own factory at Newport Pagnell? As a result, the Towns four-door saloon became a Lagonda – well almost.

Project Number MP230 was given to this new four-door car, the first to carry a Lagonda badge for five years, the previous model being the six-cylinder 4-litre Rapide of 1961–4, which had been based on the DB4 chassis, with a body produced under the Tickford banner. Only fifty-five examples were built over its three-year life and it was apparently very unpopular within the factory, for the disruption it caused to DB4 production. It is said that this disruption was a factor in John Wyer's departure from the company.

With the creation of this new Lagonda, William Towns' design philosophy was thoroughly vindicated, and though he had now left the employ of the company to set up his own design studio, he remained in contact. The car first appeared in 1969 and was instantly acclaimed as a truly elegant luxury saloon. Some even dared to compare it with Rolls-Royce, though one should hasten to add that Aston Martin Lagonda Limited never attempted to do so, at least not officially and certainly not in public.

Longer in the wheelbase by a foot, as originally designed by Towns, the new Lagonda had a roof-line which fitted the car exactly, without looking as though it had been pulled and stretched out of proportion to make a short wheelbase car into a long wheelbase one. Of course, that was because it was designed as a long wheelbase one in the first place, and so the roof-line was exactly right for the car. It *looked* as if it was designed that way precisely because it *was* designed that way. If you have any doubts about how difficult it might be to design the extended roof-line of a 'stretched' car, then try extending the line of your favourite two-seater, and

'Lagonda' was now, for the time being, a model name of Aston Martin rather than a make of car in its own right. This was the Aston Martin Lagonda built for 'DB', which demonstrated very clearly William Towns' philosophy of designing the long version of a car before the short.

you'll realize that the Towns principle of 'design the long wheelbase first' is exactly the right way. If you still have doubts, look at the stretched Jaguar 'E' Type 2+2.

Given that the roof-line is so important to the appearance of a four-door version of any two-door car (which is how the market place saw this one), the rest of the design was

The V-12 variant of the E-Type Jaguar, on the other hand, shows a car which was stretched from its original design to make more room in the back.

almost certain to fall into place, though the other aspect essential to the right 'look' is the size and outline of the doors. Being an interior designer, too, meant that William Towns had the measure of this challenge, and the doors looked the part and were sufficiently well proportioned to allow easy entry into and exit from the car.

This new model was actually called an Aston Martin Lagonda, which implied that it was an Aston Martin car with the model name 'Lagonda'. It had a Lagonda badge with 'Aston Martin' added to it, but did become known and recognized as a Lagonda – thoroughly confusing to the casual observer. This 'Chairman's carriage' had an overall length of 15ft 10¾in (4.8m) and a width of 6ft (1.8m) (the same width as the DBS). It was a large car and a heavy one, too, weighing in at 4,400 pounds (1,996kg) – almost two tons. The prototype, for that is what it ultimately proved to be, inherited the DBS wire wheels, was finished in 'cosmic fire-finish' paintwork and was, in every respect, a true luxury high-speed saloon. In fact, it was one of the fastest four-door cars around, but for five further years, LPP 5G was the only one.

THE ASTON MARTIN 'LAGONDA' GOES INTO PRODUCTION

They say that all good things come to an end, and for Aston Martin Lagonda Limited, the 'good thing' of Sir David Brown's tenure of office as chairman was to end on 16 February 1972, when the company was handed over to William Willson's Company Developments Limited. There had been good times, like winning the Le Mans 24 Hours Race and the World Sports Car Championship in 1959, and there had been downright tough times, like when £1,000 had to be lopped off the price of DB6s in 1969 in order to keep them selling, but the company had enjoyed a certain stability from having a single owner for longer than ever before – some twenty-five years in fact.

Two years after Company Developments took over Aston Martin Lagonda Limited, the four-door DBS–V8-styled Lagonda was listed as a model for sale in the product range. William Towns had already been brought back to revamp the DBS–V8 and the Vantage Saloon, the letters 'DB' no longer

The softer line of the post-David Brown cars had nothing to do with the arrival of Company Developments on the scene, for William Towns had already created the 'production' variant of the Aston Martin Lagonda Saloon.

Aston Martin DBS-V8 Saloon – 1970–1972

Vehicle construction

Steel box-section chassis with steel superstructure and aluminium bodywork

Engine

Crankcase/cylinder block material	Aluminium alloy
Cylinder head material	Aluminium alloy, twin-plug
Number of cylinders	8 in 90° V-formation, wet liners
Cooling system	Water – pump, thermostat and viscous-coupling fan
Bore and stroke	100mm × 85mm
Engine capacity	5,340cc
Number of main bearings	Five
Valve gear and operation	Two chain-driven overhead camshafts per cylinder bank; two valves per cylinder
Fuel supply method and type	Twin SU electric pumps and Bosch fuel injection system
Quoted maximum power output	310–320bhp @ 5,000rpm
Quoted maximum torque output	360lb/ft

Transmission

Clutch type and operation	Single 10¼in plate, hydraulically actuated on manual and multi-plate torque converter on automatic
Gearbox ratios	Manual: 10.27, 6.3, 4.32, 3.54, 2.99:1 (reverse 9.31:1); auto: 8.16, 4.83, 3.33:1 (reverse 7.33:1)
Final drive ratio	Manual: 3.54:1; Auto: 3.33:1

Suspension and steering

Front suspension	Independent – double wishbones, anti-roll bar and Koni shock absorbers
Rear suspension	De Dion, twin radius rods, Watts linkage, coil springs and lever-arm shock absorbers
Steering type	Adwest power-assisted rack and pinion
Wheel type and size	Cast alloy ventilated 7in × 15in
Tyre size and rating	Pirelli GR70VR × 15in
Brakes: type and actuation	Vented discs all round – 10¾in front, 10.38in rear, with split-circuit hydraulic system

Vehicle Dimensions

Overall Length	15ft 0½in (4,585mm)
Overall Width	6ft 0in (1,829mm)
Wheelbase	8ft 6¾in (2,610mm)
Track (front and rear)	4ft 11in (1,499mm)
Overall height	4ft 4¼in (1,327mm)

being used to prefix model types. Thus, the nose restyling he had done on the Aston Martins was applied to the Lagonda, except that the radiator grille shape was different in not having the 'fluted' ends of the AM–V8. Instead, it had a simple shallow arched curve across the top of the grille, a straight horizontal line across the bottom and a horseshoe-shaped Lagonda grille (much like the shape of the DB4-based Rapide grille) set in the centre.

Quite what William Willson expected of this car is not clear now, but it certainly was not destined to sell in large numbers, not least because it was announced in 1974, in the wake of Britain's three-day week and the greatest Middle-East oil crisis in history (at that time). Willson may possibly have seen Rolls-Royce's market as the target for this car, vying with the Silver Shadow (or the Bentley 'T' Series?), the Iso Rivolta Fidia and the Monteverdi for sales.

There were others in this market place, such as the Monica, a French-inspired car developed by Chris Lawrence (of Lawrence-tune fame), which had started its career using the Martin V-8 engine originally destined for Formula 1 Grand Prix use (then overshadowed by the Cosworth Ford DFV, but supplanted by the ubiquitous Chrysler engine. Then there was the Maserati Quattroporte, which simply didn't seem to have the appeal, because to many it seemed somehow out of character with everything else Maserati.

Inside, the Lagonda model was typically Aston Martin, with plush leather seating, a centre console for the rear-seat passengers, air-conditioning, headlamp wash/wipe and a stereo radio/cassette player with recording facility. Top speed remained in the area of 160mph (258kph) and the price tag, taxes paid, was just over £14,000, which put it very firmly in the Bentley 'T' league,

---

Aston Martin Lagonda V8 Saloon – 1974–1976

Vehicle construction
Steel box-section chassis with steel superstructure and aluminium bodywork

Engine

Crankcase/cylinder block material	Aluminium alloy
Cylinder head material	Aluminium alloy, twin-plug
Number of cylinders	8 in 90° V-formation, wet liners
Cooling system	Water – pump, thermostat and viscous-coupling fan
Bore and stroke	100mm × 85mm
Engine capacity	5,340cc
Number of main bearings	Five
Valve gear and operation	Two chain-driven overhead camshafts per cylinder bank; two valves per cylinder
Fuel supply method and type	Twin SU electric pumps and Bosch fuel injection system
Quoted maximum power output	310–320bhp @ 5,000rpm
Quoted maximum torque output	320lb/ft

Transmission

Clutch type and operation	Multi-plate torque convertor on Chrysler Torqueflite automatic (single 10¼in plate, hydraulically actuated on manual)
Gearbox ratios	Torqueflite 7.52, 4.45, 3.07:1 (reverse 6.75:1)
Final drive ratio	3.07:1

Suspension and steering

Front suspension	Independent – double wishbones, anti-roll bar and Koni shock absorbers
Rear suspension	De Dion, twin radius rods, Watts linkage, coil springs and lever-arm shock absorbers
Steering type	Adwest power-assisted rack and pinion
Wheel type and size	Cast alloy ventilated 7in × 15in
Tyre size and rating	Pirelli GR70VR × 15in
Brakes: type and actuation	Vented discs all round – 10¾in front, 10.38in rear, with split-circuit hydraulic system

Vehicle Dimensions

Overall Length	16ft 2in (4,928mm)
Overall Width	6ft 0in (1,829mm)
Wheelbase	9ft 6¾in (2,915mm)
Track (front and rear)	4ft 11in (1,499mm)
Overall height	4ft 5¼in (1,353mm)

The profile of the 'production' Aston Martin Lagonda shows it to be an extremely well-proportioned car, belying its size.

whether its makers wanted it to be there or not. The Ferrari 365GT 2+2 came in at just under £13,000 for a very elegant, but a lot 'less', car. The Bristol 411 was priced at just under £8,000, the Jensen at nearer £9,000, but both were also a lot less car than the Lagonda, being closer comparisons, as two-door cars, with the Aston Martin V-8.

The first of these new Lagondas was registered SWW 6. With Chairman Willson's initials being 'S.W.', it doesn't take much effort to guess whose that car was! However, as can often happen, it was a car outside its best time, and so it didn't sell as the company expected. In fact, it was even more of an intrusion into production time and space

than the early sixties' Rapide, for only seven were built, two of which had manual transmissions – ZF 5-speed gearboxes instead of Torqueflite automatics.

Over the car's official life of almost exactly two years, the price went up by over £3,000, and number seven of the series (L/12007/RCAC) left the factory in July 1976, SWW6 having been released from production in July 1974. That was not the end of the Lagonda story by far, however, for Mr Towns had been retained yet again, to produce a reincarnation of this car, clothed in a far more exciting body which better fitted the times.

4 Post David Brown – The New V-8

Project MP231 was the programme to update the DBS, instigated as the result of wind-tunnel exercises conducted by William Towns. His aim had been to reduce the lift generated by the car's nose at high speed and so improve its road-going stability. This work was well advanced by the time that Company Developments Limited took over the assets of Aston Martin Lagonda Limited, and contrary to the popular view among the uninitiated, the newly shaped car was almost ready for production as Sir David Brown relinquished control.

'DBS' BECOMES 'V-8'

Almost as though the philosophy of the new management was to be 'The King is Dead – Long Live the King', William Willson decreed that the prefix 'DB' would no longer be used to identify any Aston Martin model in the future. The introduction of the revised DBS body lines into production was the perfect opportunity for designations to be changed with the minimum of fuss or public reaction. Willson was heard to say in public that he believed the company's previous difficulties had arisen from too much enthusiasm and not enough finance, so he clearly had little heart for the sentiment of loyalty which would have caused the continuation of the 'DB' prefix.

Half of Willson's argument was, of course, correct, for Aston Martin Lagonda Limited had run short of finance, simply because of

the stretched position of the whole David Brown Corporation at that time. On the other hand, the comment about too much enthusiasm was entirely out of place. The disposal of this company in favour of others in the David Brown Group was decided upon because it was felt that it could sell its way out of its predicament, given the proper level of investment. However, that sales potential was heavily dependent upon the very kind of enthusiasm which was in abundance at Aston Martin Lagonda, to perpetuate the high standards of craftsmanship for which its products were renowned.

Philosophies apart, the new Aston Martin V-8 was released upon the world in May 1972. Its front end displayed the immediately most obvious styling change. The radiator grille was now slightly recessed into a softer, more rounded front which looked instantly more attractive than its immediate predecessor. The grille was so designed to recall a glorious past, taking a radiator shape similar to that of the DB3S and incorporating it into this production saloon. Gone were the four headlamps with their bright metal surrounds, to be replaced by two 7in (18cm) quartz iodine lamps positioned either side of, but separate from, the stylish new grille. The whole front end of the new V-8 gave the car a softer, instantly appealing, appearance.

Under the skin of this new model came more changes. Inside the body, sound deadening and heat insulation were improved from the DBS, whilst air-conditioning was

The new Aston Martin V-8 (The 'DB' prefix was now dropped), the basic styling of which was to endure for almost twenty years.

now to be a standard feature. The classic woodrim steering wheel was replaced with one of similar diameter, but with a thicker rim and bound in leather. In the engine compartment, the induction boxes were modified, though the Bosch fuel injection system was retained, for the time being, at least. However, a combination of power and legislation needs caused AML engineers to concentrate a lot of attention on the induction

Rear view of the AM V-8 – the view exhibited to most people on the road – was as elegant and businesslike as the front end.

Aston Martin V8 Saloon – 1972–1973

Vehicle construction

Steel box-section chassis with steel superstructure and aluminium bodywork

Engine

Crankcase/cylinder block material	Aluminium alloy
Cylinder head material	Aluminium alloy, twin-plug
Number of cylinders	8 in 90° V-formation, wet liners
Cooling system	Water – pump, thermostat and viscous-coupling fan
Bore and stroke	100mm × 85mm
Engine capacity	5,340cc
Number of main bearings	Five
Valve gear and operation	Two chain-driven overhead camshafts per cylinder bank; two valves per cylinder
Fuel supply method and type	Twin SU electric pumps and Bosch fuel injection system
Quoted maximum power output	310–320bhp @ 5,000rpm
Quoted maximum torque output	360lb/ft

Transmission

Clutch type and operation	Single 10¼in plate, hydraulically actuated on manual and multi-plate torque converter on automatic
Gearbox ratios	Manual: 9.66, 5.93, 4.06, 3.33, 2.83:1 (reverse 8.78:1); auto: 7.05, 4.20, 2.88:1 (reverse 6.34:1)
Final drive ratio	Manual: 3.33:1; auto: 2.88:1

Suspension and steering

Front suspension	Independent – double wishbones, anti-roll bar and Koni shock absorbers
Rear suspension	De Dion, twin radius rods, Watts linkage, coil springs and lever-arm shock absorbers
Steering type	Adwest power-assisted rack and pinion
Wheel type and size	Cast alloy ventilated 7in × 15in
Tyre size and rating	Pirelli GR70VR × 15in
Brakes: type and actuation	Vented discs all round – 10¾in front, 10.38in rear, with split-circuit hydraulic system

Vehicle Dimensions

Overall Length	15ft 3in (4,648mm)
Overall Width	6ft 0in (1,829mm)
Wheelbase	8ft 6¾in (2,610mm)
Track (front and rear)	4ft 11in (1,499mm)
Overall height	4ft 4¼in (1,327mm)

---

system at this time, with the result that a further series of revisions were to be incorporated into the car from August 1973.

NEXT STEP IN THE V-8's DEVELOPMENT

It has never been the habit of Aston Martin Lagonda Limited to describe a specification revision as a new series of car, since its policy is one of continuous improvement of any given model until it is discontinued. Because it is convenient to group together a number of improvements for the ease of manufacture, there is a temptation to view a specification revision as a new series. Therefore, some bodies, including the Aston Martin Owners' Club, have resorted to labelling cars as series for ease of identification, one specification from another. As a consequence, various cars are referred to as series,

The deeper air scoop on the bonnet of the third version of V-8 is clear to see in this front quarter view of a so-called 'Series 3' car. (Inset: the interior of an automatic V-8.)

the first revision having become known as the Series 2 V-8.

Chassis number V8/11002/RCA saw the so-called 'Series 3' V-8, with a larger 'power bulge' to conceal four Weber twin-choke carburettors, which for styling's sake extended to the rear end of the bonnet. The ventilation louvres positioned directly below the rear window on earlier models were replaced with a single horizontal lip, so eliminating a water trap. Other bodywork changes included improved seating and switches, a larger ashtray, further improved sound and heat insulation and electric door locking.

The mechanical benefits in what is now known as 'Series 3' cars included two new final drive ratios – 3.07:1 for automatic transmission and 3.54:1 for manual gearboxes, a performance improvement from the four-carburettor engine in torque and fuel consumption (the fuel consumption went up to 14–15mpg (18–20l/100km!) and a switch back to Avon tyres.

'SERIES 3' ON THE ROAD

Motor magazine road tested the new variant of the V-8, finding good and not-so-good things to say about it. For example, the tester found the clutch heavy on the ZF-gearboxed version he drove. He didn't think much of the illumination from the headlamps (a complaint often pointed at the car-maker, when in fact responsibility truly lies with the lampmaker), he thought the turning circle was too wide and didn't think much of the heating and ventilation controls.

The steering geometry had been one of the original design problems with the DBS, a factor which had much to do with the final width of the car. It must be remembered that there were problems of designing steering geometry round such a large front-mounted engine, with the exhaust manifolding adding to the clearance limitations, to say nothing of the greater tyre width than was used on the previous DB models.

Aston Martin V8 Saloon – 1973–1978

Vehicle construction
Steel box-section chassis with steel superstructure and aluminium bodywork

Engine

Crankcase/cylinder block material	Aluminium alloy
Cylinder head material	Aluminium alloy, twin-plug
Number of cylinders	8 in 90° V-formation, wet liners
Cooling system	Water – pump, thermostat and viscous-coupling fan
Bore and stroke	100mm × 85mm
Engine capacity	5,340cc
Number of main bearings	Five
Valve gear and operation	Two chain-driven overhead camshafts per cylinder bank; two valves per cylinder
Fuel supply method and type	Twin SU electric pumps and four Weber 42DCNF twin-choke carburettors
Quoted maximum power output	320bhp @ 5,000rpm (304bhp from 6/77)
Quoted maximum torque output	360lb/ft

Transmission

Clutch type and operation	Single 10¼in plate, hydraulically actuated on manual and multi-plate torque converter on automatic
Gearbox ratios	Manual: 9.66, 5.93, 4.06, 3.33, 2.83:1 (reverse 8.78:1); auto: 7.52, 4.45, 3.07:1 (reverse 6.75:1)
Final drive ratio	Manual: 3.33:1 (or 3.54); auto: 3.07:1

Suspension and steering

Front suspension	Independent – double wishbones, anti-roll bar and Koni shock absorbers
Rear suspension	De Dion, twin radius rods, Watts linkage, coil springs and lever-arm shock absorbers
Steering type	Adwest power-assisted rack and pinion
Wheel type and size	Cast alloy ventilated 7in × 15in
Tyre size and rating	Avon GR70VR × 15in
Brakes: type and actuation	Vented discs all round – 10¾in front, 10.38in rear, with split-circuit hydraulic system

Vehicle Dimensions

Overall Length	15ft 3¾in (4,667mm)
Overall Width	6ft 0in (1,829mm)
Wheelbase	8ft 6¾in (2,610mm)
Track (front and rear)	4ft 11in (1,499mm)
Overall height	4ft 4¼in (1,327mm)

Despite the criticisms, *Motor* found quite a few good things to say about this new variation of the V-8, too. Among them was the sparkling performance under both throttle and brakes. The tester found that the car could accelerate from as low an engine speed as 600rpm, with the clutch fully engaged, without 'kangarooing' and that, also with the clutch fully engaged, full throttle could be applied from around 1,300rpm without the previous tendency to 'dive', because the engine now didn't choke on the sudden influx of fuel/air mixture.

In the timed tests, 0–60mph was reached in a neck-jerking 5.7 seconds and the already seat-belt-snatching brakes were said to improve as they warmed up. However, as all these improvements were being heralded for the V-8, few people noticed the demise of the six-cylinder 'Vantage' (into which the DBS had developed), for as the 'Series 3' V-8 was announced, the Vantage was withdrawn.

The Aston Martin V8 Automatic and its Adversaries (1978)

Car and Model	Engine Type and Size	Gearbox	Max. Speed		Consumption		G.B. Price
			mph	kph	mpg	l/100km	
Aston Martin V-8 Automatic	5,340cc V-8 tohc per bank	3-Auto	145	233	11–15	19–26	£22,999 (1978)
Jaguar XJ-S	5,343cc V-12 tohc per bank	3-Auto	152	245	13–16	18–22	£15,149 (1978)
Mercedes-Benz 450SLC	4,990cc V-8 sohc per bank	3-Auto	140	225	12–18	16–24	£18,250 (1978)
Bristol 603 Coupé	5,898cc V-8 pushrod ohv	3-Auto	124	200	13–19	15–21	£29,984 (1978)
Maserati Kyalami	4,136cc V-8 tohc per bank	3-Auto	150	242	12–15	19–24	£23,975 (1978)
Ferrari 400 2+2	4,823cc V-12 tohc per bank	3-Auto	150	242	11–14	20–26	£25,500 (1978)
Porsche 928 2+2 Coupé	4,474cc V-8 sohc per bank	3-Auto	145	233	19–23	12–15	£19,499 (1978)

FRESH FINANCIAL AND POLITICAL PROBLEMS

By 1974, Aston Martin Lagonda Limited was once again encountering financial difficulties, Company Developments Limited seemingly being unable to provide the essential recapitalization from its own resources. As a result, an application for government support, under the terms of the then-recent Industries Act (an act brought in by the Labour government of the day to create financial support for deserving but ailing British businesses), was submitted to the Secretary of State for Trade and Industry.

Hardly surprisingly, with a socialist government and a left-wing Secretary of Trade and Industry, the loan application was twice rejected. One supposes there must have been rumblings in the corridors of power about the merits of subsidizing a manufacturer of such symbols of capitalism as Aston Martin Lagonda Limited. Even William Willson's contacts within government circles were of little value to him in this case, for the government wasn't listening, despite the export potential of the Newport Pagnell company.

Sadly, as a consequence of the government's intransigence, the company was forced into receivership in December 1974, with the loss of production and many jobs. It was to be June 1975 before the receiver was able to complete the sale of the business to the partnership of two Aston Martin Owners' Club members in North America. One was American Peter Sprague, and the other was Canadian car dealer George Minden.

These two put up just over a million pounds to buy the interests of the company and reform it as Aston Martin Lagonda (1975) Limited. It was about a further year before production resumed at a reasonable rate – six cars a week being 'reasonable' – by which time further modifications were seen to be needed to keep the car abreast of market needs. Thus was born the next variant, colloquially referred to as the 'Series 4' range of cars.

THE 'VANTAGE' NAME REVIVED

Before the fourth generation of the V-8 was announced to the public, a high-performance development of the previous version ('Series 3') was to revive the name 'Vantage', which had disappeared with the demise of the six-cylinder car of that name. This new car was to be based on the third series car and would be known as the V-8 Vantage. It was first revealed in February 1977, going into production the following month.

The original V-8 Vantage with the tacked-on rear spoiler and deep front air dam. These features, combined with the blanked-off radiator grille, were the immediate recognition points of the Vantage.

After all the early design and development problems encountered with this engine at its inception, particularly in the days when it was being used in the Lola-Aston Martin, it is interesting to reflect that a decade later the engine was considered to be so reliable as to merit 'tweaking' to extract more power amd justify a 'Vantage' variation in the tradition and spirit of earlier 'Vantage' six-cylinder DB Aston Martins.

With revised camshaft profiles, larger inlet valves, different spark plugs, bigger carburettors, new inlet manifolding and a new air box, the V-8 Vantage was said to provide a 40 per cent power increase and some 10 per cent extra torque over its lower-powered sibling. It has been said that the V-8 Vantage engine was capable of giving 432bhp, so substantiating the claimed 40 per cent power hike. However significant the power claims were in theory, the fact was that the Vantage engine was clearly capable of propelling the car into which it was installed at 170mph (274kph).

On the outside, this high-performance projectile acquired a number of appearance changes from the normal V-8. Firstly, there was a deep front air dam positioned under

The Aston Martin V8 Vantage and its Adversaries (1979)

Car and Model	Engine Type and Size	Gearbox	Max. Speed		Consumption		G.B. Price
			mph	kph	mpg	l/100km	
Aston Martin V-8 Vantage Saloon	5,340cc V-8 tohc per bank	5-speed	165	266	11–15	19–26	£29,000 (1979)
Ferrari 400	4,823cc V-12 tohc per bank	5-speed	150	242	11–14	20–26	£25,500 (1979)
De Tomaso Longchamp Convertible	5,736cc V-8 pushrod	5-speed	152	245	11–16	18–26	£37,600 (1979)
Jaguar XJ-S	5,343cc V-12 tohc per bank	4-speed	152	245	13–16	18–22	£15,200 (1979)
Bristol 603 S	5,898cc V-8 pushrod ohv	3-Auto	124	200	11–15	19–26	£29,985 (1979)
Maserati Khamsin 2+2	4,930cc V-8 sohc per bank	5-speed	155	250	14–18	16–20	£23,975 (1979)
Porsche 928	4,474cc V-8 sohc per bank	5-speed	145	233	19–23	12–15	£19,500 (1979)

Aston Martin V8 Volante Drophead – 1978–1986

Vehicle construction

Steel box-section chassis with steel superstructure and aluminium bodywork; power-operated hood

Engine

Crankcase/cylinder block material	Aluminium alloy
Cylinder head material	Aluminium alloy, twin-plug
Number of cylinders	8 in 90° V-formation, wet liners
Cooling system	Water – pump, thermostat and viscous-coupling fan
Bore and stroke	100mm × 85mm
Engine capacity	5,340cc
Number of main bearings	Five
Valve gear and operation	Two chain-driven overhead camshafts per cylinder bank; two valves per cylinder
Fuel supply method and type	Twin SU electric pumps and four Weber 42DCNF twin-choke carburettors
Quoted maximum power output	304bhp @ 5,500rpm
Quoted maximum torque output	320lb/ft

Transmission

Clutch type and operation	Single 10½in plate, hydraulically actuated on manual and multi-plate torque converter on automatic
Gearbox ratios	Manual: 9.66, 5.93, 4.06, 3.33, 2.83:1 (reverse 8.78:1); auto: 7.49, 4.43, 3.058:1 (reverse 6.73:1)
Final drive ratio	Manual: 3.33:1 (or 3.54); auto: 3.058:1

Suspension and steering

Front suspension	Independent – double wishbones, anti-roll bar and Koni shock absorbers
Rear suspension	De Dion, twin radius rods, Watts linkage, coil springs and lever-arm shock absorbers
Steering type	Power-assisted rack and pinion
Wheel type and size	Cast alloy ventilated 7J × 15in
Tyre size and rating	Avon GR70VR × 15in
Brakes: type and actuation	Vented discs all round – 10¾in front, 10.38in rear, with split-circuit hydraulic system

Vehicle Dimensions

Overall Length	15ft 4in (4,674mm)
Overall Width	6ft 0in (1,829mm)
Wheelbase	8ft 6¾in (2,610mm)
Track (front and rear)	4ft 11in (1,499mm)
Overall height	4ft 6in (1,372mm) (with hood raised)

the bumper; then the air scoop on the bonnet was closed off to give a cleaner air flow over the top of the car. The radiator grille was blanked off, so that cool air required through the radiator and into the induction air boxes would be drawn in under the front bumper. At the rear, a spoiler was added on to the boot lid to improve down-force there.

Other modifications which identified the Vantage from its peers included perspex headlamp covers – a feature frowned upon in the United States – and 255/60 ratio Pirelli tyres. Out of view were the Koni shock absorbers which stiffened up the suspension to match the improvement in performance. That improvement meant that the Vantage bettered the already startling 0–60mph time to an even more awesome 5.3 seconds, whilst it took a further 7.6 seconds to reach the magic 100mph.

This front-end view of the second variant of Vantage shows the blanked-off radiator grille with inset spot lamps.

David Morgan and Ray Mallock drove this Vantage, the first with an integral rear spoiler, at the Aston Martin Owners' Club St. John Horsfall meeting at Silverstone.

Aston Martin V8 Saloon – 1978–1986

Vehicle construction

Steel box-section chassis with steel superstructure and aluminium bodywork

Engine

Crankcase/cylinder block material	Aluminium alloy
Cylinder head material	Aluminium alloy, twin-plug
Number of cylinders	8 in 90° V-formation, wet liners
Cooling system	Water – pump, thermostat and viscous-coupling fan
Bore and stroke	100mm × 85mm
Engine capacity	5,340cc
Number of main bearings	Five
Valve gear and operation	Two chain-driven overhead camshafts per cylinder bank; two valves per cylinder
Fuel supply method and type	Twin SU electric pumps and four Weber 42DCNF twin-choke carburettors
Quoted maximum power output	304bhp @ 5,500rpm
Quoted maximum torque output	320lb/ft

Transmission

Clutch type and operation	Single 10½in plate, hydraulically actuated on manual and multi-plate torque converter on automatic
Gearbox ratios	Manual: 9.66, 5.93, 4.06, 3.33, 2.83:1 (reverse 8.78:1); auto: 7.49, 4.43, 3.058:1 (reverse 6.73:1)
Final drive ratio	Manual: 3.33:1 (or 3.54); auto: 3.058:1

Suspension and steering

Front suspension	Independent – double wishbones, anti-roll bar and Koni shock absorbers
Rear suspension	De Dion, twin radius rods, Watts linkage, coil springs and lever-arm shock absorbers
Steering type	Power-assisted rack and pinion
Wheel type and size	Cast alloy ventilated 7J × 15in
Tyre size and rating	Avon GR70VR × 15in
Brakes: type and actuation	Vented discs all round – 10¾in front, 10.38in rear, with split-circuit hydraulic system

Vehicle Dimensions

Overall Length	15ft 4in (4,674mm)
Overall Width	6ft 0in (1,829mm)
Wheelbase	8ft 6¾in (2,610mm)
Track (front and rear)	4ft 11in (1,499mm)
Overall height	4ft 4¼in (1,327mm)

ARRIVAL OF THE 'OSCAR INDIA' SERIES

The description 'Oscar India' was applied to the fourth generation of the V-8 Saloon though the letters are not used in the chassis numbers, nor was the term used officially. The label 'Oscar India', used to identify this latest fourth version of the V-8 internally within the factory, is credited to the enthusiasm for aviation of managing director, Alan Curtis, but in fact 'OI' actually denotes October 1st, the date the car was due for completion.

The first car in the new form was V8SOR/12032, the most obvious visible change being the integral rear spoiler brought over from the Vantage. There were several changes on the inside of the car, too. For example, wood veneer was introduced for the dashboard and the door cappings, which was a feature introduced on the Vantage a

Alan Curtis

Alan Curtis's introduction to Aston Martin came in 1971, through his then-fifteen-year-old son Paul's enthusiasm for the breed. As a birthday present to his son, Curtis bought himself a DBS-V8, then bought a new V-8 each year after that. One day in 1974, his attention was drawn to the company's collapse. After continuous pressure from young Paul to take an interest in the salvation of Aston Martin Lagonda Limited, he took steps to find out more. He learned that Peter Sprague and George Minden had secured the company, but that they wanted an English partner in order to retain the English nature of the business.

Coming from the property business, Alan Curtis's only motor industry asset was his enthusiasm and general management prowess, but that proved enough, and the company was reformed with four share-holders: Peter Sprague, George Minden, Alan Curtis and Denis Flather. In 1976, Curtis had a major hand in the creation of the most adventurous project to date – the razor-edged Lagonda V-8. This was the magnificent car designed by William Towns and engineered by Mike Loasby and his team. It was Alan Curtis, too, who was behind the creation of the Bulldog, another vehicle laden with electronic wizardry. Appointed chief executive early in 1977, he was to sponsor the creation of the V-8 Volante and the expansion of Aston Martin's U.S. market.

A keen aviator, Alan Curtis was to choose the name 'Bulldog' for that promotional vehicle, but the achievements for which he will perhaps best be remembered as Aston Martin Lagonda chief is his ever-expanding affection for the product and his realization of profit status for a company that was thought by many in the industry as never destined to make money.

year earlier. The headlining was now of leather, rather than cloth, and the seats were improved and fitted with a new design of head restraint. A new centre console was fitted between the front seats, and the air-conditioning was sustantially improved. Finally, the air scoop on the bonnet had disappeared, giving the car a smoother line, though a slight 'power bulge' remained, because it was not possible to reduce the carburettor height sufficiently to eliminate it.

By 1980, it was decided to make a few mechanical changes to the V-8. Polynomal camshaft profiles actuated 'Tuftrided' valves, which had larger and dished heads, whilst the smaller cylinder head porting of the Vantage engine was now made standard to all Aston Martin Lagonda power units. Barrel-shaped pistons were adopted and the compression ratio was increased in the standard engine to 9.3:1, whilst it was reduced from 9.5:1 on the Vantage engine to the same 9.3:1 ratio, making it standard except for cars which went to North America, where U.S. market engines had a much lower compression of 8:1, reduced from 8.5 to meet the ever-tightening emission legislation.

As time had improved the Aston Martin V-8, so other cars had improved and developed, too, with the consequence that a number were thought to be nearer to the Aston Martin in specification, performance and finish than ever before. That may have been true, but a quick comparison of the leading pretenders soon dispels the myth that they might topple the Aston Martin from its lofty pedestal.

The principal British challenger was the Bristol 412, which, by 1978, was 20 per cent more expensive and powered by an American volume-produced engine. The Jaguar XJ-S, the Ferrari 400GT and the Porsche 928 were really the only other true challengers, though there were odd one-offs and very small producers of cars that might have

The fourth variant of the V-8 became known as the 'Oscar India' series. ('October 1' abbreviated to 'O1' and written 'OI' became 'Oscar India' in aviation language. Alan Curtis, being a keen aviator, caused it to stick.)

challenged the Newport Pagnell car's supremacy in its market if they had been in serious production, but they were not and so the competition was limited.

THE MAIN CHALLENGERS

The Bristol 412 was of similar dimensions to

The supreme Grand Touring saloon? Perhaps surprisingly, the only true challenger in terms of space and performance was the Porsche 928, a car never conceived to take on anything from Newport Pagnell and built in a totally different way. This view of the V-8 epitomizes the modern English sporting saloon.

The Jaguar XJ-S continued to be the only British alternative to Aston Martin's V-8, but by being a volume-produced car, panelled in steel, it was no competitor.

the Aston Martin V-8, though a much less elegant looking car, being rather 'boxy' in design. It did have more leg-room in both front and rear, though surprisingly, in view of its less flowing shape, it had less headroom. The car was longer and narrower than the V-8, yet still looked squat and chunky. The interior of the car was the only area where it could readily be said that the Bristol was comparable with the Aston Martin, and whilst its performance was quite exciting, it was no match for the V-8.

Ferrari's 400GT was clearly a contender in the performance stakes, with a claimed higher top speed than the Aston Martin, on a litre less engine capacity. However, like most Ferraris, it was barely a four-seater and it was arguable whether the Italian car had quite the tractability or refinement of handling. Certainly, the finish of the Maranello car was now fast approaching that of its better-equipped competitors, but the charisma of that name continued to be the main motivation for its buyers, who might buy a Ferrari for its reputation above all else.

Jaguar's XJ-S continued to be the only British car which came anywhere near the Aston Martin V-8 in terms of performance and engine size. Its interior was well

finished, but not up to the standard of the Aston Martin, and it had a volume-produced V-12 engine of similar capacity to the Newport Pagnell car's V-8. The Jaguar's performance fell short of the V-8, in both top speed and road holding, but it would probably be unfair to call it a 'pretender' to the Aston Martin's 'throne' since Jaguar never sought to offer products in direct competition. The XJ-S had an all-steel pressed body, whereas the Aston Martin was of hand-crafted aluminium panelling on a steel floor-pan. The Jaguar was a volume-manufactured line-production car, whereas the Aston Martin was a very small production hand-built car. However, it is an inescapable fact that many people who bought the Jaguar XJ-S (for a lot less money than they would have paid for an Aston Martin), were those who would aspire to an Aston Martin if they could afford it.

Last in this comparison is the German Porsche 928, which, emerging into the 1980s, was powered by a 4.7-litre V-8 engine. The 928 was, and remains at the time of writing, Stuttgart's flagship. Of totally different styling (almost in the category of modern 'jelly-mould' car body styling), the 928 was a highly efficient aerodynamic tool endowed with outstanding road

Porsche's 928 had slightly more rear leg-room than the Aston Martin and a very similar performance, but was also steel-bodied and was intended to be a successor to Zuffenhausen's immortal 911.

holding and a performance envelope which came very close to that of the Aston Martin V-8. Once again, it was a car whose manufacturer did not pitch it directly against the Aston Martin as a competitor, but comparisons are inevitable in view of the Porsche's unsolicited label as 'the attainable supercar'.

Like the Jaguar, the Porsche had a steel body and its trim did not match that of the Aston Martin, but at £3,500 less than the price tag of the Aston V-8, it came awfully close to being an alternative, without ever seeking to 'take on' the Aston head-on. The Porsche was a volume-produced car with a truly sparkling performance. It fell short of the Aston Martin's top speed, but its sure-footed handling and race-bred responses made sure it was a car that was noticed. However, despite it having very similar overall dimensions to the Aston Martin, it did not enjoy quite the same interior space, being a little tight in the rear. In the final analysis, Newport Pagnell's most famous product continued to stand quite alone in the world of superb motoring.

A NEW VANTAGE

As a consequence of the fourth series V-8's introduction, a revised Vantage was announced, and the integral rear spoiler of the production car became a characteristic of both models, though the blanked-off radiator grille and front air dam remained a Vantage exclusive. All the interior features of the standard V-8 also became common between the two models. Chassis numbering of the Vantage was identified by the second 'V' appearing in the number sequence. For example, the first of the new Series 2 Vantage cars (as it has become known) was numbered V8VOR-12040.

There were few specification changes in the Vantage, only those body and interior modifications which brought the standard V-8 and Vantage together. The four twin-choke downdraught Weber 48DNF carburettors remained, and the compression ratio of the engine was reduced to make a standard through all non-U.S. market V-8 engines. Of course, the other engine improvements

Aston Martin V8 Vantage Saloon – 1977–1986

Vehicle construction

Steel box-section chassis with steel superstructure and aluminium bodywork

Engine

Crankcase/cylinder block material	Aluminium alloy
Cylinder head material	Aluminium alloy, twin-plug
Number of cylinders	8 in 90° V-formation, wet liners
Cooling system	Water – pump, thermostat and viscous-coupling fan
Bore and stroke	100mm × 85mm
Engine capacity	5,340cc
Number of main bearings	Five
Valve gear and operation	Two chain-driven overhead camshafts per cylinder bank; two valves per cylinder
Fuel supply method and type	Twin SU electric pumps and four Weber 48IDF/3 twin-choke carburettors
Quoted maximum power output	380bhp @ 6,000rpm
Quoted maximum torque output	380lb/ft at 4,000rpm

Transmission

Clutch type and operation	Single 10½in plate, hydraulically actuated on manual and multi-plate torque converter on automatic
Gearbox ratios	Manual: 10.27, 6.30, 4.32, 3.54, 3.01:1 (reverse 9.33:1)
Final drive ratio	Manual transmission only: 3.54:1

Suspension and steering

Front suspension	Independent – double wishbones, anti-roll bar and Koni shock absorbers
Rear suspension	De Dion, twin radius rods, Watts linkage, coil springs and lever-arm shock absorbers
Steering type	Power-assisted rack and pinion
Wheel type and size	Cast alloy ventilated 7in × 15in
Tyre size and rating	Pirelli CN12 255/60VR × 15in
Brakes: type and actuation	Vented discs all round – 10¾in front, 10.38in rear, with split-circuit hydraulic system

Vehicle Dimensions

Overall Length	15ft 4in (4,674mm)
Overall Width	6ft 0in (1,829mm)
Wheelbase	8ft 6¾in (2,610mm)
Track (front and rear)	4ft 11⅓in (1,507mm)
Overall height	4ft 4¼in (1,327mm)

affected the Vantage, too, and the consequence of these in a *Motor* road test seems to have been a further tenth of a second clipped from the 0–60mph time, bringing the recorded time to 5.2 seconds, whilst the 0–100mph figure came down to 11.9 seconds. That was in 1981, when the price of a Vantage had reached the best of £40,000, taxes paid.

With all of the styling modifications incorporated into both the V-8 Saloon and the Series 2 Vantage, the general specification of the Vantage remained the same, until after the introduction of the fifth specification (Series 5) V-8 Saloon, which came along in 1985. That new Vantage, however, now described as Series 3, did not appear until the Birmingham Motor Show in 1986, introduced for the 1987 Season.

The engine numbers issued for the Series

The smoother line of the revised Vantage ('Series 2' to many) did not detract from the impression of sheer power conveyed by the car. This is an automatic transmission Vantage.

2 Vantage (and the Series 4 V-8) changed in 1980, so that the prefix to the serial number changed from V/540, the '540' identifying the nominal engine size of 5.4-litres, to V/580. The '80' part of that prefix number represented the year of redesign of the engine –1980. V/580/2247/S was the first such numbered engine, which appeared in March 1980, fitted to Chassis Number V8SOR/12247. The first Vantage with the new-type engine number was V8VOR/12248, the engine number of which was V/580/2248/V.

SERIES 5 AND SERIES 3

This heading refers to the final so-called 'series' of both V-8 Saloon and Vantage, the last variation of the V-8 Saloon being disclosed in 1985, to be followed a year later by the final version of the Vantage V-8.

The gestation of the last version of the V-8 was preceded by an odd sequence of events. It began in 1983, when Peter Livanos – a member of the Greek shipping family of that name – bought a majority shareholding in

The Aston Martin V8 Saloon and its Adversaries (1982)

Car and Model	Engine Type and Size	Gearbox	Max. Speed		Consumption		G.B. Price
			mph	kph	mpg	l/100km	
Aston Martin V-8 Saloon	5,340cc V-8 tohc per bank	5-speed	150	242	11–15	19–26	£39,999 (1982)
Jaguar XJ-S HE Coupé	5,343cc V-12 tohc per bank	5-speed	120	193	13–16	18–22	£19,708 (1982)
Mercedes-Benz 500SEC	4,973cc V-8 sohc per bank	4-Auto	145	233	12–17	17–24	£28,700 (1982)
Bristol 603 Saloon	6,277cc V-8 pushrod ohv	3-Auto	140	225	12–18	16–24	£35,900 (1982)
Maserati Kyalami	4,136cc V-8 tohc per bank	5-speed	160	258	12–15	19–24	£37,000-est (1982)
Ferrari 400i 2+2	4,823cc V-12 tohc per bank	5-speed	162	261	9–18	16–31	£38,500 (1982)
Porsche 928S 2+2	4,664cc V-8 sohc	5-speed	156	251	14–29	10–20	£25,250 (1982)

The magnificent final version of the V-8 Vantage – the car known as 'Series 3' – one of the most powerful luxury sports cars of its day.

Aston Martin Lagonda Incorporated, the American arm of AML. At the same time, Victor Gauntlett had taken full-time management control of Aston Martin Lagonda Limited in Great Britain after the resignation of the previous managing director, Bill Archer. The share movements which took place after that resulted in the Papanicolaou family (also Greek shippers) buying the total holding of Pace Petroleum, of which Victor Gauntlett was previously majority shareholder, so acquiring a majority share in AML through a company called Automotive Investments Incorporated. Peter Livanos than bought out the Papanicolaou interest, so becoming a 75 per cent shareholder of AML, with Victor Gauntlett holding 25 per cent and chairmanship of the company.

Victor Gauntlett was now able to devote his whole management time to Aston Martin Lagonda Limited with a clear mind, and the model range was reviewed again in light of there being a little cash available for development. So came about the (still unofficially described) 'Series 5' Aston Martin V-8. The first public appearance of this fifth V-8 variant was at the New York Motor Show in January 1986. Its most significant specification

change was the reversion to fuel injection, though this time a Weber/Marelli system was chosen in preference to Bosch of the earlier fuel-injected second series model which replaced the original DBS-V8. This caused another revision of engine numbering, with the prefix now reading 'V/585' instead of 'V/580'. The new injection installation was an electronically controlled sequential system, and with it came a much flatter bonnet with no air scoop, though the slightly raised centre panel of the bonnet was retained for styling reasons as a continuation of the line from the radiator grille.

For the first time in a long time, the power output was quoted, now said to be 305bhp in standard form. Other feature details included the standard use of BBS 8in (20cm) alloy wheels, as on the previous version, and the length of the car increased by 3½in (9cm). It is interesting to note that the weight of the V-8 Saloon had, despite twenty years development, increased by a mere 210lb (95kg) since the introduction of the DBS-V8, and that was after the fitting of wider wheels, bigger tyres, heavier trim and air-conditioning.

The last of the V-8 Vantage versions was

Aston Martin V8 Saloon – 1986–1989

Vehicle construction

Steel box-section chassis with steel superstructure and aluminium bodywork

Engine

Crankcase/cylinder block material	Aluminium alloy
Cylinder head material	Aluminium alloy, twin-plug
Number of cylinders	8 in 90° V-formation, wet liners
Cooling system	Water – pump, thermostat and viscous-coupling fan
Bore and stroke	100mm × 85mm
Engine capacity	5,340cc
Number of main bearings	Five
Valve gear and operation	Two chain-driven overhead camshafts per cylinder bank; two valves per cylinder
Fuel supply method and type	Twin SU electric pumps and Weber-Marelli fuel injection
Quoted maximum power output	305bhp @ 5,000rpm
Quoted maximum torque output	320lb/ft

Transmission

Clutch type and operation	Single 10½in plate, hydraulically actuated on manual and multi-plate torque converter on automatic
Gearbox ratios	Manual: 9.66, 5.93, 4.06, 3.33, 2.83:1 (reverse 8.78:1); auto: 7.49, 4.43, 3.058:1 (reverse 6.73:1)
Final drive ratio	Manual: 3.33:1 (or 3.54); auto: 3.058:1

Suspension and steering

Front suspension	Independent – double wishbones, anti-roll bar and Koni shock absorbers
Rear suspension	De Dion, twin radius rods, Watts linkage, coil springs and lever-arm shock absorbers
Steering type	Power-assisted rack and pinion
Wheel type and size	Cast alloy ventilated 7J × 15in
Tyre size and rating	Avon GR70VR × 15in
Brakes: type and actuation	Vented discs all round – 10¾in front, 10.38in rear, with split-circuit hydraulic system

Vehicle Dimensions

Overall Length	15ft 4in (4,674mm)
Overall Width	6ft 0in (1,829mm)
Wheelbase	8ft 6¾in (2,610mm)
Track (front and rear)	4ft 11in (1,499mm)
Overall height	4ft 4¼in (1,327mm)

released to the public at the 1986 British Motor Show at the National Exhibition Centre in October. It now cost a little over £5,000 more than the V-8 Saloon, but brought with it an engine of much higher power output – 400bhp (with a further option of 432bhp for the stout-hearted). This higher output was achieved by the use of higher-lift camshafts, larger porting to the cylinder heads and a higher compression ratio, now up to 10.2:1.

The Series 3 Vantage had a slight 'power-bulge' on the bonnet, disturbing the smooth line of the Series 5 V-8 Saloon, and, of course, all the other features which distinguished a Vantage from a V-8. These included the front air dam and the blanked-off radiator grille into which was mounted a pair of spot lamps. The rear spoiler was now the same on both models, integrated into the line of the bodywork.

Aston Martin V8 Vantage Saloon – 1986–1989

Vehicle construction
Steel box-section chassis with steel superstructure and aluminium bodywork

Engine

Crankcase/cylinder block material	Aluminium alloy
Cylinder head material	Aluminium alloy, twin-plug
Number of cylinders	8 in 90° V-formation, wet liners
Cooling system	Water – pump, thermostat and viscous-coupling fan
Bore and stroke	100mm × 85mm
Engine capacity	5,340cc
Number of main bearings	Five
Valve gear and operation	Two chain-driven overhead camshafts per cylinder bank; two valves per cylinder
Fuel supply method and type	Twin SU electric pumps and four Weber 48IDF/3 twin-choke carburettors (optional 50IDA carburettors)
Quoted maximum power output	400bhp @ 6,000rpm (432bhp with 50IDA carburettor engine)
Quoted maximum torque output	380lb/ft @ 4,000rpm (395lb/ft @ 5,100rpm on 432bhp engine)

Transmission

Clutch type and operation	Single 10½in plate, hydraulically actuated on manual and multi-plate torque converter on automatic
Gearbox ratios	Manual: 10.27, 6.30, 4.32, 3.54, 3.01:1 (reverse 9.33:1);
Final drive ratio	Manual transmission only: 3.54:1

Suspension and steering

Front suspension	Independent – double wishbones, anti-roll bar and Koni shock absorbers
Rear suspension	De Dion, twin radius rods, Watts linkage, coil springs and lever-arm shock absorbers
Steering type	Power-assisted rack and pinion
Wheel type and size	BBS cast alloy 8in × 16in
Tyre size and rating	Goodyear Eagle 255/50VR × 16in
Brakes: type and actuation	Vented discs all round – 10¾in front, 10.38in rear, with split-circuit hydraulic system

Vehicle Dimensions

Overall Length	15ft 4in (4,674mm)
Overall Width	6ft 0in (1,829mm)
Wheelbase	8ft 6¾in (2,610mm)
Track (front and rear)	4ft 11⅓in (1,507mm)
Overall height	4ft 4¼in (1,327mm)

THE V-8 VOLANTE

Open cars of any kind suffered a decline in support for quite a number of years and by the late 1970s, there were very few built outside Great Britain, where open sports cars have always been part of the motoring tradition. With more and more Aston Martin users wanting an open version of the current model, a new drophead version of the V-8 was announced, to be called the 'Volante', a name first given to an open Aston Martin with the last few, short wheelbase, DB5 convertibles (thirty-seven to be precise).

First shown in June 1978, this new model, the V-8 Volante, received a very warm welcome, especially in the United States, where home-grown convertibles had become a thing of the past, partly due to Ralph

Nader's obsessive gnashing of teeth over vehicle safety, resulting in most American cars becoming all-enclosed centres of isolation. Market forces had driven up the prices of older Volantes, demonstrating that there was a demand, and so the company set about satisfying it.

Mechanical specifications of the Volante were in line with the then-current Series 4 V-8 Saloon. Aston Martin Lagonda published the same weights for the Volante as for the Saloon. That *may* not be coincidence because the reinforcement essential to the bodywork of a convertible to keep it hanging together could actually take the weight *above* that of a corresponding saloon, especially since the hood could well weigh in at more than that of a roof on a closed car.

Aston Martin V8 Volante Drophead – 1986–1989

Vehicle construction
Steel box-section chassis with steel superstructure and aluminium bodywork; power-operated hood

Engine

Crankcase/cylinder block material	Aluminium alloy
Cylinder head material	Aluminium alloy, twin-plug
Number of cylinders	8 in 90° V-formation, wet liners
Cooling system	Water – pump, thermostat and viscous-coupling fan
Bore and stroke	100mm × 85mm
Engine capacity	5,340cc
Number of main bearings	Five
Valve gear and operation	Two chain-driven overhead camshafts per cylinder bank; two valves per cylinder
Fuel supply method and type	Twin SU electric pumps and Weber-Marelli fuel injection
Quoted maximum power output	305bhp @ 5,000rpm
Quoted maximum torque output	320lb/ft

Transmission

Clutch type and operation	Single 10½in plate, hydraulically actuated on manual and multi-plate torque converter on automatic
Gearbox ratios	Manual: 9.66, 5.93, 4.06, 3.33, 2.83:1 (reverse 8.78:1); auto: 7.49, 4.43, 3.058:1 (reverse 6.73:1)
Final drive ratio	Manual: 3.33:1 (or 3.54); auto: 3.058:1

Suspension and steering

Front suspension	Independent – double wishbones, anti-roll bar and Koni shock absorbers
Rear suspension	De Dion, twin radius rods, Watts linkage, coil springs and lever-arm shock absorbers
Steering type	Power-assisted rack and pinion
Wheel type and size	Cast alloy ventilated 7J × 15in
Tyre size and rating	Avon GR70VR × 15in
Brakes: type and actuation	Vented discs all round – 10¾in front, 10.38in rear, with split-circuit hydraulic system

Vehicle Dimensions

Overall Length	15ft 4in (4,674mm)
Overall Width	6ft 0in (1,829mm)
Wheelbase	8ft 6¾in (2,610mm)
Track (front and rear)	4ft 11in (1,499mm)
Overall height	4ft 6in (1,372mm) (with hood raised)

The Aston Martin V8 Volante and its Adversaries (1986)

Car and Model	Engine Type and Size	Gearbox	Max. Speed		Consumption		G.B. Price
			mph	kph	mpg	l/100km	
Aston Martin V8 Volante Drophead	5,340cc V-8 tohc per bank	5-speed	135	217	12–15	19–24	£68,500 (1986)
Bentley Continental Convertible	6,750cc V-8 pushrod ohv	3-Auto	125	201	10–14	20–28	£89,940 (1986)
De Tomaso Longchamp Convertible	5,736cc V-8 pushrod	5-speed	152	245	11–16	18–26	£37,600 (1986)
Jaguar XJ-S HE Cabriolet	5,343cc V-12 tohc per bank	3-Auto	145	233	10–14	20–28	£33,600 (1986)
Bristol Beaufighter 412/S3	5,898cc V-8 pushrod ohv	3-Auto	140	225	11-15	19–26	£53,000 (1986)
Jensen Interceptor S4	5,898cc V-8 pushrod	3-Auto	140	225	10–16	18–28	£46,000 (1986)
Rolls-Royce Corniche	6,750cc V-8 pushrod ohv	3-Auto	125	201	10–14	20–28	£92,995 (1986)

Thus, it may be to Aston Martin Lagonda Limited's credit that it was able to maintain the weight, but it's just as likely that someone was looking for a figure to complete for the publication of a brochure and used what was available.

A Vantage version of the Volante came along in 1986, offering higher power for what should have been a lighter, and so brisker car (but unless we put one on a weighbridge, we'll never know). The Series 2 Vantage Volante appeared at the British Motor Show at the National Exhibition Centre, unveiled on 8 October. Whilst the Series 2 Volante used the same Weber/Marelli fuel-injection system as the Saloon, the Vantage

This is the prototype V-8 Volante (V8 COR/15001). It was first seen at the 1978 British Motor Show and was road tested by Motor *magazine on 3 March 1979.*

This is in fact a US-specification Volante with Vantage rear spoiler, but it shows the general profile of the model.

A brace of 1987 Volantes: (above) a French specification 'Series 2'; (below) a 'Series 2' Vantage.

Aston Martin V8 Vantage Volante Drophead – 1986–1989

Vehicle construction
Steel box-section chassis with steel superstructure and aluminium bodywork; power-operated hood

Engine
Crankcase/cylinder block material	Aluminium alloy
Cylinder head material	Aluminium alloy, twin-plug
Number of cylinders	8 in 90° V-formation, wet liners
Cooling system	Water – pump, thermostat and viscous-coupling fan
Bore and stroke	100mm × 85mm
Engine capacity	5,340cc
Number of main bearings	Five
Valve gear and operation	Two chain-driven overhead camshafts per cylinder bank; two valves per cylinder
Fuel supply method and type	Twin SU electric pumps and four Weber 48IDF/3 twin-choke carburettors (optional 50IDA carburettors)
Quoted maximum power output	400bhp @ 6,000rpm (432bhp with 50IDA carburettor engine)
Quoted maximum torque output	380lb/ft @ 4,000rpm (395lb/ft @ 5,100rpm on 432bhp engine)

Transmission
Clutch type and operation	Single 10½in plate, hydraulically actuated on manual and multi-plate torque converter on automatic
Gearbox ratios	Manual: 10.27, 6.30, 4.32, 3.54, 3.01:1 (reverse 9.33:1);
Final drive ratio	Manual transmission only: 3.54:1

Suspension and steering
Front suspension	Independent – double wishbones, anti-roll bar and Koni shock absorbers
Rear suspension	De Dion, twin radius rods, Watts linkage, coil springs and lever-arm shock absorbers
Steering type	Power-assisted rack and pinion
Wheel type and size	BBS cast alloy 8in × 16in
Tyre size and rating	Goodyear Eagle 255/50VR × 16in
Brakes: type and actuation	Vented discs all round – 10¾in front, 10.38in rear, with split-circuit hydraulic system

Vehicle Dimensions
Overall Length	15ft 4in (4,674mm)
Overall Width	6ft 0in (1,829mm)
Wheelbase	8ft 6¾in (2,610mm)
Track (front and rear)	4ft 11⅓in (1,507mm)
Overall height	4ft 6in (1,372mm) (with hood raised)

Volante reverted, as did the Vantage Saloon, to the use of carburettors for fuelling and helping to elevate the engine power output to either 400bhp or 432bhp.

Oddly, there was a small number of cars built to what became known as the 'PoW' specification. No, it wasn't highly secure, nor matt olive drab finish, nor did it have steel-framed webbing seats, barbed wire surrounds or searchlights! In fact, it was the 'Prince of Wales' specification. It appears that H.R.H. preferred a boot lid with no raised rear lip, a front end with no air dam and wheel arches with less pronounced flares. In keeping with the fashion, others decided they'd like the same thing, so a dozen or so were produced.

By 1988, of course, the next car in the line of Aston Martin V-8s was to be seen, in showrooms at least, so the V-8 was to cease

This publicity shot shows Volantes down the ages. From left to right the cars are: an early V-8 Volante, a DB6 Mk I, a short chassis (DB5), a DB6 Mk II and a final specification V-8 with impact bumpers. The car in front is, of course, a Zagato Volante.

production in 1989, after a life of nineteen years, including the DBS-V8. The Zagato had come into the range in 1986, with the Zagato Volante following a year later, but now the way was made clear for the next heir to the Aston Martin mantle – the magnificent Virage.

5 Enter the Towns Lagonda

It seems almost odd that it was felt essential to soften the razor-edged lines of the Aston Martin DBS-V8 with the introduction of the V-8 Saloon, when by total contrast after the initial foray into the market with the Aston Martin Lagonda of similar shape to the DBS-V8, the new square-shaped, razor-edged Lagonda V-8 Saloon appeared in 1976.

This car has become known as the 'Towns Lagonda' – a slightly silly soubriquet when one recalls that William Towns also designed the DBS-V8. Whilst this car had many features in common with its Aston Martin sibling, it truly was a 'state-of-the-art' motor car, with solid-state digital instrumentation instead of the more familiar analogue dials.

CREATING A DREAM

Before the first series of Aston Martin Lagonda reached production, William Towns was sitting at his drawing-board, working on the shape of his next creation to carry the Lagonda badge. His aim from the beginning was to create something of a 'dream car', but a practical dream car which represented all the luxury and charisma associated with the name Lagonda. Towns' principal partner in this new creation was Mike Loasby.

Mike Loasby designed the platform chassis of this new Lagonda, using – logically enough – the suspension and steering gear of the Aston Martin V-8. However, he decided that self-levelling rear dampers were essential, as this was likely to be the kind of car which would be chauffer driven, and so the variation in rear seat and luggage loads could be considerable. The engine was, of course, the now well-established Aston Martin V-8 power unit, an interesting reversal of history, in that the Lagonda LB6 engine had been the unit which powered the Aston Martin name back into the market place almost thirty years previously.

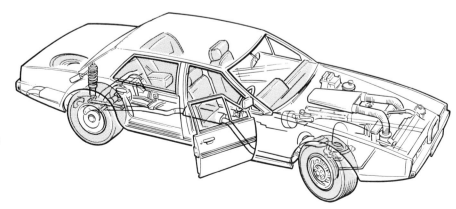

This cutaway drawing shows the Lagonda V-8's superb lines and layout.

The V-8 press car, showing the well-proportioned lines which make the car seem smaller than its 17ft (5,181mm) length. (Inset) the prototype, occupied by Denis Flather, Peter Sprague and Alan Curtis after the 1976 Motor Show. Remarkably, the solid silver motif on the radiator grille remained on the car throughout the show.

The styling task which faced William Towns was that of creating a car which was aerodynamically efficient yet appealing to the eye and which embodied the classic 'three-box' concept of engine compartment at the front, passenger compartment in the middle and a full rear luggage boot at the rear – all within a very long car (over 17ft [5m]), without appearing ungainly. Within this design ideal, Towns also had the self-set task of making his new car look different – something which would leave his mark. Announced on 12 October 1976, this new Lagonda quite certainly made an impression.

This new dream car had to be – and indeed was – a car which stood alone in innovation, style, comfort and performance. *Road and Track* summed it all up rather well in an introductory piece to a road test, when the point was made that this was a car which would be totally lost on the 'gold-chain set'. For them were the BB Porsche Turbo, the white Mercedes 500 or the Excalibur, not the subtlety of the Aston Martin Lagonda.

WHAT MADE THE LAGONDA TICK

Essentially, the engine which powered this new Lagonda was a 'softened' version of Tadek Marek's 5.3-litre Aston Martin V-8 power unit. The camshafts were designed to produce a gentler power curve and flatter

Peter Sprague making a point to Bert Brooks, craftsman supreme and paragon of the body shop, during the building of the prototype Lagonda V-8 in 1976; the car is in the background.

torque characteristics than the Aston Martin variants, whilst larger valves were fitted to both inlet and exhaust ports. The resulting power output was said to be 280bhp and the torque, though not quoted, was said to have been aimed at providing greater flexibility and smoothness on the road. This lower power rating allowed the use of a smaller air box, which in turn permitted a much lower bonnet line than was found on the Aston Martin cars.

Chrysler's 'Torqueflite' automatic transmission was matched up to this new Lagonda's engine – the same drivetrain selected for use on the earlier Aston Martin Lagonda Saloon of DBS/V-8 styling. Drive was

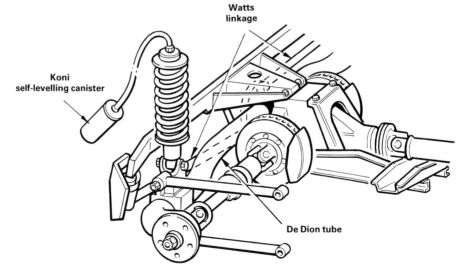

This drawing of the final drive and rear suspension assembly shows the de Dion tube located transversely by Watts linkage and longitudinally by twin trailing links. The Koni self-levelling shocks sat inside the coil springs and brakes were inboard vented discs.

Lagonda V8 Saloon – 1977–1986

Vehicle construction

Steel box-section chassis with steel superstructure and aluminium bodywork

Engine

Crankcase/cylinder block material	Aluminium alloy
Cylinder head material	Aluminium alloy, twin-plug
Number of cylinders	8 in 90° V-formation, wet liners
Cooling system	Water – pump, thermostat and viscous-coupling fan
Bore and stroke	100mm × 85mm
Engine capacity	5,340cc
Number of main bearings	Five
Valve gear and operation	Two chain-driven overhead camshafts per cylinder bank; two valves per cylinder
Fuel supply method and type	Four Weber 42DCNF twin-choke carburettors
Quoted maximum power output	280bhp @ 5,000rpm
Quoted maximum torque output	360lb/ft

Transmission

Clutch type and operation	With Chrysler Torqueflite automatic transmission – multi-plate torque convertor
Gearbox ratios	7.52, 4.45, 3.07:1 (reverse 6.75:1)
Final drive ratio	3.07:1

Suspension and steering

Front suspension	Independent – double wishbones, anti-roll bar and Koni shock absorbers
Rear suspension	De Dion, twin radius rods, Watts linkage, coil springs and lever-arm shock absorbers
Steering type	Adwest power-assisted rack and pinion
Wheel type and size	Cast alloy ventilated 7in × 15in
Tyre size and rating	Avon GR70VR × 15in
Brakes: type and actuation	Vented discs all round – 10¾in front, 10.38in rear, with split-circuit hydraulic system

Vehicle Dimensions

Overall Length	5,283mm
Overall Width	1,816mm
Wheelbase	2,916mm
Track (front and rear)	1,499mm
Overall height	1,302mm

conveyed through this 3-speed unit to a 3.07:1 ratio limited slip differential, which was mounted in a de Dion rear suspension with self-levelling rear dampers. Steel wheels, 7in wide and 15in diameter were fitted with stainless steel hubcaps, these being so designed as to direct cooling air onto the brake discs through the wheel naves. The intermediate drive ratios of the Torqueflite were 4.45:1 and 7.52:1, whilst reverse was 6.75:1, and there was no manual gearbox option on this car. On the road, the transmission gave 26mph (42kph) per 1,000rpm in top ratio.

The electronic wizardry of the Lagonda was one of its most amazing features, pioneering as it did so many things that we take for granted today. Everything was intended to operate 'at the touch of a button'. The only problem was that Cranfield Institute of Technology, developers of the computer to control all of these gadgets, took longer to perfect the system than anyone could ever have anticipated. The result of that delay was that the first car delivered was over a year late, and even at that it could not be driven because it did not have its computer fitted. The consequence of this delay was a

As this drawing shows, the dashboard of the original design was a space-age nightmare, with a plethora of touch-sensitive switches that would have done justice to Concorde. Needless to say, the complications of persuading the computer to work consistently finally caused its abandonment for a simpler solution.

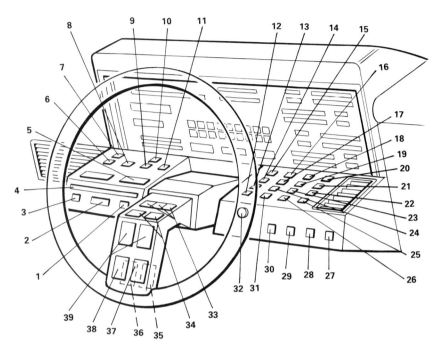

Lagonda Facia – Key

1 Hazard warning	10 Fast wipe	20 Minutes/days	30 Fog lamps
2 Second gear and Drive	11 Bonnet	21 Mph/Kph	31 Display
3 First gear	12 Start/stop	22 Average consumption	32 Dimmer
4 Visual gear legend for	13 Reset	23 Average speed	33 Cruise control switches
night driving	14 Date	24 Mode	34 Indicators
5 Neutral, Reverse, Park	15 Set clock	25 Test	35 Headlamp flash
6 Left fuel filler	16 Hours/months	26 Essential instruments	36 Screen wash
7 Heated rear window	17 Interior lights	27 Headlamps	37 Dip/main beam
8 Right fuel filler	18 Set date	28 Side lamps	38 Wiper on/off and single wipe
9 Fuel reserve	19 Trip	29 Spot lamps	39 Town and country horns

considerable extra cost burden on Aston Martin Lagonda Limited, combined with a major loss of cash flow arising from the inability to deliver finished cars.

Cynicism aside, one of the major features of the Lagonda V-8 were the forty-six switches installed to cover every possible aspect of the car's operation, except for driving it. Elevating and switching on the 'pop-up' headlamps, opening the windows, operating the air-conditioning or changing gear ratios were all performed 'at the touch of a button'. The steering wheel was connected to its hub by means of a very wide single spoke and beyond was the digital read-out instrument panel – a feature common today but then an electronics engineer's nightmare.

At the end of all this ingenuity and advanced techology, what really made this new Lagonda attractive to its potential buyers? The state-of-the-art electronics had a great deal to do with it, though the space-age lines were a large part of it, too. However, even that wasn't all of it. It was very much because this advanced technology 145mph (233kph) projectile was hand-crafted. Indeed, the combination of traditional craftsmanship and leading-edge design and engineering left the car with no direct competitors. Clearly, its character and price put

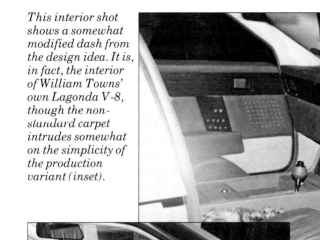

This interior shot shows a somewhat modified dash from the design idea. It is, in fact, the interior of William Towns' own Lagonda V-8, though the non-standard carpet intrudes somewhat on the simplicity of the production variant (inset).

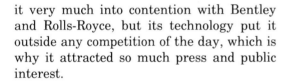

it very much into contention with Bentley and Rolls-Royce, but its technology put it outside any competition of the day, which is why it attracted so much press and public interest.

PRESS REACTION IN AMERICA AND AUSTRALIA

An early target market for the Lagonda V-8 was of course, the United States of America, where British craftsmanship has long been held in high esteem. Combined with the latest in gadgetry, the Lagonda provided that craftsmanship in a package which many journalists found little less than startling. The combination of leather headlining,

walnut trim and a fully digital solid-state instrument panel (which used light-emitting diodes to relay information to the driver instead of moving needles), together with the clean space-age lines, made this car a head-turner like few others, even in its price class. One correspondent made the comment: '. . . if you can't lip-read the question "What the hell is that?" now, you'll soon be able to after twenty minutes in a Lagonda'.

The same correspondent made the point that the interior of this car might have been described as 'plain', though he preferred the term 'simply elegant'. Its hide seats were typical of British quality cars, in that they were soft and comfortable, without the firmness of German car seats. In this appraisal, the Lagonda was being compared with the Mercedes-Benz 450SEL. Apart from similarities in length and width, he came to the conclusion that there was really no contest, with little to compare after dimensions, the Mercedes being a volume-produced car in a totally different idiom.

Other American road testers and reviewers found the low roof-line of the Lagonda hard to believe, since when they sat inside it, they discovered that head-room was not skimped, except perhaps for the tallest of drivers or passengers. Again, the opulent simplicity of the interior design drew comment, with the soft hide seats putting it well ahead of its rivals on comfort. The mixture of walnut trim, digital read-outs and touch-button controls would have been hard to accept from many other manufacturers, but that these were integral features of Aston Martin's new Lagonda seemed not only accepted but expected.

Americans seem to have a concern for luggage space, so one aspect of the car's design was almost bound to attract adverse comment. This was the limited boot size, though no one actually said it was unusable, just '. . . a little limited, especially with a briefcase full of tools in there already'. It is

rather odd, in fact, that whilst the Lagonda was designed as a long-legged luxury conveyor of its occupants from Point A to Point B, the U.S. reviewers saw it more as a prestigious town car. After all, if you were going to spend $85,000 (in 1978) on an imported luxury car, as opposed to $20,000-odd for a Cadillac limousine (just to put it into perspective), then you wanted your $85,000-worth to be on maximum public view!

The Australians took a little longer to put their views into print, perhaps because the car was even more expensive there in 1982 than a Rolls-Royce! A 1982 review made that point, stating that the Lagonda was Australia's most expensive luxury car (putting it at about twenty-five times the price of an up-market Jap-mobile) and setting it head-on in competition with a Crewe-built car. That the two had totally different design ideals from the outset and were aimed at totally different owner profiles didn't seem to make much difference in 'Oz'. However, the similarity in price and

'The most expensive car in Australia', is how the press there reviewed the Lagonda. This is an early production car.

presentation of the two car-makes made the comparison almost inevitable.

The Aussies found it highly amusing that it was American capital that had saved the Newport Pagnell company and funded this new car, given that they had already bought the Queen Mary and London Bridge. However, they couldn't fault the Lagonda on the open road – even *their* open roads – for it was one of a very few high-speed super-luxury machines that ate Australian miles without the feel of doing it by kangaroo! They did criticize the boot space though, for they did not see this as a town car, rather as a means of getting from somewhere like Adelaide to Perth, when of course luggage does become a point for concern. After all, you do need somewhere to put your tucker bag!

CONTINUING DEVELOPMENT

Development of this new Lagonda was not without its problems, one of the major early setbacks being to achieve absolute reliability from the computer which fed all the electronic instruments. Sadly, Cranfield Institute seemed unable to beat the problem, with the result that AML took it across the Atlantic to a man named Brian Refoy, who ran a company in Dallas, Texas, called the Javelina Corporation. Mr Refoy's company had long experience of making computers work in the aerospace industry, so it was a fair prospect that it would be able to produce a reliable unit for the Lagonda.

Finally, the job was done, and a reliable computer was delivered. It is interesting to note that L.J.K. Setright observed that it seemed the automotive environment was much more hostile to computers than the cockpit of a high-performance combat aircraft – a comment which seemed to have more than a grain of truth to it! Anyway, the

William Towns

Ask anyone who knows about modern Aston Martins for what he best remembers the name William Towns, and he will almost certainly tell you: 'The Lagonda V-8'. Whilst regarded in many circles as the pinnacle of his design achievements, it is by no means his most important design. Indeed, as far as Aston Martin Lagonda is concerned, Towns' most important project was, without doubt, MP227, which resulted in the longest line of Aston Martins, the DBS, which led to the DBS-V8 and the V-8.

William Towns joined the Rootes Group at Coventry in 1954 at eighteen and spent his early career designing small fittings, like door handles. He did produce pilot designs for the Hillman Hunter saloon but left, leaving its development to others, to join the Rover Company in 1963. There, he worked on the original 2000, a design he thought quite odd, then progressed to being given charge of the Le Mans Rover-BRM Gas Turbine car's styling.

After three years at Rover, he joined Aston Martin Lagonda Limited in 1966 as a seat designer, working under the supervision of Engineering Director Harold Beach. Towns didn't like the DB6 and sketched his own ideas in the form of dummy brochures, which found their way on to Chairman David Brown's desk and met with his strong approval. The ultimate result was the DBS, followed by the Lagonda and the outline of 'Bulldog', though now as a freelance designer.

William Towns also did design work on the Jensen Healey, a Lotus design which had a profound effect on the ultimate line of Elite, Eclat and Esprit models, then the abortive Aston Martin MG and Reliant's SS2 and SST models. Sadly, he died at the age of fifty-six in 1993.

reliability was now such that it was possible to programme a situation where, at night, only the essential instruments were illuminated (reducing the risk of distracting the driver's attention). However, if an emergency or a fault arose, then the instrument relating to the problem would immediately light up, warning the driver that something was not as it should be.

Within a year or so of this Lagonda going on sale, there was a quest for more power to offset the escalating weight, which was damping down the design performance. As a consequence, by 1980, the Newport Pagnell engineering team had developed a twin-turbocharged version of the V-8 engine and installed it into Chassis LOOR/13004. The idea was to retain the more docile characteristics of the Lagonda engine's camshafts (a Vantage engine would have been a simpler solution to the power problem, but would almost certainly have made the car too hairy!), but give the necessary power boost to bring the car back to its intended performance envelope.

Whilst remaining a one-off, the turbo Lagonda was a most interesting project and could possibly have found its way into production if the performance improvements had justified the cost. Compression ratio of the engine was reduced to 7.5:1, using special Cosworth pistons, and the two Garrett T03 turbochargers were accommodated down in the nose of the car, as the under-bonnet space was already pretty full. Using the standard 42DCNF Weber carburettors and a boost pressure of 10lb/psi, the power output of the Lagonda engine was estimated at 380bhp, whilst torque was reckoned to be over 450lb/ft in an engine speed range of between 2,500rpm and 4,500rpm.

Motor magazine performed a brief road test of this car in the spring of 1980 and were impressed, reckoning that the turbo Lagonda left a Jaguar XJ-S gasping for breath. However, the car was not to reach

production, no doubt partly due to the high cost. It was also almost certainly felt that the Lagonda buyer would not demand this level of performance in the way that an Aston Martin buyer might – and he did have the choice of a Vantage Saloon as an option, the sales of which could possibly have been adversely affected by the offering of a turbo Lagonda. Thus, the idea was still-born.

By 1983, Tickford, a one-time subsidiary of Aston Martin Lagonda Limited (and whose original premises the parent now occupied), introduced a 'stylized' version of the Lagonda V-8 Saloon, with a deep front air dam, deep side-skirts, BBS wheels and colour-coordinated (instead of plated) radiator grille, door handles and exterior mirrors. This treatment elevated the price of the car from £66,000 to £85,000. It may seem, therefore, a little less than surprising that only five were sold, most of those to the Middle East, where they could be afforded without too much concern for the damage their cost might do to the housekeeping budget.

THE LAGONDA ACQUIRES A VOICE

By 1984, the Lagonda V-8's electronic wizardry had acquired two new facets – computerized instrumentation transmitted to three 5in (12.7cm) cathode ray tubes in the instrument panel and a voice synthesizer to relay that information. This meant that one could be given warnings of impending problems without looking down at the instruments. It also meant one could be reminded to fasten the seat-belts, that a door was not properly closed, or any of a number of other bits of news.

The car had already been viewed with considerable interest in the Middle East, from where several early orders came for the original version anyway, but now there was

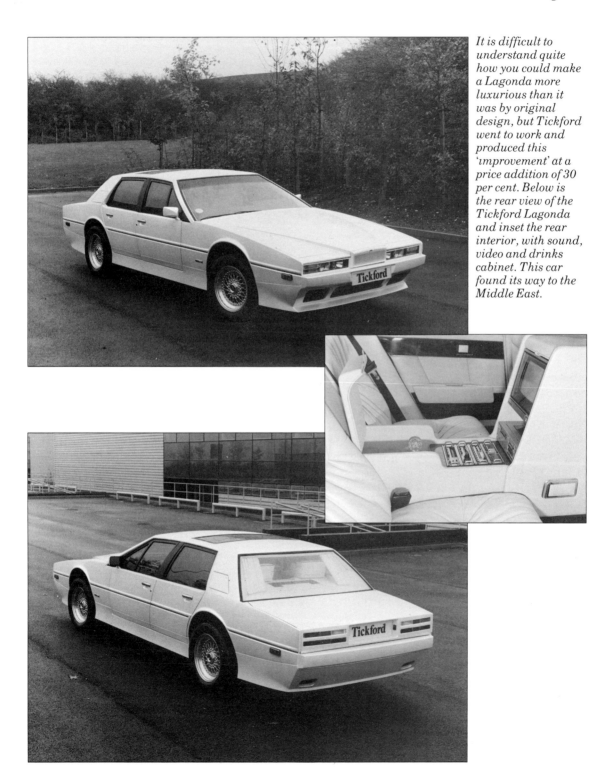

It is difficult to understand quite how you could make a Lagonda more luxurious than it was by original design, but Tickford went to work and produced this 'improvement' at a price addition of 30 per cent. Below is the rear view of the Tickford Lagonda and inset the rear interior, with sound, video and drinks cabinet. This car found its way to the Middle East.

a new interest. After all, if you were going to have a prestige car to mark your position in local society, one that talked was so much more attractive – especially if it spoke Arabic! The Lagonda's voice synthesizer was programmed in four languages: English, French, German and Arabic.

In Saudi Arabia, the new 'talking Lagonda' caught on, and with keen support from the local agent was soon vying with other supercars for sales. However, delays occurred during this time, when certain management changes were taking place at Newport Pagnell, and as the Arabs are not noted for their patience when it comes to waiting for something they want to buy, they turned their attention to other cars which were available off the shelf. The few that did find their way into that market seemed to attract considerable attention, and as long as the air filters were given proper regular attention they ran reliably despite the talcum-like desert dust.

The voice synthesizer was also popular in North America, so the U.S. version found considerable enthusiasm among the buying public because it was another gimmick to boast about in that $100,000-plus (by 1984) new car. It's amusing now to reflect that many a driver switched off the voice synthesizer once the novelty had worn off because it became an intrusion on driver concentration and conversations in the car. It is a fact that the flat tones of a synthesized voice do become irritating after a time, and there is a strong inclination to answer the automated comment 'Door not fastened' with an abrupt 'I know, stupid!'

At about the same time as the 'Talking Lagonda' was announced to the world, Tickford, who had produced a stylized version of the standard Lagonda a year before, now came back to the market with another development from the factory standard. This was a long wheelbase limousine version of the 'Talking Lagonda', which was aimed at

Rocker switches took over a number of the functions in the Lagonda as the electronics were modified, though the simplicity of the interior was unspoiled by this change.

attracting petro-dollars (nobody else would have been able to afford it!) into the Newport Pagnell coffers. Sadly (but perhaps predictably now, as the Middle Eastern economies were going through a period of change and down-turn), the project did less well than the 1983 exercise on the standard wheelbase, selling only three examples at the somewhat stunning price for the time of £110,000 – definitely a very expensive motor car, even in its class.

Thus the state of the Lagonda art remained for a couple of years, with the specification of the car being somewhat stable and sales plodding on at a rate of one or two cars a week, alongside the production

Tickford's second adventure with the Lagonda V-8 was the limousine version, seen here. Even with a longer wheelbase, the car still looks in proportion, though with a £110,000 price tag, it's hardly surprising that it didn't reach production numbers.

of Aston Martin models. By 1986, however, because it was decided to standardize the newest variant of Aston Martins with fuel injection, replacing the Weber carburettors, the Lagonda followed suit and so became known as the Series 3, the first razor-edged Lagonda being Series 2 and the original DBS-shaped car Series 1.

SERIES 3 AND SERIES 4

With a constant eye on the ever-tightening emission control regulations in the United States, fuel injection was deemed to be a necessary change for the Series 5 Aston Martin and Series 3 Lagonda models, so a Weber/Marelli Type was fitted, to raise the domestic Lagonda version's power output to a genuine 300bhp, whilst the American specification offered 60bhp less. This change was introduced to the public at the New York Motor Show in January 1986, along with a few other features.

As 1987 approached, the Series 3 Lagonda was advertised as having 'vacuum fluorescent instrumentation', which was a new way to describe the three cathode ray tubes in the dashboard. The kerb weight had now risen to 4,622lb (2,080kg) and the final drive

ratio had risen slightly, to 3.058:1 from a previously quoted 3.07:1. An interesting quote in the press release of early 1987 states the width of the car to be 5ft 8½in (1.79m). One has to wonder if that was an option on the width, for 1.79 metres actually comes out two inches more than that (it is 5.87 feet, which is marginally under 5ft 10½in). It's an easy enough mistake to make, but not for the press.

The Series 3 car didn't last very long, in fact, because William Towns had already begun work on softening the design to fit the market demands of the time. The sharp razor-edge had had its day, now, just as it had back in the early 1950s. People wanted softer, less intrusive lines, and so Towns's task was to 'take the edge off' the Lagonda. The result was announced at the Geneva Motor Show in March 1987.

The fourth generation of V-8 Lagonda featured numerous detail changes inside and a number of noticeable styling changes on the outside. For example, the nose was redesigned and the four 'pop-up' headlights disappeared, relocated on the front valance, alongside a pair of spot lamps, whilst a pair of fog lamps appeared in the valance below the slightly chunkier front bumper. The sills were made deeper, and the wheels went

Lagonda V8 Saloon – 1986–1987

Vehicle construction
Steel box-section chassis with steel superstructure and aluminium bodywork

Engine

Crankcase/cylinder block material	Aluminium alloy
Cylinder head material	Aluminium alloy, twin-plug
Number of cylinders	8 in 90° V-formation, wet liners
Cooling system	Water – pump, thermostat and viscous-coupling fan
Bore and stroke	100mm × 85mm
Engine capacity	5,340cc
Number of main bearings	Five
Valve gear and operation	Two chain-driven overhead camshafts per cylinder bank; two valves per cylinder
Fuel supply method and type	Weber-Marelli Fuel injection
Quoted maximum power output	300bhp (240 in USA) @ 5,000rpm
Quoted maximum torque output	320lb/ft

Transmission

Clutch type and operation	With Chrysler Torqueflite automatic transmission – multi-plate torque convertor
Gearbox ratios	7.49, 4.43, 3.058:1 (reverse 6.73:1)
Final drive ratio	3.058:1

Suspension and steering

Front suspension	Independent – double wishbones, anti-roll bar and Koni shock absorbers
Rear suspension	De Dion, twin radius rods, Watts linkage, coil springs and lever-arm shock absorbers
Steering type	Adwest power-assisted rack and pinion
Wheel type and size	Cast alloy ventilated 7in × 15in
Tyre size and rating	Avon GR70VR × 15in
Brakes: type and actuation	Vented discs all round – 10¾in front, 10.38in rear, with split-circuit hydraulic system

Vehicle Dimensions

Overall Length	5,283mm
Overall Width	1,816mm
Wheelbase	2,916mm
Track (front and rear)	1,499mm
Overall height	1,302mm

from 15in to 16in alloys to take advantage of current trends in tyre design.

Tyres on the car were quoted in the original brochure as being 255/60VR 16 Avon Turbospeed CR27s, but a note at the foot of the same brochure made it clear that from April 1988, the tyres would change to 'Z' rating. The spare wheel was, of course, a 'get-you-home' type, known in the car market as a 'convenience' wheel, with a maximum speed limit of 50mph (80kph). Can you imagine a car like this being driven on a high-speed motorway at that speed?

The great skill of this redesign were the very minor changes made necessary to the forming bucks for the body panels, for it looked quite different in many ways, yet the actual changes in line were of the minimum. It is interesting, too, to observe that this last version of the Lagonda was actually still being described in sales literature as the 'Aston Martin Lagonda', though the badge on the front of the car had read only 'Lagonda' since somewhere around the middle of 1982, when the earlier stock of badges ran out, and new ones were bought in.

Lagonda V8 Saloon – 1987–1990

Vehicle construction

Steel box-section chassis with steel superstructure and aluminium bodywork

Engine

Crankcase/cylinder block material	Aluminium alloy
Cylinder head material	Aluminium alloy, twin-plug
Number of cylinders	8 in 90° V-formation, wet liners
Cooling system	Water – pump, thermostat and viscous-coupling fan
Bore and stroke	100mm × 85mm
Engine capacity	5,340cc
Number of main bearings	Five
Valve gear and operation	Two chain-driven overhead camshafts per cylinder bank; two valves per cylinder
Fuel supply method and type	Twin SU electric pumps and Weber-Marelli Fuel injection
Quoted maximum power output	289bhp @ 5,000rpm
Quoted maximum torque output	321lb/ft @ 3,000rpm

Transmission

Clutch type and operation	With Chrysler Torqueflite automatic transmission – multi-plate torque convertor
Gearbox ratios	7.52, 4.45, 3.07:1 (reverse 6.75:1)
Final drive ratio	3.07:1

Suspension and steering

Front suspension	Independent – double wishbones, anti-roll bar and Koni shock absorbers
Rear suspension	De Dion, twin radius rods, Watts linkage, coil springs and lever-arm shock absorbers
Steering type	Adwest power-assisted rack and pinion
Wheel type and size	Cast alloy ventilated 7in × 16in
Tyre size and rating	255/60VR × 16in Avon CR27
Brakes: type and actuation	Vented discs all round – 10¾in front, 10.38in rear, with split-circuit hydraulic system

Vehicle Dimensions

Overall Length	5,283mm
Overall Width	1,816mm
Wheelbase	2,916mm
Track (front and rear)	1,499mm
Overall height	1,302mm

The Series 4 car brought a number of changes in specification with it. Apart from eliminating the weight of the motors to raise and lower the headlamps, the actual appearance was improved by the repositioning of the headlamps and spots – and, of course, a control circuit was disposed of in the process. The touch-button switches also went, in favour of more orthodox push-button ones, all fitted into an improved dashboard. The steering wheel had already changed with the Series 3 car to a two-spoke design, and this was retained in the newer model, whilst the leather and walnut trim remained much as before in appearance and quality.

The company had now returned to quoting power outputs for its engines and the power of the Series 4 Lagonda was said to be 289bhp, with a 321lb/ft torque rating at 3,000rpm. Fuelling was by Weber electronic digital sequential fuel injection and the tank capacity was now 23g (104l). The final drive quoted was another change, with 3.062:1 given for all markets except the U.S.A. and Japan, which were lower at 3.54:1, no doubt to accommodate the more sluggish

By 1987, the razor-edged variant of the Lagonda had reached its zenith. This is a 'Series 3' car destined for France with, inset, an interior shot of a right-hand drive car.

performance of the lower-powered engine for those markets.

WHAT THE ROAD TESTERS SAID

One of the first 'men-of-the-press' to drive the razor-edged Lagonda V-8 Saloon did so almost two years after the announcement of the car to the world at large. The man was Michael Bowler, then editor of *Thoroughbred and Classic Car* magazine and later to become a director of Protech, the company formed with Richard Williams at its helm to race the AMR-1. The result of Mr Bowler's experience was published in April 1978, and he was clearly impressed.

One very interesting observation that

Michael Bowler made was that it took him a 250-mile (400km) drive to familiarize himself with the functions and locations of all the switches – and even then, it took the occasional sneak visual check to be sure of some of them! If it took a man of that experience so long to acquaint himself with the switchery of this car, imagine how long it would take the average Lagonda buyer ('average' being a relative term, you understand).

It was this same correspondent who commented that it was such a pity Jaguar got the slogan first, for 'Grace, Space and Pace' so perfectly described this particular magnificent machine. Mr Bowler's conclusion was that the Lagonda was no four-wheeled gimmick, but a serious 'super-barouche'. This was perhaps not quite the right descriptive expression, when the original horse-

The final version of the Lagonda V-8 was a remarkably skilful piece of styling, incorporating a softening of the razor-edged lines of the original design without, as so often happens in the 'updating' of a car, detracting from its original character.

Gone were the pop-up headlamps on the outside and (inset) gone were all vestiges of the touch-sensitive switches, as well as the single-spoke steering wheel.

drawn barouche placed the four internal occupants facing each other and the driver up on an outside seat, but we all know what he was getting at.

John Lamm, of *Road and Track* in the United States, was next to report a drive in a Lagonda. He was clearly almost mesmerized by the instrumentation of the car, demonstrated by his constant desire to keep looking down at the speedometer until 100mph (160kph) came up, and that was in a country where a 55mph (90kph) national open-road limit applied. Mr Lamm achieved this speed on a two-lane road of mediocre surface, which led him to make a very strong point of how completely secure the car felt with its uncanny ability to adapt to all road surfaces, smoothing out patches and lumps to stay steady at 100mph (160kph). Praise indeed.

The reviewer moved on then to compare the Lagonda with the current 6.9-litre Mercedes-Benz saloon and a Rolls-Royce (presumably a Shadow, but he didn't specify the model), commenting that the seating in the rear of the Newport Pagnell car was more comfortable than either of the other two. He regretted that the rear doors of the Lagonda didn't open as far as those of the other two cars, so found it less easy to step into and out of the car.

The only comment which spoiled John Lamm's eulogy was the comparison of prices which he drew between the Lagonda and the Mercedes-Benz, saying that the latter cost almost $35,000 less, with no reference to price positions between the Lagonda and the Rolls-Royce (which would have been a fairer and closer comparison). The point here is, of

The AM Lagonda V8 and its Adversaries (1979)

Car and Model	Engine Type and Size	Gearbox	Max. Speed		Consumption		G.B. Price
			mph	kph	mpg	l/100km	
Lagonda V8 Saloon	5,340cc V-8 tohc per bank	3-Auto	143	230	13–16	18–22	£37,500 (1979)
Bentley T-Series Saloon	6,750cc V-8 ohv pushrod	3-Auto	118	190	12–15	19–24	£34,500 (1979)
Cadillac Eldorado	5,737cc V-8 ohv pushrod	3-Auto	112	180	13–17	17–22	£19,000-est (1979)
Chrysler New Yorker	5,211cc V-8 ohv pushrod	3-Auto	107	172	12–16	18–24	£21,000-est (1979)
Bristol 603	5,210cc V-8 pushrod ohv	3-Auto	112	180	13–19	15–22	£29,000-est (1979)
Daimler Double-Six Saloon	5,343cc V-12 tohc per bank	3-Auto	140	225	12–19	15–24	£15,750 (1979)
Mercedes-Benz 450 SEL 6.9	6,834cc V-8 sohc per bank	3-Auto	140	225	12–18	16–24	£27,500 (1979)

course, that the Mercedes-Benz *should* have cost $35,000 less, as it was a steel-bodied volume-produced car, whilst the Lagonda was an alloy-bodied hand-crafted one-a-week-out-of-the-door product with much more to offer in the form of tangible quality and specification, quite apart from the charisma factor.

THE FIRST TRUE ROAD TESTS

It was to be 1980 before a Lagonda V-8 was finally fully road tested, when *Motor* magazine presented what it described as '. . . the first full road test of Aston Martin's sensational Lagonda, fifty thousand pounds worth of sporting luxury in a shape that draws crowds like no other saloon in the world'. That comment set the scene for what the reader was about to learn of this car, which, unlike many, retained its fascination even four years after the initial announcement to the world of its existence.

Motor uses a long-established star-grading system for expressing its qualitative view of cars, running from one at the bottom end of the scale up to five at the top – and it is a magazine which has the reputation of being quite critical of what it sees, so this road test has a certain extra poignance about it for that. It makes especially interesting reading

for the fact that two aspects of the Lagonda are marked down to two stars, though on the up-side there are five four-star ratings and three five-stars, all reflecting more important qualities of the car.

Whilst Mr Lamm, in his earlier assessment of the Lagonda, was entranced by the instruments, it is quite clear that the *Motor* staff was not. In fact, some very unkind things were said, starting with the statement that Lagonda's use of space-age technology earned a chorus of raspberries from *Motor*'s testers, because they felt they were not aesthetically pleasing, nor practical in that when bright sunlight struck the instrumentation panel, they were illegible. They did feel, however, that the instrumentation was, if nothing else, very comprehensive, and one wonders how much of this criticism was centred on unfamiliarity.

The other two-star rating that the Lagonda won was concerning fuel economy, but when you have a two-ton projectile, powered by a 5.3-litre lump, you can hardly expect 39 miles per gallon (8 litres per 100 kilometres)! In fact, this car turned in about one third of that, going up to as much as 20mpg (14l/100km) at relatively low constant speeds (up to 60mph [97kph] was what *Motor* quoted). The testers accepted the point about weight, engine size and performance potential, so the low rating on fuel is actually a little surprising.

The engine was rated highly as a performer, with four stars, as was the Chrysler Torqueflite automatic transmission. A slightly spongy feel to the brakes reduced the rating here to four stars, and the dashboard, of which the testers definitely did not approve, reduced the judgement on the interior and 'at the wheel' to four as well. Air-conditioning, noise intrusion and visibility all scored only three. However, the road holding, ride comfort and equipment of the car all score five well-deserved stars. At the end of it all, *Motor* had to admit that the Lagonda was '. . . a car that is a pleasure both to drive and to ride in'.

Motor Sport, also renowned for its critical road tests down the years, noted that the seat squabs might be too short for longer-legged passengers and that after a trip into deepest Wales, the car became filthy and the tyres didn't exactly like wet, narrow and not-the-best-surfaced country lanes that one finds in large parts of that country. The car was thought not to be so silky-silent as a V-12 Jaguar, nor so refined as a Rolls-Royce, but an excellent conveyor of people over long distances without a hint of them suffering travel fatigue. One interesting comment was about driving along winding roads, where it was felt the driver of the Jaguar XJ-S V-12 might feel reasonably happy keeping up, but that the chauffeur in the Rolls would certainly have left his passengers feeling less than well!

When *Road and Track* came back formally to road test this car, in 1983, it described it as 'Ferrari performance and Rolls-Royce luxury at a price you can't afford'! That's a slight mis-statement of the situation, for the point was that if you could afford the Ferrari performance or the Rolls-Royce luxury, then you could definitely have afforded the Lagonda. Thus, it became then only a question of preference.

Interesting spot comparisons were made by *Road and Track* between the Lagonda and the Maserati Quattroporte and the Rolls-Royce Silver Spur. The Lagonda was the lightest of the three, had the shortest 0–60mph time (8.9 seconds), the best standing quarter-mile time (16.9 seconds), the second-best stopping distance (to the Rolls-Royce) and the best fuel consumption (12.5 miles per U.S. gallon). It also scored the highest speed at the end of the quarter-mile but had the dubious distinction of producing the highest interior noise at 50mph (80kph). Even at this, the tester observed that a perfectly normal conversation could be conducted at 120mph (193kph). How he proved that point in the 55mph (88kph) U.S.A.-limit would be a most interesting revelation!

END OF THE ROAD FOR THE V-8 LAGONDA

By 1990, as the recession bit deeper into Britain, it was becoming clear that not many Lagondas were going to sell each year, thanks largely to lots of the wrong kind of involvement by politicians in the management of 'Great Britain Limited' and not enough of the right kind of interest and support. The car had, in some ways, had a good run for its money, in that it was around for fourteen years before Victor Gauntlett finally cried 'Enough'.

After three variations of this superb car, which received all the accolades it deserved from the press, but not enough opportunities to sell because of economic pressures, it was decided to lay it to rest, with the promise that there might be another Lagonda in the future. Some 645 'Towns' Lagondas had left Newport Pagnell, many finding their way to the Middle East, where this author was first acquainted with them at close quarters. Therefore, it must be said that the car was certainly not a failure, though it probably didn't make Aston Martin Lagonda Limited any money.

The Vignale Lagonda was unleashed on the motoring world at the 1993 Geneva Motor Show. Aerodynamically superbly 'clean', it's a far cry from the razor-edged Lagonda that took the world by surprise in 1976.

However, in March 1993, at the Geneva Motor Show, a new Lagonda, a design exercise produced by Italian coachbuilder Vignale, was unveiled. It looked, at first glance, a bit like a giant pre-war design you might have found on an American chassis, or a Mercedes-Benz, but on closer inspection, you found that the light fittings on the outside

Inside, the Vignale Lagonda is almost as brash as the Towns Lagonda was demure, but there's a long way to go yet.

Strictly offered as conversions from production Aston Martin Virages, the Lagonda four-door Saloon and five-door Shooting Brake were revealed in late 1993. The Saloon doesn't seem to gain too much from the stretch, but there's a certain improvement for the Shooting Brake.

could not possibly have been from the 1930s, then you spotted the Lagonda badge.

This new projectile was the outcome of a chat between Walter Hayes, Chairman of Aston Martin Lagonda Limited, and Jack Telnack, Ford Motor Company's Chief Designer. Telnack, it seems was working on a revamp of the Lincoln Town Car, and the suggestion that a Lagonda badge might enhance it lit his lamp! Soon afterwards, Scotsman Moray Callum, working at Vignale in Turin, was given the task of designing a prototype. His brother, Ian, had moved to TWR Design from Ghia and was credited with the styling of the beautiful Aston Martin DB7, so there seems to be some design talent there.

We have to wait for what Lagonda has in store for us in the long term, but at the end of 1993, two new Lagondas were announced. Essentially stretched four-door versions of the Virage Saloon and Shooting Brake with the Lagonda badge upon them (déjà vu?), perhaps the V-8 Lagonda isn't dead after all. Conversions to existing Virages were made available, and the price of these two

variations on the theme was assessed at around £115,000 over whatever the original Virage cost (the ultimate price for such a Lagonda built from scratch must be in the order of £200,000). It was suggested in some quarters that the value of used Virages could lift in the face of demand for conversions, though that is hardly likely in view of the limited numbers available anyway.

The story of the Vignale version is that it *could* arrive at the production stage, no doubt modified in styling to a greater or lesser degree, with a 7-litre (Ford-derived?) V-12 engine. At present, the prototype is running around with a 4.6-litre Ford power unit which must, by the law of averages, cry 'enough' before too long.

It is of course all speculation, but the fact that Ford has designated its new Lincoln Town Car chassis as the basis for the new big Lagonda (bigger, incidentally, than a Rolls-Royce Silver Spur, though it doesn't look it), means it is serious about developing the Lagonda name. It hopefully augurs well for the overall future of the Newport Pagnell company.

6 The V-8 Zagato

Approach most motoring enthusiasts and say the word 'Zagato', and many will respond 'Alfa Romeo', for that is the company which probably did more to establish the name of Carrozzeria Zagato's worldwide reputation than any other. Say it to an Aston Martin enthusiast and *he* will reply 'DB4GT', because it was the DB4GT bodied by Zagato which brought that company's name to the fore in Great Britain in the 1960s, and what a magnificent brute it was.

THE ORIGINAL ZAGATO ASTON MARTIN

The 1960 London Motor Show saw the début of the DB4GT Zagato, bathing in the blaze of glory of the previous year's Le Mans 24 Hours win and Aston Martin's World Sports Car Championship. The car was born out of the DB4GT, a shortened wheelbase – by 5in (12.7cm) to 93in (236.2cm) – version of the DB4 Saloon. The production GT had the same basic style of Touring Superleggera bodywork as the Saloon, so the two were very similar in appearance.

Then, along came Carrozzeria Zagato, who took the DB4GT chassis, cropped off the extreme rear end to reduce the overhang and created a tubular-framed light alloy body which was much more rounded – some said bulbous – and shorter overall than the GT. The sharpest edges on the bodywork of this new car were at the rim of the radiator grille. It was a compound series of curves that combined to create the appearance of a wild animal just waiting to spring into action. When it did, what an action.

This angry beast was powered by the 3.7-litre six-cylinder engine, with a twin-plug head and a power output of 314bhp. The car weighed in at just under 2,800lbs (1,270kg) in kerb trim, so the result was very close to the magic 300bhp per ton. More spectacular was the top speed – just over 150mph (240kph). There's little wonder, then, that the DB4GT Zagato established a charisma for itself remarkably quickly, especially in the wake of the company's 1959 racing successes – Le Mans and the World Sports Car Championship. These factors combined with the appearance of the car to create an image in the mind of the observer that here was another Grand Touring Racer, which was, of course, to be the ultimate rôle of the car.

Nineteen DB4GT Zagatos were built in all, and most were raced. It was a way for the factory to keep faith with the sporting world whilst being seen to have officially withdrawn from team racing. This way, it could support private entrants, who would buy the Zagato – probably at subsidized prices – then go out and fly the Aston Martin flag without the company having to give further major financial support or commit a team of people it couldn't spare from production work. It was not to be long before that philosophy was proved right, and the launch charisma of the Zagato converted into solid reputation. With a 0–60mph time of 6.1 seconds on a 4-speed gearbox, the car would prove its pedigree with top speeds of 50mph (80kph) in first, 80mph (129kph) in second and 120mph (193kph) in third to accompany that 150mph (240kph)+ top speed.

All nineteen cars are reckoned to have

2 VEV is one of the most famous and most raced DB4GT Zagatos. This was the most evocative post-war closed Aston Martin, inspiring the V-8 Zagato.

been raced at one time or another, but two particularly famous Zagatos were John Ogier's Essex Racing Team examples, 1VEV and 2VEV, which were a regular sight on the circuits of Britain and Europe, starting with the 1961 Le Mans 24 Hours Race. They didn't fare well there, but in the Tourist Trophy Race at Goodwood, Aston Martins followed the invincible V-12 Ferraris of Stirling Moss and Mike Parkes to finish third, fourth and fifth. Roy Salvadori and Jim Clark drove 1VEV and 2VEV. The fifth-place car was a DB4GT driven by Innes Ireland. DB4GT Zagatos became the flag-ships of Britain in sports and GT car racing for years – now they dominate much of the Classic Sports Car scene.

BIRTH OF A NEW ZAGATO

Twenty-five years after the DB4GT Zagato,

Aston Martin Lagonda Limited and Carroz-zeria Zagato did it again, this time using the V-8 Vantage chassis as the basis. It seems it began with Victor Gauntlett, then Chair-man of AML, visiting the 1984 Geneva Motor Show. He saw the announcement of the limited-edition Ferrari GTO, of which 200 were to be built, and decided that if one manufacturer could offer a car for sale unseen and take advance orders and deposits, then so could Aston Martin. He had been toying with the idea of a new Zagato Aston Martin anyway, so he did no more than set up a meeting with Gianni and Elio Zagato at that very show.

Victor Gauntlett and Peter Livanos had put their heads together and reasoned that the original DB4GT Zagato was now selling at silly high prices, largely due to the growing investor interest in classic and cur-rent supercars. If Ferrari could pre-sell the GTO and Porsche the 959, then a V-8 Zagato must be viable. The ingredient in such a

These artist's impressions from Carrozzeria Zagato show the basic line from which the V-8 Zagato was developed and upon which a number of cars were sold.

programme that made the whole thing attractive was that Aston Martin Lagonda already made exclusive cars on a very small production level, so the idea of limiting the production number of a specific model in order to secure advance orders and deposits was already realistic. The cash flow advantage needed no explanation.

Messrs Gauntlett and Livanos took their thoughts to the Zagato brothers at that same 1984 Geneva Show. The idea was met with enthusiasm, and a few months later Giuseppe Mittino, Zagato's Chief Stylist, travelled to Newport Pagnell with some design outlines, charged with the task of acquainting himself thoroughly with the

The Porsche 959 was one of the so-called 'supercars' that provided additional motivation to create the V-8 Zagato. After all, if Zuffenhausen and Modena could pre-sell limited editions, then so could Newport Pagnell.

Vantage V-8 chassis. It would be important to produce a car which could break the psychological 300kph (186.4mph) barrier (to equal the anticipated performance of the Ferrari GTO and the Porsche 959) and give a 0–60mph time of less than 5 seconds! It was decided also, despite the intention to build only fifty examples of this super-exclusive car for sale worldwide, that the body-design calculations would be by computer.

Mittino returned to Milan, knowing exactly what he had to do and what he had with which to do it. Using the 432bhp Vantage engine, fuelled by four Weber 50IDF carburettors, the 5-speed gearbox and the Vantage chassis as built, the Zagato task was to produce a car that weighed in at 10 per cent below the existing Vantage Saloon and with a drag coefficient of 0.29 to improve aerodynamic penetration. The final drive ratio determined for the job was 3.06:1 in the existing limited slip differential.

During the development of the car's design, a number of prospective customers

This V-8 Vantage (VNK360S) was used as the development car for the Zagato model.

101

were flown to Milan to see the prototype under development. It appears not everyone liked the shape of the car instantly, but it still attracted enough buyers to ensure that all fifty would be sold long before the finished article would be on display at Geneva. After extensive to-ing and fro-ing in the design stage, the car came together to be exhibited in the metal at the 1985 Geneva Motor Show, exactly a year after the project was first discussed.

SALES BUILD-UP AND THE LAUNCH AT GENEVA

Leading up to the 1985 introduction of the new Zagato, Aston Martin Lagonda Limited let it be known that the car was in development. Amazingly, perhaps, there were people out there in the world at large who were so taken with the prospect of a new Zagato Aston Martin, that they put down their £30,000 deposits and accepted the £87,000 selling price. It didn't take too long to generate the fifty customers needed for every car in the limited edition to be sold unseen and without even the complete specification.

Such was the degree of trust people were prepared to place in this new car and its maker.

Finally, the prototype was complete. From the full-scale mock-up, several people knew what to expect from the shape, but it still drew gasps of excitement as it rolled out of the workshop for the first time. Hardly surprisingly, the car was red. Some thought it a little bland in certain aspects and too aggressive in others, much because of the colour, but in fact the new Zagato Aston Martin was very much in the idiom of its predecessor, except for one thing – few would be raced.

The prototype, V8ZGR20010, was brought to Geneva for the 1985 Motor Show and it was a show-stopper. It was to be another year, though, before customer cars could be made available, not least because of the movement back and forth of chassis between Newport Pagnell and Milan and, of course, there was still development work to be done. However, the whole design idea had taken into account the need to retain as much of the standard specification of the chassis, so as to eliminate having to go through approvals all over again.

By the 1986 Geneva Show, there were

Prototype of the Zagato Coupé in Milan upon completion. Note the lack of a rear spoiler at this stage.

After the fully built and road-tested chassis arrived in Milan, the framework was attached and the panels fitted in very similar fashion to the construction of a car at Newport Pagnell.

three Zagatos available to be seen – two in the exhibition halls, and one on display on top of the Beau Rivage Hotel, overlooking Lake Geneva. The two on show inside the halls were customer cars, whilst the one on top of the hotel was the development prototype. All three were finished in red, and they were a spectacular success in promoting the names 'Aston Martin Lagonda' and 'Zagato'. Indeed, before the production run was complete, there were rumours of cars, or rather car orders ahead of delivery, changing hands at up to double the original asking price.

PRODUCING THE GOODS

Once all the development work was complete, the Vantage Zagato went into production, and each chassis was built at Newport Pagnell. They were then shipped over to Milan for Carrozzeria Zagato to build on the bodies. There was no pre-construction of bodies, so it wasn't just a matter of dropping on a body as a chassis arrived. Each chassis

was road tested in Britain before being shipped, then it was received at Milan and checked over to ensure that there was no damage or missing parts. At this point, the body frame was built up on to the chassis, and the panels were then added in a very similar fashion to the process of body build-up at Newport Pagnell.

The alloy body panels were finished every bit as one would have expected from either Aston Martin Lagonda Limited or from Carrozzeria Zagato. The super-smooth panels were accompanied by super-flush fitting glassware, so that the drag coefficient was met by each and every car as it left Milan. The wheels upon which the chassis left Newport Pagnell were treated as 'slaves' and replaced with Speedline rims of Zagato design of 16in diameter and 8in width.

A spoiler was fitted to the front valance, as an air dam, and two spoilers appeared on the car at the rear. That sounds a bit blatant, but these spoilers were nothing like the 'whale-tail' of the Porsche Turbo, or the things fitted to many a mass-produced car, such as the Ford Sierra Cosworth. On the Aston

---

Aston Martin V8 Zagato Coupé – 1986–1987

Vehicle construction

Steel box-section chassis with Zagato designed superstructure and aluminium bodywork

Engine

Crankcase/cylinder block material	Aluminium alloy
Cylinder head material	Aluminium alloy, twin-plug
Number of cylinders	8 in 90° V-formation, wet liners
Cooling system	Water – pump, thermostat and viscous-coupling fan
Bore and stroke	100mm × 85mm
Engine capacity	5,340cc
Number of main bearings	Five
Valve gear and operation	Two chain-driven overhead camshafts per cylinder bank; two valves per cylinder
Fuel supply method and type	Four twin-choke Weber Type 50IDF carburettors
Quoted maximum power output	432bhp @ 6,000rpm
Quoted maximum torque output	395lb/ft @ 5,100rpm

Transmission

Clutch type and operation	Single 265mm plate, hydraulically actuated
Gearbox ratios	ZF 5-speed manual: 8.88, 5.45, 3.73, 3.062, 2.60:1 (reverse 8.05:1)
Final drive ratio	3.062:1

Suspension and steering

Front suspension	Independent – double wishbones, anti-roll bar and Koni shock absorbers
Rear suspension	De Dion, twin radius rods, Watts linkage, coil springs and lever-arm shock absorbers
Steering type	Power-assisted rack and pinion
Wheel type and size	8J × 16in cast alloy Speedline
Tyre size and rating	255/50ZR × 16in Goodyear Eagle
Brakes: type and actuation	Vented discs all round – 10¾in front, 10.38in rear, with split-circuit hydraulic system

Vehicle Dimensions

Overall Length	4,390mm
Overall Width	1,860mm
Wheelbase	2,610mm
Track (front and rear)	1,499mm
Overall height	1,295mm

Martin Vantage V-8 Zagato, the lower of the rear spoilers blended into the deformable rear panel, whilst the other sat unobtrusively on top of the boot lid. This combination created 120lb (54kg) of down-force at the rear of the car when driven at 150mph (240kph), so giving considerable stability to the Zagato on the road.

Once finished at Milan, the completed cars were very carefully protected and packed for shipment back to England, where, upon arrival at Newport Pagnell, they were closely inspected and road tested prior to delivery to their proud new owners. The Zagato was a truly 'magic' car, in that whilst it didn't possess all the electronic gadgetry of the Lagonda, it had all the charisma of the DB4GT Zagato. A string of customers stood ready and anxious to buy one. It is interesting that the aerodynamics had been very carefully worked out with Computer-Aided Design (CAD) techniques, though the full-size body drawings themselves were apparently manually produced, it being thought more cost-effective and, of course, it added a little to the car's 'magic'.

This was the finished product, as offered for sale. A truly magnificent 300kph (185mph) luxury projectile.

In proving tests, the Zagato achieved everything asked of it. The drag coefficient actually came out at 0.286 and the 0–60mph time beat the design target by 0.2 seconds, coming in at 4.8 seconds. Top speed in trials proved to be 186mph (300kph), so all in all the car had met its objectives with flying colours. Remembering that this car, albeit 10 per cent lighter than the Vantage Saloon, still weighed in at almost 1½ tons, that performance is electric. Its stopping power was just as startling. With a slightly heavy pedal, it was still possible to stop this great brute in a very short distance. The gear change, too, was reckoned to be super-fast – up and down – and certainly equalled that of any car in a similar performance bracket.

As the car was beginning to become

Inside, the Zagato was airy, light and thoroughly functional.

The Aston Martin V8 Zagato and its Adversaries (1987)

Car and Model	Engine Type and Size	Gearbox	Max. Speed		Consumption		G.B. Price
			mph	kph	mpg	l/100km	
Aston Martin V-8 Zagato Vantage	5,340cc V-8 tohc per bank	5-speed	189	304	11–15	19–26	£87,000 (1987)
De Tomaso Pantera Coupé	5,736cc V-8 pushrod	5-speed	170	274	11–16	18–26	£47,600 (1987)
Lamborghini Countach Quattrovalvole	5,167cc V-12 tohc per bank	5-speed	183	295	9–14	20–31	£69,600 (1987)
Bristol Beaufort	5,277cc V-8 pushrod ohv	3-Auto	150	242	12–18	16–24	£53,000 (1987)
Ferrari Testarossa	4,943cc Flat-12 tohc per bank	5-speed	181	292	9–18	16–31	£69,900 (1987)
Porsche 911 3.3 Turbo Sport	3,929cc Flat-6 tohc per bank turbo	5-speed	182	293	14–29	10–20	£86,443 (1987)

available for delivery, in July 1986 in fact, Aston Martin Lagonda Limited and Carrozzeria Zagato announced to the world that AML had acquired a 50 per cent stake in the Zagato business. This was shortly after the prototype had demonstrated in public its ability to come up to the mark in terms of what had been promised of it. Needless to say, when Ford Motor Company acquired its stake in Aston Martin Lagonda Limited, the Zagato deal did not go with it, and Carrozzeria Zagato returned to an independent state.

THE V-8 ZAGATO VOLANTE

It has been said that it was not surprising an open development of the V-8 Zagato came about, but that seems to be a slightly oversimplified view, since one has to consider that a car like the Zagato Coupé was a very high performance car in anybody's book and was originally perceived only as a logical successor to the DB4GT Zagato, which was only ever a coupé. Before the decision to create a Zagato Volante from the V-8 car would have been made, several questions would have had to be answered.

The first question of significance would have been 'Can we sell enough Volantes to make the project worthwhile?' The answer was almost certainly 'Yes', before the

question was asked in public. The next question would surely have been 'Is it practical to make such a car?', to which the answer would have been less precise, because practicality ranges from 'practical to build' to 'practical to own' to 'practical to drive'. Therefore, some design explorations had to be made before the sales question could be posed. The other aspects of practicality were, it might be supposed, for the intending owners to ask and answer.

Guiseppe Mittino, therefore, returned to his computer and drawing board. He had to find the structural strength in his car to replace the roof. He then had to address the weight question and the drag coefficient. After that, he had to try to make an open car as comfortable and useable as possible. It certainly didn't seem to make a lot of sense that an open car should be created out of a 186mph (300kph) coupé, when the driver of the open car would hardly be able to – or want to – drive his or her car at that road speed with the hood down! Even so, the work commenced, and the car was offered for sale in November 1986.

Twenty-five Zagato Volantes were to be sold, and the orders were soon in at a British tax-paid price of £125,000 – an incredible figure for a car. You could have bought a very reasonable house in Newport Pagnell for that price at the time. However, those interested in buying this new car would probably not have been satisfied to live in

---

Aston Martin V8 Zagato Volante Drophead – 1988–1989

Vehicle construction

Steel box-section chassis with Zagato designed
superstructure and aluminium bodywork

Engine

Crankcase/cylinder block material	Aluminium alloy
Cylinder head material	Aluminium alloy, twin-plug
Number of cylinders	8 in 90° V-formation, wet liners
Cooling system	Water – pump, thermostat and viscous-coupling fan
Bore and stroke	100mm × 85mm
Engine capacity	5,340cc
Number of main bearings	Five
Valve gear and operation	Two chain-driven overhead camshafts per cylinder bank; two valves per cylinder
Fuel supply method and type	Weber-Marelli fuel injection
Quoted maximum power output	305bhp @ 5,000rpm
Quoted maximum torque output	320lb/ft

Transmission

Clutch type and operation	Single 10½in plate, hydraulically actuated
Gearbox ratios	ZF 5-speed manual: 8.88, 5.45, 3.73, 3.062, 2.60:1 (reverse 8.05:1)
Final drive ratio	3.062:1

Suspension and steering

Front suspension	Independent – double wishbones, anti-roll bar and Koni shock absorbers
Rear suspension	De Dion, twin radius rods, Watts linkage, coil springs and lever-arm shock absorbers
Steering type	Power-assisted rack and pinion
Wheel type and size	8J × 16in cast alloy Speedline
Tyre size and rating	255/50ZR × 16in Goodyear Eagle
Brakes: type and actuation	Vented discs all round – 10¾in front, 10.38in rear, with split-circuit hydraulic system

Vehicle Dimensions

Overall Length	4,480mm
Overall Width	1,860mm
Wheelbase	2,610mm
Track (front and rear)	1,499mm
Overall height	1,302mm

---

such a house, so the point is a little academic. The real point is that there were people prepared to pay such a price for an Aston Martin, as opposed to other makes of cars.

The first V-8 Zagato Volante was, in fact, a conversion from a coupé (Chassis number V8ZGR 20042). It was shown at the Geneva Motor Show (Geneva and the Zagato Aston Martin had by now established a certain affinity) in March 1987, and like its closed sibling before it, it received rave reviews. The car was almost 60lb (27kg) heavier than the coupé, caused by the extra reinforcement needed around the doors to compensate for no roof, and had an engine which gave about 100bhp less than that in the coupé, so its performance envelope was closer to that of the standard V-8 Volante.

The power output was influenced by a styling decision, in that it was decided to reduce the large 'power-bulge' on the bonnet, so as to smooth out the body line – and recover a little of the lost drag coefficient figure forfeited by the missing roof. Whilst the opening side windows on the coupé were

Then came the Zagato Volante, which bore a different radiator 'grille' and lacked the 'power-bulge' of the coupé.

smaller than the total glazed area because the rest of the glass could be retained within the door frame, on the Volante, the opening side windows were of full door length, again aimed at helping to recover a bit of that essential drag coefficient. The final aerodynamic feature aimed in that direction was a change in the radiator grille design, which meant that the 'grille' was much more symbolic on the Volante, again to improve air flow. It wasn't a grille at all, in fact – just a shaped panel.

The standard engine in the Volante produced 100bhp less than the Coupé's Vantage engine and had no 'power-bulge', though several owners sought a conversion to Vantage specification and accepted the bulge.

This rear view of the Zagato Volante shows the simplicity and elegance of line from any angle.

There is no doubt that the Zagato Volante was a huge success, so much so that the company relented and allowed thirty-five cars to be built instead of the original twenty-five limited edition planned. It is interesting to note that several of the Zagato Volantes were returned by their owners to the factory for modification because they felt the car merited the 432bhp Vantage engine. The higher-rated engine was fitted in those cases, bringing with it, of course, the larger 'power-bulge' of the Weber-carburettored unit. At the same time, some customers also asked for the coupé-style radiator grille to be fitted. The result would have played havoc with the drag co-efficient, but it is reasonable to say that as a consequence of these retrospective changes the owners of these modified cars would own examples of probably the fastest production convertibles in the world! Whether they were capable of coming up with a 186mph (300kph) top speed is another question, though it is probably doubtful that any owner has ever tried to find out. One wonders how many of these cars will acquire the label 'V-8 Zagato Vantage Volante' in the future.

THE 'MAGIC' COMES TO AN END

Somehow, whilst the original intention was to build only seventy-five V-8 Zagatos in total, there were actually some ninety cars made, of which thirty-five were Volantes. This leaves fifty-six coupés, including the one which was converted to the Volante prototype. It is interesting, too, that apparently no two coupés were identical but for every car to be different in some detail makes it a most interesting 'limited edition'.

Whilst Ford pressure was not yet apparent at Newport Pagnell, the writing must have been on the wall for any future relationship between Aston Martin and Zagato as these cars were being built, simply by virtue of the fact that Ford already owned Ghia and – through that company – Vignale as well. The Zagato connection was now clearly dead – or was it? In 1990, there was just a very small number of DB4GT Zagatos built, under the label of 'Sanction II'. These were six-cylinder cars built in the exact specification of the original 1960s Zagato model – but for the V-8, it seems that connection will never again be made.

7 Into the Nineties with the Virage

As the V-8 Zagato was being made much of in the mid-1980s, Aston Martin Lagonda Limited was looking for its next production model, as it was felt that the William Towns V-8 Saloon was getting just a bit long in the tooth, and a new model would be needed for the 1990s. With that view in mind, the company went out to a number of design houses and asked for design submissions to meet that need.

Among those invited was William Towns, who was now working as an independent design consultant and who had done so much Aston Martin work in the past that he was a natural candidate. John Heffernan and Ken Greenley, designers of the Panther Solo project and the Bentley 90 were invited to submit a design, too, as was Richard Oakes, designer of the Midas Coupé, a sports car design which used much of the Austin Metro as a base. Then John Evans, who had been heavily involved in work on the Aston Martin Bulldog and Nimrod projects, asked if he could submit a design and was allowed to do so. Finally, right at the last minute, Mike Gibbs and Associates was given the go-ahead to submit a design, making it a contest of five.

Each design consultancy was asked to produce a quarter-scale model of its projected idea, and the deadline given for the models' submission was 13 August 1986 (no, it wasn't a Friday), just three months after the original invitations went out. This actually gave Evans and Gibbs only six weeks in which to complete their ideas. For a car which was to carry Aston Martin Lagonda Limited through the nineties, the first completely new car from that company in twenty years, this was a ludicrous time limit, but it was met by all entrants in the design contest.

None of these designers had the slightest chance to think twice about what he was doing. He simply had to conceive an idea, and it had to work for him or he would fail anyway. That was perhaps part of Victor Gauntlett's strategy, for he was always a great believer in concentrating the mind, and concentrate the mind this project certainly would for those bent on coming out with the development contract.

Once all the models were received at Newport Pagnell, Victor Gauntlett invited a selected number of people – dealers, customers and others – to visit the factory and view them. He had them put on display in the Service Department workshop one evening and invited those present to vote for the design they liked best. By this means, the outline of the Virage, which had not yet been named, was decided.

Winners of that vote were Heffernan and Greenley, who had submitted two models against everyone else's one, with Richard Oakes' design coming a close second. It seems that there was then quite a gap between the top three models and the rest, Evans' and Gibbs' designs not being sufficiently 'evolutionary', whilst William Towns was disappointed not to have done better. By October 1986, the design contract was

This was the design model submitted by John Heffernan and Ken Greenley for the new generation Aston Martin.

awarded to John Heffernan and Ken Greenley and Design Project 2034 began its gestation.

DESIGN OF A WINNER

Despite having submitted two scale models, one for a fastback and the other for a notchback, Heffernan and Greenley realized that their task had really only just begun, for much would change about the detail of their accepted model before it became a real car in the metal. The Factory Design Team also had a fierce task ahead of it, for Victor Gauntlett, in his inimitable way of focusing attention, had given the public début deadline as the 1988 British Motor Show, to be at the National Exhibition Centre in Birmingham in October. There were now just two years available to go through all the design, development and proving stages and bring the car to the show stand for the world to see.

From the Factory Design Team's point of view, a great deal had been learned in the exercise of developing the V-8 Zagato, which had given extremely valuable lessons in updating technology, as well as working with outside designers on bodywork. Quite apart from that, the Zagato had put some £6,250,000 in cash flow through the till at Newport Pagnell, though of course much of that went out in costs. None the less, a handsome profit had been made on the project, and the charisma had also been very valuable, for the Zagato had kept the Aston Martin name in the public eye, especially the buying public.

The task was to select which of Heffernan and Greenley's designs was to be adopted for DP2034. Feeling that the fastback would have made a much better Chevrolet Corvette than an Aston Martin, Victor Gauntlett decided on the notchback. His view was that there were more Aston Martin 'signatures' on the selected design, and so it would receive a much warmer reception from those who would ultimately pay for the car – the customers.

There is the story that immediately after securing the design contract John Heffernan almost lost it again – and all for a brief holiday! He had been under a great deal of pressure in 1986 and decided to take four days in Spain with his wife and daughter

The headlamp unit that replaced the 'pop-ups' in the new design was an existing production unit from Audi.

before getting down to serious work on the Aston Martin project. A meeting had been arranged with Victor Gauntlett and the Factory Design Team for the day he returned to England. However, he was caught up in a huge traffic jam on the way to Marbella airport and missed the flight. Questions were asked about how seriously he took this project, and he had quite a few 'moments' in the process of convincing everyone that he was. Thankfully, he managed it.

Having put that problem behind him, Heffernan went into discussions with the Engineering Team. Those discussions are on record as having been quite 'firm', in that his intention about headlights was firmly rebutted. There was no way that Aston Martin Lagonda Limited wanted to produce a new car with 'pop-up' headlamps. It had already been proven with the Lagonda that they were a source of constant problems. Occasionally they didn't work, and the weight of the motors to power them was excessive, as was

the cost. It was thought serious enough for the owner of a much less expensive sporting car to have the problems of failing headlamp motors, but it was unthinkable for that of a £100,000-plus car such as DP2034.

John Heffernan was not very pleased to lose this first battle because he had wanted to use a very low front end, in keeping with his idea of a sports car. However, he had to give in and begin the search for a suitable headlamp which would fit into a revised front end and be legal in Great Britain, Europe and the United States. That – surprisingly – was not easy, and the lamp finally chosen came from central Europe, from Audi. Now he had to adapt that lamp to the grille, whilst retaining an acceptable grille in the eye of Victor Gauntlett's engineers – and, of course, the man himself.

In the matter of the radiator grille, which was actually no such thing since air did not pass through it to the radiator at all, Heffernan and Greenley agreed with the Newport

The Virage front end as it reached production, with the definitive shape of the radiator grille clear to see here, as well as the front spoiler. This is not one of the prototypes, as can be seen from the lack of side vents (which were built into the first cars).

Pagnell thoughts, in that the identity of certain cars is expressed through their radiator grilles (whether air passes through them or not), and Aston Martin was just such a car. The design task was to create a grille, front bumper and headlamp combination which would be aesthetically pleasing, aerodynamically clean, capable of providing the forward lighting essential to safe high-speed night driving and impact legal in all the countries where the new Aston Martin was expected to be sold. After the use of much wood and clay, the task was satisfactorily completed.

The finished line of the Virage presented Victor Gauntlett with a truly magnificent successor to the V-8 series of cars, though in the process of forming and achieving it, the roof-line had to be raised to satisfy certain legal requirements, and the front spoiler changed shape almost as many times as John Heffernan changed shirts. The rear end from Heffernan's sketches had to be extensively modified and, in the eyes of some, including this author, it was perhaps a pity that the rear end was not made into a hatchback, to match the magnificent idea first pioneered in the DB2/4.

One of the Aston Martin 'signatures' that was seen in the Heffernan/Greenley prototype were the classic side-vents, pioneered in Aston Martin terms by the DB4 and carried all the way through to the V-8. This characteristic was featured in the early prototypes, but was abandoned as a production feature, probably for no other reason than that they served no actual function and proved to be an expensive item of decoration.

DEVELOPING THE CHASSIS OF DP2034

While the body lines of the new car were being sorted out, the chassis needed extensive design and development work, which involved the Engineering Team in burning a lot of midnight oil. The Team was headed by Rob Robinson, reporting to Bill Bannard, who carried overall responsibility for the Virage project. The enthusiasm was beyond measure, and this small band of experts together created a chassis, drawn up by Malcolm Pearson and his team, which was then built in model-form from balsa wood to establish what it looked like in three dimensions.

Much of the actual engineering design work was validated by the company's Computer-Aided Design/Computer-Aided Manufacture (CAD/CAM) system, which was installed over the winter of 1986/87, by which time the design work needed to be well advanced. Cranfield Institute of Technology (which had produced the prototype computer system for the Lagonda V-8 Saloon) was asked to evaluate the merits of CAD/CAM to Aston Martin Lagonda Limited, and after its report was completed, a system was installed and taken charge of by Peter Rang, who had come to AML from ISTEL, a Coventry-based CAD consultancy business.

Once that system was in, the rather Heath-Robinson practices of balsa models and a lot of hand drawing were eliminated in favour of the whole car design being concluded on CAD/CAM. Even the work already done was validated on the system, just to be sure that nothing had been missed. Bearing in mind the limited training time available and the extensive learning curve required to become competent in the use of such systems, it was a very brave decision by the Board of AML to pursue that route – but one that paid off in the end.

The Lagonda chassis was used as the basis for the new car because it was felt that the V-8 unit was too heavy and a bit long in the tooth. As soon as the Lagonda base was considered, it was thought that it would not be torsionally stiff enough as it stood, partly because the square tube sections didn't extend the total length of the chassis. There was also the accommodation of a newly designed front suspension to consider, so whichever path the engineers followed, there was a fair bit of original design work to be done.

From the beginning, it was always intended to build a Volante version of the Virage, so when it came to final chassis design, the torsional stiffness required for

an open car was engineered in. The whole project assumed a car without a roof, so that when the roof was added, it brought with it further rigidity. This solid philosophy also brought the bonus of allowing the stylists a little latitude in their design of the glazed areas of the car. The whole idea of this chassis was to create a strong, stiff structure on to which could be hung the mechanical components before the body – one of the lessons learned from the Zagato project.

THE LAGONDA 'MULE'

Development of the chassis for the new Virage required road testing, and it was decided that this new shape was not to be seen by the world outside until Aston Martin Lagonda Limited decreed it was ready. As a consequence, the first chassis built found itself clothed (or is it 'cloned'?) as a two-door Lagonda. Simply, the Lagonda V-8 panelwork used on this chassis was adapted to become a two-door car. To the world at large, as it drove by, or sat wherever it might stop on the roadside, this prototype would be a Lagonda V-8 Saloon, not a brand new Aston Martin in Lagonda clothing.

As part of the process of developing the rear suspension for the new car, it was agreed by the Board that the company should purchase an Alfa Romeo GTV6 in order to assess the performance of the de Dion rear suspension unit which used triangulated radius arms on a central pick-up for longitudinal location of the axle. Aston Martin engineers had come up with this idea as an original, thinking they had a 'first', but then they discovered that Alfa Romeo had actually used the same basic idea on the Alfetta GTV6. Whoops!

The principle of this design is that by using triangulated radius arms connecting to a central pivot point all the forces can be contained within the triangle and are

An example of the Alfa Romeo GTV6 was bought by Aston Martin Lagonda to assess the performance of its de Dion rear end with triangulated radius arms. The GTV6 in this picture took seventeen new speed records at MIRA's high speed track in 1983.

therefore not transferred into the car's body structure. The GTV6 is no slouch, and much of its handling quality is due to the careful design work which went into the installation of that particular de Dion rear end. On a

'Why re-invent the wheel?' philosophy, the Aston Martin engineers decided that the Alfa was worth investigation, which is a tremendous compliment to the Italian firm.

Having done all their investigations, the

This is the car which did so much of the development work for the Virage, the shortened Lagonda 'Mule'.

rear suspension was designed for the new Aston Martin. Surprise, surprise, it was the de Dion the team had designed, but now built from aluminium, so as to keep weight to a realistic minimum. The aluminium bit and the triangulated radius arms were what was new to Aston Martin Lagonda, for de Dion rear ends had been fitted to its cars since the very first DBS-V8. However, this one was different and new, so it needed testing and proving on the road, despite the comfort of CAD/CAM validation checks.

Once the new suspension had been fitted to the chassis, the Lagonda 'Mule' was driven slowly around Newport Pagnell, where it could be quickly recovered if anything went wrong, until everyone felt sure enough that this was the design for serious rig testing. It was then taken to the Leyland Technical Centre at Preston and put on a test rig to assess performance under all kinds of conditions, to predict fatigue life and generally establish the suspension's reliability and durability.

That Lagonda covered 35,000 miles

(56,316 kilometres) in testing all over mainland Britain to prove the new de Dion unit, and it did so with flying colours. The rear end was subjected to all kinds of abuse, both on rigs and on the road, and never made a murmur of complaint. Thus, the theory of using a triangulated radius arm, similar to the Alfa Romeo one but not identical, was now fully proved. The next step was the Virage prototype itself.

THE FIRST VIRAGE

Chassis DP2034/1 was ready by 1987, by the time of the Ford takeover in fact, to be fitted with its front suspension and taken out for testing. The bodywork had been completed and approved, but the front suspension did not yet exist. Somebody had to go to work pretty quickly and produce one! A Jaguar-based front suspension had been contemplated, but it was thought imprudent now, in light of the Ford involvement. Finally a variation on the Lagonda V-8 front end was

In near-profile, the smooth clean lines and superb proportions of the Virage belie the size of the car.

116

Aston Martin V8 Virage Coupé – 1990–

Vehicle construction

Steel box-section chassis with steel superstructure and aluminium bodywork

Engine

Crankcase/cylinder block material	Aluminium alloy
Cylinder head material	Aluminium alloy, twin-plug
Number of cylinders	8 in 90° V-formation, wet liners
Cooling system	Water – pump, thermostat and viscous-coupling fan
Bore and stroke	100mm × 85mm
Engine capacity	5,340cc
Number of main bearings	Five
Valve gear and operation	Two chain-driven overhead camshafts per cylinder bank; four valves per cylinder
Fuel supply method and type	Weber-Marelli fuel injection
Quoted maximum power output	330bhp @ 6,000rpm
Quoted maximum torque output	350lb/ft @ 4,000rpm

Transmission

Clutch type and operation	Single 265mm plate, hydraulically actuated for ZF 5-speed manual, or multi-plate torque convertor on Chrysler Torqueflite automatic
Gearbox ratios	Manual: 8.874, 5.540, 3.736, 3.062, 2.587:1 (reverse 8.053:1)
Final drive ratio	3.062:1

Suspension and steering

Front suspension	Independent – double wishbones, anti-roll bar and co-axial dampers
Rear suspension	Alloy de Dion, alloy triangulated radius arms, Watts linkage, dual-rate coil springs and telescopic dampers
Steering type	Adwest power-assisted rack and pinion
Wheel type and size	8J × 16in cast alloy
Tyre size and rating	255/50ZR × 16in Avon Turbospeed
Brakes: type and actuation	Vented 13in front and solid 11.3in rear vacuum-servo assisted discs, with split-circuit hydraulic system

Vehicle Dimensions

Overall Length	4,737mm
Overall Width	1,854mm
Wheelbase	2,610mm
Track (front and rear)	1,511mm/1,524mm
Overall height	1,321mm

settled upon. It required a new front upright to be connected to the existing Lagonda upper wishbones and lower link with a co-axial spring damper unit running through the middle.

Having established the requirements of the suspension design, the practical aspect was to find or make a new stub axle, a new upright, a new steering rack, steering arm, track rod and ball joints, because the prototype was to go to Germany for high-speed ride and handling tests. Finally, with all the new components in place, the Virage itself went to Germany, performed with flying colours and returned to a rigorous programme at Bruntingthorpe, a testing ground that was once an airfield (how many weren't?).

Now the details had to be sorted out. The interior was laid out with the help of a firm

Even looking down on the Virage, it maintains its elegance. So many cars are let down by this angle of view, but not this one.

called Anglo-Swedish Consultants and finally the production form was agreed upon. The prototype was examined again and again, then finally changed into something nearer to the production variation. The radiator grille was wrong. Victor Gauntlett walked into the workshop one day and is said to have commented 'Bloody hell, it's an Opel!', then a few days later was appeased by the change sufficiently to comment that it now looked like an Aston. The dummy side-vents disappeared, and the second Virage finally took shape, looking a little different from its predecessor.

Road testing, road testing, road testing – that was all that seemed to be done through the winter and into the spring of 1988. However, it was all to be worth while, for the car came together, piece by piece, and finally was able to be offered as a viable Grand Touring Saloon. 'Offering' is the operative word, of course, for a little of the technique that had worked so well with the Zagato was also tried here. Advance deposits were taken on sales of a car that was not yet built.

THE VIRAGE ENGINE

Barry Rowledge and Arthur Wilson are two men given the task of developing the V-8 Aston Martin engine for installation into the production version of this magnificent new car. Their task began with the job of making the engine capable of running on unleaded fuel and improving breathing by means of new four-valve-per-cylinder heads. The unleaded bit was probably not quite so difficult as producing a four-valve head. Our duo went to work with no experience of designing four-valve heads, and so someone else was going to have to help with that.

Hearing 'on the grapevine' that Aston Martin was looking for someone to design four-valve heads for the V-8, an American named Reeves Callaway, whose business, Callaway Engineering, was located in a small new England town called Old Lyme, Connecticut, came along and offered a proposal. He was competing against such companies as Porsche Design, Cosworth Engineering and Lotus Engineering, but

Lift the bonnet of a Virage and you suddenly realize just how big the power unit really is.

had the advantage of having done more four-valve head work than anyone else in the U.S.A. and that he could give a full two years to the project, at an economic cost and within Aston Martin Lagonda Limited's required timetable.

The Callaway contract called for an engine rework that involved the least possible interference with the design of the engine's bottom end, to achieve international emission control standards with a single-engine specification, to reach 300bhp power output from the one standard engine and to provide a basis for continuous development. At the end of all that, the cylinder heads were to be of four-valve-per-cylinder configuration. The man he brought in to help with the cylinder head design was Hans Herrmann, a German living in California, who had designed BMW's Formula 2 cylinder head in the 1960s.

Callaway's initial self-imposed target, having looked closely at the competition and decided that the Porsche 928 engine was the one to beat, was to achieve 70bhp per litre.

On a 5.3-litre engine displacement, that meant 371bhp, a chunk more than the originally targetted 300bhp of his contract. This was, as much as anything else, because the Porsche's 5-litre engine was proved at 61bhp per litre, or 305bhp. On the bench, Herrmann's cylinder head on the Aston Martin V-8 gave 65bhp per litre on the first run-up, which was a very reassuring 344bhp for the whole engine.

BRINGING IT ALL TOGETHER

Now that the suspension, the engine, the body shape and the interior were all resolved and the car was ready to 'go to work', it was time to bring it all together into one car and put it all to the test. Literally 'to the test', for type approval and impact testing were a very critical stage in the process of making the Virage legal for use in all parts of the world.

Aston Martin Lagonda Limited had

Unlike many Grand Touring cars of today, the rear end of the Virage is clean and unencumbered.

managed to secure exemptions from much of the developing emission, noise and lighting legislation in the motoring world, simply because the V-8 had been around for twenty years. However, a new car meant new compliance – not only with existing regulations, but with anticipated new ones, too, A fellow called Roy Goldsmith was appointed to the task of ensuring that each and every Aston Martin and Lagonda car which left the

An atmosphere of opulent space combined with simplicity of line inside one of the most elegant cars around.

Newport Pagnell factory complied with its destination country's requirements.

The list of items requiring testing and approval seems almost endless but particularly includes end-, side- and roof-impact yield limits, seat-belt anchorage standards, seat deformity limits, noise limits, exhaust emission standards, lighting regulations and rear-view mirror requirements. Chassis Number DP2034/2 was sent to the Motor Industry Research Association's proving ground at Nuneaton, where it was subjected to the side-impact and roof-impact tests required of it before it was driven, remotely, into a concrete wall at 30mph (48kph), to prove it would not bend too far in an accident.

After all these tests, the car was then subjected to the final humiliation of being checked for fuel leaks, battered again in the rear and the side and turned over once more through 360° to see if the fuel system leaked now. As one might expect, it did not, and the car was declared legal and more importantly safe to be sold in a wide range of countries throughout the world. The Virage had passed its tests.

'Bringing it all together' was now the final task before the launch of Development Project DP2034 as the Aston Martin Virage at Birmingham's National Exhibition Centre in October 1988, for the British Motor Show. The usual combination of simplicity and elegance were the hallmarks of the Virage's interior, with Connolly hide-covered seats (the front ones were adapted from Rover patterns) and walnut veneer dashboard and door trims. A two-spoke leather-rimmed steering wheel and leather-covered gear-lever knob were part of the driver comforts, whilst a quad-speaker stereo gave entertainment on the road.

The instrument panel had electro-luminescent back-lighting and a computerized information unit, with fault-finder. Security was a high priority with the Virage, for having spent your £110,000, you would not want to step outside and find your car gone without trace. Once the key was removed from the ignition, the car automatically shut down all of its systems so that only a genius would have been able to start the engine. In fact, the car even locked itself automatically after the key was out of the ignition for a particular period of time.

How did the name come about, you ask? Well, Victor Gauntlett can take the credit for that. He wanted a name which continued the letter 'V' as in 'Vantage' and 'Volante', and after asking around for suggestions, finally came up himself with 'Virage', a fine-sounding name, though in the original French, it means 'turn' or 'about turn'.

On display at the Birmingham Motor Show were two examples, both saloons, one finished in silver, the other in dark metallic green. Despite Jaguar showing its new

The Aston Martin V8 Virage and its Adversaries (1992)

Car and Model	Engine Type and Size	Gearbox	Max. Speed		Consumption		G.B. Price
			mph	kph	mpg	l/100km	
Aston Martin V-8 Virage Coupé	5,340cc V-8 tohc per bank	5-speed	155	250	11–15	19–26	£132,000 (1992)
BMW 850i Coupé	4,988cc V-12 sohc per bank	6-speed	157	253	14–19	15–20	£67,250 (1992)
Bentley Continental R	6,750cc V-8 pushrod	4-Auto	145	233	10–14	20–28	£175,000 (1992)
Jaguar XJ-S 5.3	5,343cc V-12 tohc per bank	3-speed	152	245	13–16	18–22	£50,000 (1992)
Bristol Britannia	5,898cc V-8 pushrod ohv	3-Auto	150	242	11–15	19–26	£91,000 (1992)
Jensen Interceptor Mk V	6,600cc V-8 pushrod ohv	3-Auto	140	225	12–16	18–24	£100,500 (1992)
Porsche 928GTS	5,397cc V-8 sohc per bank	5-speed	175	282	17–21	13–17	£67,000 (1992)

*Aston Martin's
Virage was a
sensation at the
1988 British Motor
Show, rivalling even
the Jaguar XJ220
and the Ferrari F40
for spectator
interest.*

XJ220 and Ferrari displaying the F-40, the Aston Martin Virage was a show-stopper in every sense. In fact, whilst the first customer car was not delivered until early 1990, the first two years production, at six cars per week, were sold long before the first one was out of the doors. Once again, there was a long waiting list, deposits were paid in advance and Aston Martin Lagonda Limited was moving towards a profitable state.

EXPANSION OF THE RANGE

True to its promise, the company unveiled the Virage Volante at the 1990 British Motor Show in the National Exhibition Centre at Birmingham. This original Volante was a two-seater in which the hood (fully lined of course) was power-operated and which, when lowered at the touch of a button, receded into its purpose-designed container between the passenger compartment and the boot. There was a platform just behind the two seats, upon which a very temporary and hardy passenger might have sat for a brief journey.

This magnificent machine was said to be capable of propelling its occupants along at a remarkable 155mph (250kph). As AML itself said: 'Setting new standards in soft-top elegance, the Virage Volante has recaptured the spirit of the golden age of grand touring ... The Virage Volante is a monument to the finest tradition of British cars'. One criticism is that the hood sat so high when lowered as to restrict rearward vision when reversing the car – so much so that the driver had either to know exactly the length of the car or be very good at guessing. This was all on a price-tag of £150,000-odd.

The year 1992 brought four very significant Aston Martin announcements. The first, revealed in January, was the 6.3-litre engine option. This engine was available as an option in new cars and also as a conversion to existing vehicles. It consisted of an increased bore and stroke, a revised fuel injection system, special Cosworth pistons,

The first open two-seater Aston Martin for many a long year, this is the original Virage Volante, the only two-seater built and displayed at the 1990 British Motor Show. The car is now in Sweden.

Aston Martin V8 Virage Volante Drophead – 1990–1993

Vehicle construction

Steel box-section chassis with steel superstructure and aluminium bodywork

Engine

Crankcase/cylinder block material	Aluminium alloy
Cylinder head material	Aluminium alloy, twin-plug
Number of cylinders	8 in 90° V-formation, wet liners
Cooling system	Water – pump, thermostat and viscous-coupling fan
Bore and stroke	100mm × 85mm
Engine capacity	5,340cc
Number of main bearings	Five
Valve gear and operation	Two chain-driven overhead camshafts per cylinder bank; four valves per cylinder
Fuel supply method and type	Weber-Marelli fuel injection
Quoted maximum power output	330bhp @ 6,000rpm
Quoted maximum torque output	350lb/ft @ 4,000rpm

Transmission

Clutch type and operation	Single 265mm plate, hydraulically actuated for ZF 5-speed manual, or multi-plate torque convertor on Chrysler Torqueflite automatic
Gearbox ratios	Manual: 8.874, 5.540, 3.736, 3.062, 2.587:1 (reverse 8.053:1)
Final drive ratio	3.062:1

Suspension and steering

Front suspension	Independent – double wishbones, anti-roll bar and coaxial dampers
Rear suspension	Alloy de Dion, alloy triangulated radius arms, Watts linkage, dual-rate coil springs and telescopic dampers
Steering type	Adwest power-assisted rack and pinion
Wheel type and size	8J × 16in cast alloy
Tyre size and rating	255/50ZR × 16in Avon Turbospeed
Brakes: type and actuation	Vented 13in front and solid 11.3in rear vacuum-servo assisted discs, with split-circuit hydraulic system

Vehicle Dimensions

Overall Length	4,737mm
Overall Width	1,854mm
Wheelbase	2,610mm
Track (front and rear)	1,511mm/1,524mm
Overall height	1,346mm

higher-lift camshafts and a new crankshaft which not only accommodated the longer stroke, but was of a much higher specification. The cylinder heads were reworked and the net result of all this was an engine pushing out 465bhp, 460lb/ft of torque and a 0–60mph time below 5.5 seconds.

There were other modifications, too, to the chassis and to the bodywork. The suspension was endowed with higher-rate springs and shock absorbers, together with revised roll bar and wishbone mountings. Tyres were now 285/45ZR rated Goodyear Eagles on 10.5in × 18in rims and the wheel arches were enlarged and flared to accommodate the change. Anti-lock brakes (ABS) also came as part of the package, and these included the largest-ever disc brakes to be fitted to a production car, at 14in in diameter. For around £50,000 to cover the cost

1992 saw the 6.3-litre conversion option announced. This is the rather more fierce-looking 6.3 Virage, complete with chunky wheels and tyres, side vents and rear aerofoil spoiler.

of this conversion, the proud Aston Martin owner had a 174mph (280kph) projectile to drive.

March and the Geneva Motor Show was

when and where the next Aston Martin revelation was to take place. This was the Virage Shooting Brake – the fastest estate car (station wagon) in the world. In the past,

This is the Shooting Brake version of the Virage, looking from this angle rather like Volvo's 480ES, but somewhat more purposeful and quite a bit bigger.

125

Aston Martin V8 Virage Shooting Brake – 1992–

Vehicle construction
Steel box-section chassis with steel superstructure and aluminium bodywork

Engine

Crankcase/cylinder block material	Aluminium alloy
Cylinder head material	Aluminium alloy, twin-plug
Number of cylinders	8 in 90° V-formation, wet liners
Cooling system	Water – pump, thermostat and viscous-coupling fan
Bore and stroke	100mm × 85mm
Engine capacity	5,340cc
Number of main bearings	Five
Valve gear and operation	Two chain-driven overhead camshafts per cylinder bank; four valves per cylinder
Fuel supply method and type	Weber-Marelli fuel injection
Quoted maximum power output	330bhp @ 6,000rpm
Quoted maximum torque output	350lb/ft @ 4,000rpm

Transmission

Clutch type and operation	Single 265mm plate, hydraulically actuated for ZF 5-speed manual, or multi-plate torque convertor on Chrysler Torqueflite automatic
Gearbox ratios	Manual: 10.26, 6.40, 4.32, 3.54, 2.99:1 (reverse 9.31:1); auto: 8.67, 5.133, 3.54:1 (reverse 7.79:1)
Final drive ratio	3.54:1

Suspension and steering

Front suspension	Independent – double wishbones, anti-roll bar and coaxial dampers
Rear suspension	Alloy de Dion, alloy triangulated radius arms, Watts linkage, dual-rate coil springs and telescopic dampers
Steering type	Adwest power-assisted rack and pinion
Wheel type and size	8J × 16in cast alloy
Tyre size and rating	255/50ZR × 16in Avon Turbospeed
Brakes: type and actuation	Vented 13in front and solid 11.3in rear vacuum-servo assisted discs, with split-circuit hydraulic system

Vehicle Dimensions

Overall Length	4,745mm
Overall Width	1,856mm
Wheelbase	2,610mm
Track (front and rear)	1,511mm/1,524mm
Overall height	1,320mm

coachbuilder Harold Radford had created the only shooting brake Aston Martins – and only eighteen of them – on the DB5 and DB6 chassis. This was the first time ever that Aston Martin Lagonda Limited had designed and built its own version – and it looked exactly right, not the least as though a bit had been 'stuck on' to the coupé. The tailgate was basically Ford, but by the time it had been blended into the body line, it looked made for the job. This beautiful car was hardly the place for dogs in the back, but ideal for holiday luggage and despite the slight increase in overall weight, the car's performance fell little short of that of the Coupé.

Third on the list of 1992 surprises was the next stage in the evolution of the Virage

The Volante 2+2 version with, below, the interior.

Volante, which was now made into a 2+2 drophead, with a slightly shortened rear deck to accommodate two rear seats, slightly restricted for size, but nonetheless of a luxury standard typical of Aston Martin. However, it was the fourth of these revelations that was, in a number of ways, the most significant, for it concerned the most

Aston Martin V8 Virage Volante Drophead – 1993–

Vehicle construction

Steel box-section chassis with steel superstructure
and aluminium bodywork

Engine

Crankcase/cylinder block material	Aluminium alloy
Cylinder head material	Aluminium alloy, twin-plug
Number of cylinders	8 in 90° V-formation, wet liners
Cooling system	Water – pump, thermostat and viscous-coupling fan
Bore and stroke	100mm × 85mm
Engine capacity	5,340cc
Number of main bearings	Five
Valve gear and operation	Two chain-driven overhead camshafts per cylinder bank; four valves per cylinder
Fuel supply method and type	Weber-Marelli fuel injection
Quoted maximum power output	330bhp @ 6,000rpm
Quoted maximum torque output	350lb/ft @ 4,000rpm

Transmission

Clutch type and operation	Single 265mm plate, hydraulically actuated for ZF 5-speed manual, or multi-plate torque convertor on 4-speed automatic
Gearbox ratios	Manual: 8.874, 5.540, 3.736, 3.062, 2.587:1 (reverse 8.053:1); auto: 4-speed
Final drive ratio	Manual: 3.062:1; auto: 3.54:1

Suspension and steering

Front suspension	Independent – double wishbones, anti-roll bar and coaxial dampers
Rear suspension	Alloy de Dion, alloy triangulated radius arms, Watts linkage, dual-rate coil springs and telescopic dampers
Steering type	Adwest power-assisted rack and pinion
Wheel type and size	8J × 17in cast alloy
Tyre size and rating	255/55ZR × 17in Avon CR228D
Brakes: type and actuation	Vented 13in front and solid 11.3in rear vacuum-servo assisted discs, with split-circuit hydraulic system

Vehicle Dimensions

Overall Length	4,737mm
Overall Width	1,854mm
Wheelbase	2,610mm
Track (front and rear)	1,548mm/1,566mm
Overall height	1,346mm

---

powerful Aston Martin road car ever offered for sale as a production model. This was the twin-supercharged 550bhp Vantage, a car which could deliver 500lb/ft of torque and a performance on the road that was simply awesome. It was a new-generation Aston Martin which would simply put every other so-called 'supercar' into the shade.

Development Project DP2055 began as long ago as 1990, almost as the original Virage Coupé was going into production. Styling models originally featured a separate aerofoil rear spoiler, a deep front air dam, side-vents (recollections of earlier Aston Martins) and five-spoke cast wheels. The final reality produced an extended,

With the Vantage came the return of the side vents. Here also are the five-spoke cast wheels.

integral, rear boot lip spoiler, large round tail lights replacing the originals, front and rear 'bib'-type lower spoilers, five-spoke cast wheels of a different design and size – and those side-vents.

Under the bonnet was a 5.3-litre 32-valve engine boosted by two Eaton superchargers, drawing fuel through a Bosch injection system. Each supercharger fed one cylinder bank, and each cylinder bank had its own throttle body, so it was almost like having two 2.75-litre engines running on a common crankshaft. All this was done in the name of reliability, as was the introduction of water-cooled intercoolers. The result was 550bhp at 6,500rpm and 500lb/ft of torque above 4,000rpm, though on the bench, it seems, engines have produced 580bhp on test.

To convey all this power and torque on to the road, the car was fitted, for the first time in an Aston Martin, with a 6-speed dual overdrive gearbox (that is to say that both fifth and sixth were overdrive ratios), which

in turn was connected to a 3.77:1 final drive. Sixth speed, however, was 0.5:1, so the effective final drive in top was an incredible 1.885:1. All this was transmitted to a set of 285/45ZR Goodyear Eagle tyres fitted to a set of 10.5in × 18in five-spoke alloy wheels, though there was no spare supplied with the car.

This most magnificent of supercars was apparently capable of going up to 191mph (307kph), though on a road test it was only taken to 177mph (285kph) on the Millbrook proving ground – probably for no other

---

Aston Martin V8 6.3-Litre Virage Coupé – 1992–

Vehicle construction

Steel box-section chassis with steel superstructure and aluminium bodywork

Engine Conversion

Crankcase/cylinder block material	Aluminium alloy
Cylinder head material	Aluminium alloy, twin-plug
Number of cylinders	8 in 90° V-formation, wet liners
Cooling system	Water – pump, thermostat and viscous-coupling fan not quoted
Bore and stroke	not quoted
Engine capacity	6,347cc
Number of main bearings	Five
Valve gear and operation	Two chain-driven overhead camshafts per cylinder bank; four valves per cylinder
Fuel supply method and type	Weber-Marelli fuel injection
Quoted maximum power output	456bhp @ 6,000rpm
Quoted maximum torque output	460lb/ft @ 4,000rpm

Transmission

Clutch type and operation	Single 265mm plate, hydraulically actuated for ZF 5-speed manual, or multi-plate torque convertor on Chrysler Torqueflite automatic
Gearbox ratios	Manual: 8.874, 5.540, 3.736, 3.062, 2.587:1 (reverse 8.053:1)
Final drive ratio	Manual: 3.062:1

Suspension and steering

Front suspension	Independent – double wishbones, anti-roll bar and coaxial dampers
Rear suspension	Alloy de Dion, alloy triangulated radius arms, Watts linkage, dual-rate coil springs and telescopic dampers
Steering type	Adwest power-assisted rack and pinion
Wheel type and size	10.5J × 18in cast alloy
Tyre size and rating	285/45ZR × 18in Goodyear Eagle
Brakes: type and actuation	Vented 14in front × 1.4in discs all round with vacuum-servo assistance and split-circuit hydraulic system

Vehicle Dimensions

Overall Length	4,737mm
Overall Width	1,944mm
Wheelbase	2,610mm
Track (front and rear)	1,548mm/1,566mm
Overall height	1,321mm

---

reason than that the driver on the day found himself running out of space. The Vantage is so far unequalled for power and raw performance combined with simple, elegant luxury, heading up a family of four cars which surely must convey Aston Martin Lagonda Limited into the second millenium with pride.

IMPRESSIONS FROM THE PRESS

The initial press reaction to the Virage was universal praise. No one thought it looked anything less than the new Aston Martin by right should look. No one thought ill of it. John Lamm, of *Road and Track* in the

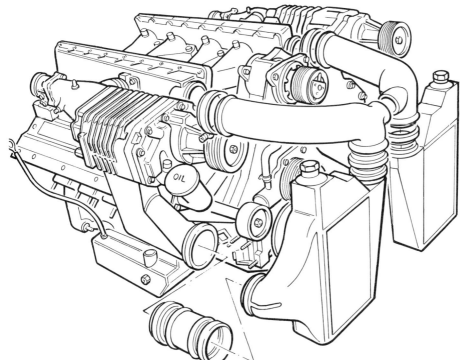

*This is the business
end of the Vantage.
The neatness of
layout can be seen
from this drawing of
the Vantage engine,
with its twin
superchargers
positioned as though
they were always
intended to be there.*

*The view familiar to
most of us of the
Vantage is the rear,
with the large
individual tail
lights and direction
flashers and the
integral spoiler.*

131

Aston Martin V8 Vantage Coupé – 1992–

Vehicular construction

Steel box-section chassis with steel superstructure
and aluminium bodywork

Engine

Crankcase/cylinder block material	Aluminium Alloy
Cylinder head material	Aluminium alloy, twin-plug
Number of cylinders	8 in 90° V-formation, wet liners
Cooling system	Water – pump, thermostat and viscous-coupling fan
Bore and stroke	100mm × 85mm
Engine capacity	5,340cc
Number of main bearings	Five
Valve gear and operation	Two chain-driven overhead camshafts per cylinder bank; four valves per cylinder
Fuel supply method and type	Weber-Marelli sequential fuel injection and twin Eaton superchargers
Quoted maximum power output	550bhp @ 6,500rpm
Quoted maximum torque output	550lb/ft @ 4,000rpm

Transmission

Clutch type and operation	Single 265mm plate, hydraulically actuated ahead of ZF 6-speed manual
Gearbox ratios	10.10, 6.786, 4.836, 3.77, 2.827:1 1.885:1
Final drive ratio	3.77:1

Suspension and steering

Front suspension	Independent – double wishbones, anti-roll bar and gas-filled dampers
Rear suspension	Alloy de Dion, alloy triangulated radius arms, Watts linkage, dual-rate coil springs and gas-filled dampers
Steering type	Adwest power-assisted rack and pinion
Wheel type and size	10.5J × 18in cast alloy
Tyre size and rating	285/45ZR × 18in Goodyear Eagle
Brakes: type and actuation	Vented 362mm front and 285mm rear discs with anti-lock system (ABS) and split-circuit hydraulic system

Vehicle Dimensions

Overall Length	4,745mm
Overall Width	1,944mm
Wheelbase	2,610mm
Track (front and rear)	1,548mm/1,566mm
Overall height	1,320mm

The Aston Martin Vantage V8 and its Adversaries (1993)

Car and Model	Engine Type and Size	Gearbox	Max. Speed		Consumption		G.B. Price
			mph	kph	mpg	l/100km	
Aston Martin Vantage	5,340cc V-8 tohc per bank, supercharged	6-speed	191	308	12–15	19–24	£177,600 (1993)
BMW 850CSi	5,576cc V-12 sohc per bank	6-speed	155	250	15–20	14–19	£77,500 (1993)
Mercedes-Benz 600SL	5,987cc V-12 sohc per bank	3-Auto	159	256	15–18	16–19	£96,400 (1993)
Bristol Brigand Turbo	5,898cc V-8 pushrod ohv, turbocharged	3-Auto	150	242	12–14	20–24	£105,040 (1993)
Bentley Continental R	6,750cc V-8 pushrod ohv	4-Auto	150	242	12–15	19–24	£168,940 (1993)
Ferrari 456 GT2+2	5,474cc V-12 tohc per bank	6-speed	186	299	12–16	18–24	£150,000+ (1993)
Porsche 928 GTS Coupé	5,397cc V-8 sohc per bank	5-speed	170	274	15–20	14–19	£69,875 (1993)

Another view of the Virage Volante, showing how well the open line suits the car.

United States, thought the car to be a dream and expressed great delight in 1989 at the thought that this car would be the flagship of AML into the 1990s. He commented that, when asked by someone at Newport Pagnell, during his visit there 'Will the car sell well in America?' he felt there was little reason to think that the Virage would not be a hit in the U.S. He went on to say 'Although Aston seems strong and healthy today, it wasn't that long ago that it was slowly crawling back from the brink. With the Virage, it should be able to roar away in top gear!'

A year later, Lamm returned to print about the Virage and eulogized again. He observed how unostentatious this car was, how luxuriously comfortable it was to sit in. He commented on the wood trim, the full instrumentation, the electronic back-up of information (though nothing like the complication of the V-8 Lagonda of a few years earlier). Performance was quoted as 0–60mph in 6 seconds with a top speed of

155mph (250kph) – even with a catalysed, unleaded-fuelled 'clean' engine. Fuel consumption was not quoted, and there wasn't much true driving impression quoted either, so presumably Mr Lamm had to wait in line for his chance of a thorough road test.

In Great Britain, it was in early 1990 that the first road test reports came out. The new suspension was the subject of considerable interest, and an early road test for *Performance Car*, described it in some detail, explaining how it was intended to keep both suspension loads and road noise isolated from the body of the car. The tester went on to observe that, as well as a higher level of comfort refinement, the Virage's suspension sustained higher peak cornering forces than its predecessor.

The tester went on to talk of tradition and how it was all there: the big front-mounted V-8, rear drive, the style and opulence of the hand-crafted alloy body. He wrote of the understatedly elegant ambience of the deep leather seats, the thick-piled carpets, the wood that looks like wood. Clearly, this tester was impressed, though there were no tables to confirm any of his findings. He simply concluded that the car had a potential for 155mph (250kph), 0–60mph in the near-5-second bracket and 0–100mph in 15 seconds.

The *'Daily Express' Guide to World Cars for 1993* (published in 1992) told of the Volante convertible's arrival to accompany the Coupé and showed a beautiful yellow example. They talked of the Ford acquisition and how it had benefited AML by giving it access to Ford finance, research and development facilities and buying muscle. The *Guide* also told of the introduction of the Virage Shooting Brake and Vantage Coupé, whilst the 6.3-litre engine option was touched on briefly – if almost as though it was insignificant.

By August 1993, the twin-supercharged Vantage was made available to *Autocar & Motor* for a comprehensive road test. Hardly surprisingly, the testers were impressed, though it didn't stop a little nit-picking along the way. Using the good old star-rating system from *Motor* (these two magazines were, by now, one), only one five-star award was made this time, which was really rather curious as it was for performance. However, the car scored four stars for handling, brakes, 'at the wheel', build and safety and noise – five four-star ratings and one five-star can't be too bad.

Marked down severely – and curiously – was the ride of the car, which only scored one star (don't know how you only score one star for ride in a five-star rating for performance?). It was made the more curious when the score for accommodation and comfort went back up to three stars! Build quality and safety might have scored five, but for odd little body rattles found in the test car, which would almost certainly have been bashed and battered around by the press so much as to make it an unrepresentative example. The equipment and value score is also curious, as the equipment level of the Virage in any form is beyond reproach, and one doesn't exactly buy a car like this with pure 'value for money' in mind. That's the kind of mentality that perpetuates the Fiat Panda and the Citröen 2CV.

All-in-all, this road test was odd because of its anomalies, but despite them, the tester could not hide the fact that he was in awe of this superb motor car. It's almost as though he had to look for faults to show he was

The Ferrari 456GT is seen as the nearest competitor to the Vantage as a super luxury 2+2 Grand Tourer.

The 550bhp Vantage is arguably the most powerful production GT available. It is almost certainly also the most luxurious.

doing his job and to hide the level of enthusiasm he felt. For example, the styling of the car, inside and out, clearly captured his imagination. Describing it as staggeringly fast, the braking was found to be spectacular, almost as though a huge hand just grabbed the car as one touched the brake pedal. Inside, the tester's only criticism were the Ford-sourced switches on the dashboard

— not much to shout about if that was the only notable fault he could find. He went on to write that after one look at the overall result, he was hooked! You may, therefore, conclude that the press found the Aston Martin Vantage to be what it truly is: one of the finest high-perfomance cars of its time available anywhere in the world.

8 Aston Martins and Lagondas at Play

For almost as many years as these two great names have existed, they have been active participants in motoring sport, either by full factory entries, by private sponsorships of factory entries, or simply at the hands of private entrants who have believed fervently in the ability of their cars to perform, quite apart from the belief that the world's race tracks are the rightful place of Aston Martins and Lagondas.

Nowhere has this commitment been better demonstrated than at the French circuit of Le Mans, a collection of ordinary country roads in western France which, when closed off for racing, become the most charismatic sports car racing venue in the world. Nowhere is the atmosphere leading up to a race so electric, so full of anticipation or so demanding of involvement from all who attend, be they competitors, officials or spectators.

We should not forget, however, that there have been, and are, other events organized by various clubs which include Aston Martins and Lagondas of a wide variety of ages and models among their competitors, to say

The date is uncertain, but this picture of Wilbur Gunn and passenger is clearly of an early Lagonda tri-car since, by the position of Mr Gunn's hands, it is a handlebar-steered machine. Judging by the vehicle in the background, the year is probably 1905, as the other machine is a 6hp Riley.

Count Louis Zborowski behind the wheel of one of the first Aston Martins built for international racing, one of the French Grand Prix cars of 1922, which was later named 'Green Pea' and survives to this day.

nothing of the Aston Martin Owners' Club itself, which puts on events for all makes of cars, if for no other reason than to prove the superiority of their own cars.

TO LE MANS – THE GREATEST RACE ON EARTH

Despite selling only a few Aston Martin 'T' Types between their introduction and the spring of 1928, 'Bert' Bertelli embarked on an ambitious plan to field two cars in that year's Le Mans 24 Hours Race. He was convinced that racing was a very good way to promote car sales, so a pair of competition three-seaters was created for that event. Drivers were Bertelli himself and Captain George Eyston aboard LM1 and Jack Bezzant with Cyril Paul (who later made a name for himself with Freddie Dixon driving Rileys) in LM2. Both cars retired, but not before Aston-Martin was awarded a special Rudge-Whitworth prize of one thousand

Francs for putting up the fastest lap by a 1½-litre car in the first 20 laps of the race.

Lagonda, in that same Le Mans, also its first time at the event, took four cars to the race. Two of the drivers, Captain Samuelson and Baron d'Erlanger, had a rather spectacular coming together with each other in the first couple of hours, when Samuelson skidded into the sand at Mulsanne and rolled into a fence, reversed onto the track, only to be shunted back into the fence by d'Erlanger. Both cars were damaged, Samuelson's going out of the race with a broken gearbox casing and a bent front axle. However, d'Erlanger's Lagonda finished eleventh overall to qualify for the following year's Rudge-Whitworth Biennial Cup.

There were many other racing successes achieved and much competition elsewhere between Aston-Martin and Lagonda, but Le Mans was the most spectacular – and a favourite of both manufacturers. It was also to be an event which Lagonda would win before the clouds of Hitler's war brought a halt to such sporting events.

LM1, A.C. Bertelli's first racing Aston Martin, prepared for the 1928 Le Mans 24 Hours Race, its first event.

LAGONDA'S GREAT VICTORY

Aston-Martin had done rather better than Lagonda at Le Mans up to 1935, finishing in fifth place, three years running between 1931 and 1933, when Riley's spectacular near-win and procession in 1934 pushed that team down the placings. Alfa Romeo had won every Le Mans since the last Bentley victory of 1930, but 1935 was Lagonda's year when, in a car sponsored by Arthur Fox (BPK202 – one of the 1934 Tourist Trophy Race cars), J.S. Hindmarsh and Luis Fontes produced a convincing win aboard the 4½-litre M45.

A single entry was submitted by Arthur Fox initially, with a second entry going in only at the last minute – too late in fact to be accepted as a full entry, so it was placed on

BPK203 was the second Lagonda entered for the 1935 Le Mans 24 Hours, driven by Dr J.D. Benjafield and Sir Ronald Gunter to thirteenth place. It is seen here in the slightly more leisurely pursuit of hill climbing at Shelsley Walsh during a Vintage Sports Car Club event.

the reserve list. However, as often happens, not all the entries made the start-line, so a second Lagonda was listed among the final fifty-eight starters, this one being driven by Dr J.D. Benjafield, who also owned the car (though it was run as Fox and Nicoll Team vehicle), and Sir Ronald Gunter. It finished the race in thirteenth place.

Aston-Martin, on the other hand, had no fewer than six cars cross the finish-line, the first of which (driven by Charlie Martin and Charles Brackenbury) was third, behind the winning Lagonda and the Heldé/Stoffel second-place Alfa-Romeo. The others placed eighth, tenth, eleventh, twelfth and fifteenth. Considering the weather and the huge entry list, this was a magnificent result, for there were sixty cars originally entered and several downpours through the event. It was also the longest list of British cars entered ever. There were Aston-Martins, Austins, Frazer-Nashes, Lagondas, MGs, Rileys and Singers. Better yet, seven of the first ten cars across the line were British.

Because of nationwide strikes in France and considerable unrest, there was no Le Mans 24 Hours Race in 1936, and 1937 saw only a single Aston Martin cross the finish line. This was LM20, an Ulster Two-Seater and the third-place car of 1935, now driven by Skeffington and Murton-Neale to fifth place overall and first in the 1,500cc Class.

Neither Aston Martin nor Lagonda had a car in the finishers' list for the 1938 Le Mans, for both firms had plenty of other problems to address at the time. Only fifteen cars finished that year, which could hardly be described as a vintage year for Le Mans, but Lagonda had achieved its finest hour back in 1935 and it was still being talked about as the entry list for the 1939 event was being prepared – especially since there were two Lagondas listed among that year's competitors.

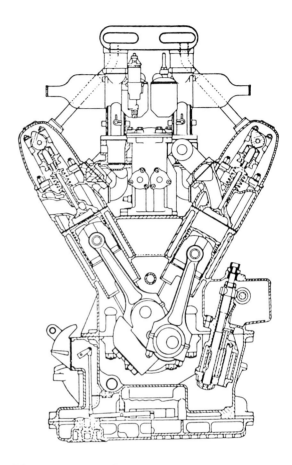

This cross-section drawing shows off W.O. Bentley's V-12 Lagonda engine well, except that it doesn't show the complicated exhaust-heated hot spot for the inlet manifold.

THE V-12 GOES TO THE SARTHE

As events developed, it turns out that less than three months before Neville Chamberlain declared war on Adolf Hitler's Germany, another pair of Lagondas was to appear at Le Mans. These Lagondas were different from anything that had preceded them, for they were powered by twelve-cylinder engines, and they had been designed by the man whose cars had already won the 24-hour classic race five times before. The man was W.O. Bentley; the cars were the 4½-litre V-12 Rapides.

By March 1939, Bentley had finally put the first Le Mans V-12 engine onto a test bed and was ironing out the bugs. It was to have four carburettors, an unusual feature for the time, which were to help the power output to 206bhp ar 5,500rpm, whilst the torque was 224lb/ft at 4,000rpm. The cars, of which there were to be two in the race, were also now in build, much attention being given to achieving the lightest possible weight within the rules. Finally, it was announced that Arthur Dobson and Charles Brackenbury would drive the Works car, whilst the other (a private entry) would be driven by the Lords Waleran and Selsdon.

Before the race, in order to attract the maximum publicity to Lagonda, Alan Good, then Managing Director of the company, threw a cocktail party to show off the new cars. W.O. Bentley was, of course, in attendance and so were several racing drivers, including a number of former 'Bentley Boys'. This was all aimed at prodding Rolls-Royce who, it seems, had made some publicity a few months earlier by exhibiting a Lagonda chassis in an article about testing. Rivalry between the two companies was strong, largely because of the presence of 'W.O.' at Lagonda, but it was to pale into insignificance as the race drew near, and minds were focussed on the business in hand.

British cars at Le Mans in 1939 were not numerous, but made their presence felt in the list of finishers. The two Lagondas (HPL448 – numbered 5 – and HPL449 – numbered 6) were accompanied to the line by single examples of Aston Martin, HRG, Morgan, Riley (French-bodied, this was a Pourtout-bodied example, one of the cars that had won the team prize on the 1937 Coupé de la Commission Sportive) and Singer. Of a field of forty-two cars that went to the start, only twenty were to make it to the finish on the Sunday.

Car No. 6 at Le Mans was the car driven by the Lords Selsdon and Waleran. It is seen here in a super-clean state in the pits before the race (no car could look that clean after 24 hours at Le Mans)!

Bentley's aim was not to win the race this day, simply to finish, and so he set a speed limit for the works car of just 1mph (1.6kph) faster than the previous year's race winner's average – just over 83mph (134kph). In the event, the cars were lapping at that kind of speed at night, but at something over 87mph (140kph) in daylight. Then problems began to crop up. The Dobson/Brackenbury car (Number 5) was reported to have a sticking clutch, making gear changes difficult, but it battled on, with Bentley's philosophy proving wise, as other cars were going down one after another.

At the finish, a Bugatti won, with Jean-Pierre Wimille and Pierre Veyron at the wheel, followed into second place by the Louis Gerard/Georges Monneret Delage. Fractionally over 3mph (5kph) behind the winner came the Dobson/Brackenbury Lagonda, followed into fourth place by Number 6, the Waleran/Selsdon car at a ¼mph (0.5kph) slower! Now came the 'ifs'. If Bentley had set a slightly faster pace, if the clutch had not tightened up, if, if! None the less, they came a very creditable fourth and fifth.

AS PEACE RETURNS

After the Second World War and the acquisition of both Aston Martin and Lagonda by David Brown, there was a brief settling period, then a man named St John Ratcliffe Stewart ('Jock') Horsfall, who had been associated with Aston Martins since the early 1930s, was now to be involved in the development of a new post-war car for entry in the 1948 Spa 24 Hours Race in Belgium. With David Brown's blessing, Horsfall and Claude Hill, then Engineering Director of Aston Martin, built LMA/48/1 as an open two-seater with more than a passing resemblance to Horsfall's pre-war C-Type Aston Martin. The car was actually finished at the track, last-minute bits being screwed on and adjustments made in the pits before the start of the race.

The Spa 24 Hours was, like Le Mans, a sports car event starting at 4 o'clock in the afternoon, though in the view of some it was a more gruelling race on this shorter circuit. Car number 54 in the race was LMA/48/1, driven by St John Horsfall and Leslie Johnson. The car to be feared most was Chinetti's

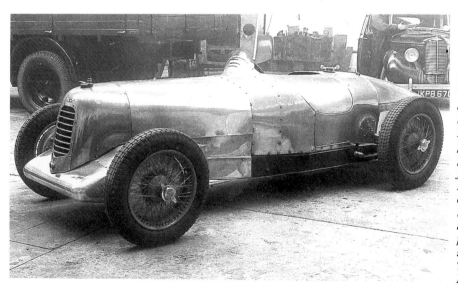

This is the famous 'Spa Special' of St John Ratcliffe Stewart ('Jock') Horsfall, without paint and clearly, from its condition, just completed. Horsfall drove this car alone for 24 hours at the 1949 Spa race to finish fourth overall and second in his class. That's Aston Martins for you.

V-12 Ferrari 166, though it was soon out with a blown cylinder head gasket. Horsfall and Johnson didn't put a tyre wrong, winning outright, the first Aston Martin victory of post-war years and the first race win for David Brown's company. They were later awarded the ERA Trophy, for 'The Best Performance by a British Racing Car and Crew in a Continental Event'.

The 1949 Le Mans 24 Hours was next, for which David Brown approved a team of three Aston Martins to be built. These were fixed-head coupés and the forerunners of the definitive DB2. Two (LMA/49/1 and /2) had 2-litre sports engines fitted, whilst the other (LMA/49/3) was fitted with the Lagonda 2.6-litre engine. LMA/49/1 was driven by Lance Macklin and Pierre Marechal (Marechal was involved in a fatal crash when a brake pipe broke, so that car did not finish its race). LMA/49/2 was driven by Arthur Jones

and Nick Haines to third place in the 2-litre Class and seventh overall, whilst Leslie Johnson and Charles Brackenbury drove the Lagonda-engined LMA/49/3, but retired with loss of coolant.

ENTER JOHN WYER

Aston Martins were now competing with increasing success. Lance Macklin drove a DB2 to second place in the 1949 Inter-Europa Cup at Monza. In the 1949 Spa 24 Hours Race, Leslie Johnson and Charles Brackenbury were second in the up-to-3-litre Class, whilst Lance Macklin and Nick Haines came third. In the meantime, a man named John Wyer was emerging as a force to be reckoned with in racing circles, having prepared a C-Type Aston Martin for Dudley Folland, which had almost won the 1948 Spa

Peter Collins and Pat Griffith drove this DB3 (DB3/5) to win the first Goodwood Nine Hours Race in 1952. The DB3 was the car which marked the beginning of Aston Martin's path to glory at Le Mans and in the World Sports Car Championship.

24 Hours Race ahead of 'Jock' Horsfall. Wyer had already established for himself an enviable reputation, based upon a military-like precision of teamwork, which had not escaped the notice of David Brown, so when the opportunity arose, he recruited Mr Wyer to the ranks of Aston Martin at Feltham, as works Team Manager, his task being to put Aston Martin in the forefront of sports car competition. The success of John Wyer's mission is today a matter of record.

John Wyer took Aston Martins to the pinnacle of success in his career with them. In the first race under his management, two cars were fifth and sixth overall, winning their Class and tying for the Index of Performance with a 611cc Monopole-Panhard. Teamwork was beginning to pay, as events showed. As the 1950s progressed, Aston Martins finished in the placings more and more. Their ascent to supremacy had begun, and John Wyer was making his mark on the world of international motor sport. It was to be an eight-year struggle against the odds and limited budgets, but finally John Wyer pulled his team through and achieved the one goal he and David Brown had aimed for

all along – they finally won at Le Mans.

1959 was the true glory-year for Aston Martin. It had enjoyed success and endured failure on the way, but now came the race everyone had been waiting for: Le Mans 1959. Three DBR1s were entered, as well as the prototype DB4GT. DBR1/2 was crewed by Roy Salvadori/Carroll Shelby, DBR1/3 by Stirling Moss/Jack Fairman and a new car, DBR1/4, by Maurice Trintignant/Paul Frère. The DB4GT was in the hands of Hubert Patthey and Jean Calderari. Two cars retired, the first being the DB4GT with a bearing failure after 21 laps, the other, the Moss/Fairman car after dropping a valve, causing an engine failure. Two Ferraris were out of the race by midnight and the other by ten o'clock on Sunday morning. The Salvadori/Shelby car won, with the Trintignant/Frère car just ³⁄₁₀mph (0.5kph) slower in second place. The Feltham team was delirious – victory at last!

As a result of their Le Mans victory and a little bit of luck along the way, Aston Martin found itself with the opportunity of winning the World Sports Car Championship, only a couple of points separating them from the

1959 was peak year for Aston Martin Lagonda Limited in competition, winning the coveted Le Mans 24 Hours Race with DBR1/2, seen here during the race, driven by Roy Salvadori and Carroll Shelby, and then going on to win the World Sports Car Championship.

When Aston Martin returned to competition with DP218, the V-8 engine, it started life in the Lola T70 Mk III. This example is seen at Tower Bend at Croft in August 1967, driven by Denny Hulme.

other contenders, Ferrari and Porsche. Victory at Goodwood sealed it, with a win from Stirling Moss, who was followed into fourth place by Maurice Trintignant and Paul Frère. This was it. Now Aston Martin were Le Mans winners and in the same year World Sports Car Champions.

AFTER RETIREMENT – THE PRIVATEERS

Despite the fact that Aston Martin Lagonda Limited had formally retired from racing, there were still Aston Martins being raced, and the company gave considerable support, even racing cars itself before retiring again in 1963. At this point, Aston Martin withdrew from racing having fielded Projects 214 and 215 in a bid for the 1963 Le Mans, after pressure from dealers around the world to go back to racing. With the offer of running Ford's new racing programme, to be spearheaded by the GT40, John Wyer

decided it was time for pastures new. That Aston Martin did not look set to race again for a long time, and that Ford's offer was very lucrative, meant he needed little persuasion. Even so, he was sad to leave, despite the new challenge and greater rewards.

It was to be 1967 that Aston Martin next went motor racing, and this time it was only with an engine. Whilst it was motor racing with serious intent, it was not Aston Martin's main purpose, for here the objective was only to prove, and if necessary de-bug, Tadek Marek's new V-8 engine. The result was the alliance with Eric Broadley's Lola T70. The association was valuable, in that it certainly helped to bring about the V-8, without which Aston Martin Lagonda's racing future would not have happened, but the combination was not a roaring success.

Another ten years were then to pass before anyone went racing again in an Aston Martin. That was 1977, when Robin Hamilton decided to take an Aston Martin V-8

This is Robin Hamilton's RHAM/ 001, a completely rebuilt V-8, competing at Le Mans and driven by Hamilton himself, Mike Salmon and Dave Preece.

racing from his home base near Burton-on-Trent, in Staffordshire. His target was Le Mans, and he managed to secure the financial backing of a wide range of sponsors. The 5¼-litre car, with new chassis number RHAM/001, was driven by Hamilton himself, supported by long-time Aston enthusiasts Mike Salmon and Dave Preece. Without full-scale factory support, which was not available at the time, it is hardly realistic to have expected Hamilton to win the race against the might of such factory teams as Porsche, who were wiping the board with the opposition at the time, but the gallant British trio kept their car going right to the end to finish seventeenth.

After rebuilding his car and fitting it with twin turbochargers in the process, Robin Hamilton took it back to the Sarthe Circuit for another attempt two years later. A pilot run in the BRDC Silverstone 6 Hours Race gave a chance to prove the car and boost confidence. Derek Bell and Dave Preece gave RHAM/001 a thorough shake-down in preparation for the big event, the 1979 Le

Mans 24 Hours Race. Drivers were to be Robin Hamilton, Dave Preece and Mike Salmon, as in 1977, but the car did less well than expected and retired after just two and three-quarter hours.

NIMROD – THE MIGHTY HUNTER

Next came Nimrod. The Book of Genesis tells us that Nimrod was the great grandson of Noah and that he was indeed a mighty hunter. It was a symbolic name for the car in which Aston Martin's engine was next to seek victory. In 1981, Robin Hamilton – a man who was clearly not a quitter – set up a new company called Nimrod Racing Automobiles Limited specifically to design and build a Group C racing team of two cars. One was to be fielded by Nimrod Racing Automobiles Limited and the other by Viscount Downe with the support of Pace Petroleum Limited, whose Chairman then was a certain Victor Gauntlett.

145

In 1982, Nimrod No. 32, entered at Le Mans by Viscount Downe (President of the Aston Martin OC) and partially sponsored by Victor Gauntlett's Pace Petroleum, finished seventh overall to be the first British car home, winning the Motor *trophy. The car was driven by Ray Mallock, Mike Salmon and Simon Phillips.*

The Nimrod was unveiled late in 1981 and was first driven in the Pace Petroleum-sponsored Silverstone 6 Hours Race in May 1982. Bob Evans and Geoff Lees drove the Nimrod-entered car, Number 31 in the race, whilst Ray Mallock and Mike Salmon drove Number 32, the Viscount Downe/Pace Petroleum car. Evans and Lees went out with a distributor failure, but Mallock and Salmon went on to finish a creditable sixth in a race which everybody expected to be a Lancia/Porsche benefit.

Under the same race numbers, the two Nimrods arrived at the Sarthe Circuit for the 50th Grand Prix de l'Endurance des Vingt Quatre Heures du Mans, the Le Mans 24 Hours Race. This time Number 31 was driven by Bob Evans, Geoff Lees and Tiff Needell, with Ray Mallock, Mike Salmon and Simon Phillips in Number 32. Both cars were well over the 800kg minimum weight limit, at 1,047kg and 1,051kg. However, these figures compared quite well with other production-engined cars, BMWs scaling 1,073kg and the Ferraris 1,075kg.

With Avon tyres, another old association was renewed, for Aston Martins had always raced on Avons, but as with John Wyer's experience in the 1955 Le Mans the 1982 Nimrod-Aston Martins had problems with

tyres. For some inexplicable reason, Number 31 came into the pits twice with a badly deflated rear tyre. All Avon could suggest was that they should raise the pressure in the hope that it would hold the tyre on the rim, as everybody had decided it wasn't a slow puncture, nor were the rims at fault. That solution had disastrous results later. By the time the fault was diagnosed, as the tyre was being sucked off the rim at high speeds, so allowing air to escape, Tiff Needell in car Number 31 had the problem in the race, spinning for almost 200 yards (180m) on the Mulsanne Straight and smashing rearwards into the crash barriers on lap 55.

Solid driving and fine teamwork meant that the other Nimrod was gaining as the race advanced, so after four hours it was in tenth place. At five hours it lay eighth, and by seven hours it was up to sixth position. During the tenth hour, the Nimrod gained another place as the result of the leading Rondeau retiring. Now, incredibly, it was fifth behind four Porsches, the only non-turbocharged car in the placings. Luck wasn't with Nimrod that day, however, for just after eighteen hours, the engine went flat. It had been using oil at an alarming rate for almost nine hours and after several pit-stops, it was still using oil, so fell back to seventh place. None the less, it held on to cross the finish-line behind five Porsches and a Ferrari.

EMKA JOINS THE FRAY

After another year, in 1983, the Nimrod was ready to race again, accompanied this time by a newcomer, an EMKA-Aston Martin. The new car was built for a man named Steve O'Rourke, a close colleague of the pop group leader Nick Mason (whose exploits are well known on the vintage racing scene). Designed by Len Bailey, whose experience included the Ford GT40, the Gulf-Mirage and Ford's C100, the fuel-injected Aston Martin EMKA first raced in the Silverstone 1,000 Kilometres in May, where the Nimrod finished seventh. The EMKA went out with a wheel bearing failure on the last lap.

At Le Mans, Ray Mallock, Mike Salmon and Steve Earle drove the Nimrod-Aston Martin, whilst Steve O'Rourke, Tiff Needell and Nick Faure drove the EMKA. They drove with caution, and by quarter-distance, despite the Nimrod's charging system having boiled a battery, the two cars were running well, the Nimrod lying eighteenth and the EMKA twenty-ninth. Just over half-way, the EMKA broke a suspension wishbone, causing a two-hour pit-stop, whilst the Nimrod had reached thirteenth position. However, '13' was unlucky that day, for the engine threw a connecting rod and finished the Nimrod's race. The EMKA kept going though, and despite its long pit-stop it managed to finish the race in seventeenth place overall, the highest placed British car in the race. Whilst everybody expected Porsche to win the race, they perhaps didn't expect the Stuttgart cars to fill ten of the first twelve places!

Nimrod and Aston Martin came up for more in 1984. Two cars this time, again prepared under the close scrutiny of Ray Mallock, went to the Sarthe Circuit to test their fortune against, among others, an old adversary, Jaguar. The two Nimrod-Astons were 31 (Chassis 005) and 32 (Chassis 004), crewed by Ray Mallock/Drake Olsen and

The EMKA-Aston Martin in the scrutineering bay at the 1983 Le Mans. Second from the right is Michael Cane, the EMKA team manager.

Mike Salmon/John Sheldon/Richard Attwood. Because FISA undermined its own commitment to stability of regulations and changed the fuel allowances (increasing them) just a month before the new season began, it meant that the Aston Martin engine could be turbocharged. With the recent experience of the Bulldog project, as well as the Tickford Ford Capri, Newport Pagnell set to and fitted a pair of Garrett AiResearch T04B turbochargers to the engine for Chassis 005. However, there were problems in testing and at the Silverstone 1,000 kilometres, so the whole installation was stripped and a naturally aspirated engine fitted.

Finally, the two cars, now in Bovis Construction colours, arrived at the circuit. The race plan was that the two cars would lap ten seconds apart, Number 31 leading, so as to allow pit crews to be fully prepared for scheduled stops. The early race ran to plan, Mallock coming in for fuel first, followed by Mike Salmon, but just before the third hour, Ray Mallock came back for a tyre change, having punctured a front one, as well as for fuel. Car 32 was now a lap behind, and the race was running reasonably well. By four hours, Number 31 was ninth, but then Number 32 lost ground because a left rear tyre was losing air, so another wheel change accompanied its fuel stop. Bad luck struck Number 31 again at six hours when Drake Olsen had another rear tyre failure just beyond the pits. His options were to retire or stagger on another full lap at much lower speed for another tyre change. He chose the latter course and managed to stay in the race, but not for long. Tragedy was just around the corner.

Three cars were in line astern on Mulsanne Straight: John Sheldon in Nimrod Number 32, Jonathan Palmer about 40 yards (35m) behind in a Canon-Porsche 956 and Drake Olsen in Nimrod Number 31 about 250 yards (230m) farther back.

Suddenly, Sheldon's car spun at high speed, smacking the barriers on his right. The car disintegrated, and bits flew everywhere. Then came the one thing all racing drivers fear most: the fuel tank split, and the car burst into flames. The Porsche and the other Nimrod were both put out of the race, though mercifully, Sheldon survived. However, two marshalls were struck by the car as it flew apart, and one died instantly.

Apart from the tragic death and injuries of that day, it was also a great shame that Nimrod and Aston Martin lost their chance once again to shine at Le Mans. 1984 had seen their best result for a long time and, based on the performance at the time of the crash, the Mallock/Olsen car could well have finished third. As it was, the team went home much chastened and Viscount Downe worse off to the tune of a Nimrod-Aston Martin.

Having not been seen on the circuits since Le Mans 1983, Steve O'Rourke's EMKA re-emerged at the 1985 Silverstone 1,000 Kilometres Race. The maximum fuel allocation was now 510 litres, which had a profound effect on the race speeds of many cars, as well as the tactics of driving. However, the Porsches had more to worry about than fuel allocation, as they seemed to be losing wheels at an alarming rate! Jonathan Palmer and Jan Lammers were in the lead when their 956 threw a front wheel after 102 laps. Thierry Boutsen's car lost two wheels and Jo Gartner, in another 956, also lost one. In all this turmoil, the EMKA-Aston Martin, in its smart new Dow Corning livery, was barely noticed when it retired. At least it had turned out and would re-appear at Le Mans in a few weeks' time.

The customary shake-down in the Silverstone 1,000 Kilometres was successful for the EMKA-Aston Martin in 1985, because it did well at Le Mans on 15 and 16 June. Team manager Michael Cane spent a lot of time on it and on perfecting his pit techniques. Driven

*Aston and Jaguar
. . . twenty five years
on.*

*The 'office' of
Nimrod.*

by Steve O'Rourke, Tiff Needell and Nick Faure, the EMKA was quickly up in the placings, so fifty minutes into the race Cane called the car in for fuel. The objective was to give Tiff Needell the chance of the lead as all the others stopped for fuel. Even after the stop, he was in third place, with the car running like a sewing-machine.

However, as everybody familiar with sports car racing knows, Le Mans produces strange twists of fate when they are least expected. Well into the race, while the EMKA was comfortably ahead of the two Jaguars entered by Bob Tullius, a split in the hydraulic pipe to the clutch slave cylinder took half an hour to fix and cost the team

its chance of finishing in the first ten. Nevertheless, it did finish eleventh, behind a clutch of eight Porsches and a pair of Lancias – not a bad performance for a privately entered team running on a shoestring budget. Once again, the EMKA-Aston Martin was the first British car home in the race.

For four years, there were to be no more Aston Martin cars or engines in endurance racing. The Union Jack was flown by the Jaguar team, run by Tom Walkinshaw Racing, which finally managed to win a magnificent race in 1988. Then it was 'Watch out Jaguar', for Aston Martin was to make a comeback with the magnificent AMR-1.

9 Back to Racing – The Protech AMR-1

Finally, Victor Gauntlett could resist the temptation no more. He had yielded to one of his quietly nursed ambitions and revived the Aston Martin/Zagato connection, and it had succeeded admirably. Now, he was to pursue another ambition that he had been pondering for long enough – to return to sports car racing, with the target of ultimately achieving a second World Sports Car Championship for Aston Martin Lagonda Limited.

August 1987 brought the announcement to the world that Aston Martin Lagonda Limited and the Scottish racing team, Ecurie Ecosse, were to work together to develop a new sports racing car for Group C. Discussions about the project had begun in the summer of 1986, when Victor Gauntlett, Peter Livanos and Hugh McCaig (the Chairman of Ecurie Ecosse) met and agreed they could jointly produce the new car, to be known as the AMR-1. Just one month after the press release which carried this news, Ford Motor Company took a controlling interest in Aston Martin Lagonda Limited, and a lot of people were now asking questions about the project's future. However, Ford gave tacit approval, subject to someone picking up the costs.

Thus, the project was to proceed, funded largely by Peter Livanos and Victor Gauntlett, with support from a limited number of sponsors. Once it was decided to go ahead, Max Boxstrom, the founder of the Dymag Wheel Company, was given the task of producing a chassis and body design, whilst

Reeves Callaway, of Callaway Engineering in the United States, had the job of developing a 700bhp 6-litre version of the Aston Martin V-8 in his Connecticut workshop. Ecurie Ecosse and Ray Mallock took on a development contract for the complete car, it having been decided at a very early stage that if the car didn't show enough promise in testing, then it would be abandoned. Some insurance against failure was the appointment of Richard Williams as the development team manager. He came to the project from a highly successful period with Ecurie Ecosse.

CREATION OF A NEW DREAM

As 1988 advanced, so did the new Aston Martin Group C contender for the World Sports Car Championship. It became clear to the world that this new car was in fact all Aston Martin and that Ecurie Ecosse's relationship was akin to that of Tom Wallkinshaw Racing and Jaguar. The team was essentially the managing agent for the manufacturer. A quarter-scale model had been built for wind-tunnel testing in September 1987, and design development for the body components progressed alongside improvements in aerodynamics. To the world at large, the AMR-1 Group C Car was about to take shape.

Design of the body unit consisted of a driver capsule – the 'tub' – built from Kevlar,

As with Grand Prix cars, the 'tub' of the AMR-1 was the driver capsule and the bit to which everything was anchored. Considering the finished size of the car, it looks pretty insignificant in this view.

which featured integral anchor points for the rear structure (to carry the engine, gearbox and rear suspension) and the front suspension. Body panels would be clipped individually to the assembly and so the whole would be relatively easy to assemble and dismantle. FISA regulations were, as ever, fluid to the last and no one knew for certain what size the final racing engine would be, so the first two built were of 5.3-litre capacity and two of these were available for testing by the beginning of May 1988. On test, they produced 550bhp at 7,000rpm, which boded well for the 6-litre units that were ultimately expected to power the AMR-1 in action.

Because FISA (typically, said some) could not or would not make up its mind about the regulations for the Group C World Sports Car Championship, three different engine sizes had to be considered for the AMR-1 to ensure its eligibility on the day. These were the production capacity 5.3-litre, the

Callaway-developed 6-litre, and a 6.4-litre. As rules became clearer, the 6.4-litre unit was abandoned for all but development purposes, leaving the 5.3-litre and the 6-litre as the race units. The first two arrived from Connecticut in June and July, then two 6-litre units followed soon after.

Upon receipt, the two 5.3-litre engines were tested up to their quoted 550bhp at 7,000rpm and were found not to be wanting. In fact, they were capable of yielding 600bhp at 8,500rpm. The 6-litres were, on the basis of the experience with the 5.3s, reckoned to be likely to produce 650–700bhp. Now the task in hand was to prepare a complete car for testing and to have the engines capable of running with restrictions, should that prove necessary in the event that FISA did not grant homologation. For this, the manufacturer had to prove a capacity to build up to 200 engines and, whilst the Technical Commission could accept the intention to manufacture in such number as justification

This is the power pack of the AMR-1. Doesn't look much sitting on a trolley, does it?

for homologation, they were not bound to do so and could have insisted on the number being built before certification.

DEVELOPMENT OF THE DREAM

Brian Redman was drafted in as a test driver for the AMR-1 project, which was now beginning to take shape, in support of team drivers Ray Mallock and David Leslie, whose combined experience of driving high downforce cars was somewhat limited. Peter Livanos was said to favour Redman's arrival on the scene because of his much greater experience and because press coverage in the United States was likely to be broad and attract a lot of interest. Not unreasonably, Mr Livanos was anxious that the attention given the project from that quarter would be positive.

With Ted Cutting (a name which conjures

up memories of Aston Martin's glorious days of the DBR-1) conducting technical audits on the project, and Michael Bowler (previously editor of *Thoroughbred and Classic Car* magazine) representing AML at the FISA manufacturers' meetings, progress was being made towards a June 1988 testing objective. This target had been set in April, in typical Gauntlett attention-focusing manner, with the car's first race meeting planned for the Spa-Francorchamps 1,000 Kilometres Race in September. However, Richard Williams went on record to say that a complete and fully competitive car by the year was far more important than a rushed first race at Spa, especially if it proved unsuccessful.

Whilst the strength of the mighty Ford Motor Company's buying power was put to use as far as was possible with component suppliers, it was also realized that many of the parts being made for the AMR-1 were not exactly standard production items. The delays resulting from slower manufacture of components than first anticipated meant that the AMR-1/01 was unveiled to senior Ford and Aston Martin management in late October, making its first test run at Silverstone almost a month after that.

PROTECH TAKES OVER AMR-1

The formation of Proteus Technology came about as part of the strategic policy to separate the racing programme from the business of production and selling of cars. Ford wanted the world to see that Aston Martin Lagonda Limited was a serious manufacturer of luxury cars, so whilst willing to go along with the AMR-1 programme, it was important that the world at large saw the two as being different interests with different objects in life.

Thus, Protech, as it became known, was established to take over the whole AMR programme. Early in 1989, the Aston Martin Group C1 project was declared to be official, when it was also announced that it was primarily to be underwritten by Peter Livanos, whose 12½ per cent stake in AML was to remain entirely independent of the £26 million he'd committed to a six-year development programme for AMR-1 and for funding the creation of a 3½-litre engine in preparation for the anticipated Group C Formula change.

The official announcement of AMR-1 and Protech's formation to manage the project was made on 25 January 1989. There were sighs of great relief amid genuine cheers of support from all areas of industry and the sport for the revival of one of Britain's great motor sporting names. Work on the AMR project was now transferred from Ray Mallock's workshop in Roade, Northamptonshire to the new site in Milton Keynes, where Protech was to be based. Now – under the direct control of Richard Williams – the AMR-1's development would go into top gear.

Technically, this new car was a collection of tremendous innovations combined with thoroughly sound engineering. The body was created around Grand Prix design practice, in that it used a central 'tub' to accommodate the driver, with everything else anchored or clipped to it. The panel work and 'tub' were made from carbon fibre and Kevlar composites, the monocoque being created from just these mouldings. The engine was attached to the rear wall of the 'tub' and coupled to a gearbox of Aston Martin Lagonda's own design (in preference to buying one in and de-bugging it), behind which, integral in the gearbox casing, was the differential. The design concentrated on keeping the polar moment of inertia as low as possible, thus maintaining maximum performance in hard cornering under high 'G' forces.

The 'coke-bottle' shape (or 'area rule' as it is properly described) was one proved many years ago in aeronautical engineering (and probably best recognized as a feature of the fuselage of the RAF's Buccaneer aircraft). It only becomes obvious when one looks at the car from behind and sees the 'waisting' of the side panels into what appears to be just a gap at the rear of the front wings, but Max Boxstrom had given it more thought than that!

The design objectives were to achieve maximum aerodynamic efficiency in terms of penetration though the air, whilst maintaining maximum stability on the surface, seeking the best possible 'ground-effect' available within the rules, whilst also providing maximum cooling. Boxstrom gave a great deal of thought to cooling – of brakes, of the driver and of the engine. They were all accounted for in the ultimate shape he gave the car. He endowed it with superb aerodynamics and created a very shallow

This cutaway drawing shows clearly the neat, businesslike layout of the AMR-1 and whut a tight package it was.

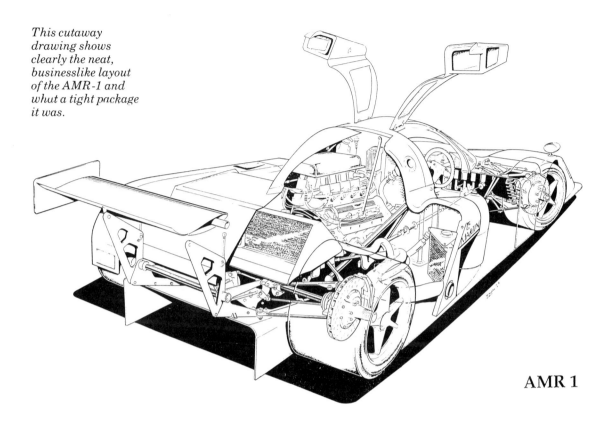

AMR 1

'tunnel' underneath the 'tub', into the engine compartment and out underneath the car, which provided a combination of highly efficient cooling and 'ground-effect'.

DEVELOPING THE AMR-1 ENGINE

Engine development was very much the task of Reeves Callaway, whose Connecticut-based workshop had created the four-valves-per-cylinder heads for the basic production 5.3-litre Virage engine. Engine performance in racing situations had always been seen as a limiting factor until Callaway's four-valve head was perfected, 7,000rpm being the previous practical maximum engine speed.

Early development problems were soon overcome and the new cylinder heads were completed, having achieved much improved water flow for efficient cooling and centrally located spark plugs for a more efficient fuel burn. Attention then turned to crankshaft damping and lubrication, the first problem being solved with a fluid damper and the second by dry-sump lubrication. Determining the best oil scavenging and baffling took a lot of time and attention, but the resulting engine durability proved it all worth while. The engine mounting was inclined to the right (facing forward) so as to allow for the provision of Max Boxstrom's under-body air tunnel. The engine management system came from a British company called Zytec, which had proved it was able to provide prompt back-up support.

According to Richard Williams, the biggest problem attached to producing this

The engine of the AMR-1 fills the space allocated to it with no room to spare. Now it does begin to look the part!

revolutionary racing car was its actual design and production. He explained his point by saying that '. . . the biggest problem of the design is getting the drawings out, because you're constantly thinking of the Mark 9 version while you're trying to finish the Mark 1!' A profound, but very relevant statement, with so many new ideas to embody in one car. However, modifications were, naturally, being made as AMR-1/02 and AMR-1/03 progressed into the build stage.

Testing continued at Donington Park, and during the programme, David Leslie suffered a hub failure in AMR-1/01, which sent him careering off the circuit, damaging the 'tub' and so demanding the speeding up of completion of AMR-1/02. Despite the damage, there was enough test data for Richard Williams to decide that despite the prototype being overweight, lap times were competitive with those of Formula 3,000 cars, as well as comparing well with the Jaguar

XJR-9, which was also testing at Donington. However, there had yet to be a Group C race at Donington Park to give real and direct comparisons between types.

Protech now acquired a fully equipped transporter with which to move about these magnificent new racing machines, with the objective of starting Aston Martin's 1989 racing programme off on the right foot. It consisted of a tractor unit and 12m semi-trailer, the trailer being capable of carrying two cars and a lot of tools and spares. The first journey to be undertaken by this brand new transporter was to Dijon-Prenais for the Dijon 480 Kilometre Race.

OFF TO THE RACES

The 1989 Dijon 480 Race was held on 20 and 21 May, and the Aston Martin team turned up in its brand new transporter, with AMR-1/02 on board. Nobody expected miracles, for

These two views of the AMR-1 show its clean lines and functional appearance – it's also bigger than it looks! The black diagonal stripe on the front left wing was applied as a mark of respect to John Wyer, who died in 1989.

Here's the way to go racing! In this picture are two of the AMR-1s, the support team and the two transporters which were used in the 1989 season.

during testing, two of the 6-litre Callaway engines had blown up, rather unexpectedly and totally out of character. The team had already missed the first round of the World Sports Car Championship at Suzuka in Japan, which had cost a fine of £250,000 because the entry was for a series of races.

Come Race Day at Dijon, Brian Redman and David Leslie found the car to be suffering the problem of having too much downforce and so not enough pace. Other shake-down problems were easily solved, but the car's uncompetitive speed would need a little more work at home. Even so, despite running on the circuit described by many as 'the most taxing in the Championship', the AMR-1 came home in seventeenth place out of thirty-six starters and ahead of five Porsche 962s. The two Jaguars went out of the race altogether, leaving the Aston Martin to cross the finish-line as the first British car home.

The Le Mans 24 Hours Race was next, with two cars entered. AMR-1/02 was numbered 18 for the race, to be driven by Brian

Redman, Michael Roe and Costas Los, whilst AMR-1/03 was numbered 19 and was to be crewed by David Leslie, Ray Mallock and David Sears. Number 19 was seemingly riddled with gremlins and so wasn't out to practise until after the start of the second session. This limited the time available for de-bugging, in addition to which Number 19 was the last car of the race to go for scrutineering. After tracing a vibration problem in Number 18 to a stone caught in a vent hole of one of the rear brake discs, the cars were finally ready for the race and were taken out to the start.

After a couple of minor pit-stops, both cars went into the night in good form, though not high in the placings, but Number 19 did not emerge. Just after 2.30 a.m., it had blown its engine in a major way and came to a somewhat abrupt stop near Mulsanne whilst in twentieth position. Number 18 continued into daylight and caused a bit of a flutter in the Aston Martin pit when Brian Redman reported a broken suspension rose joint. Once repaired, he went back out into twelfth

Despite the overall width of the car, there's not an awful lot of room inside an AMR-1.

This was Brian Redman's first finish at a Le Mans 24 Hours – and it was a very creditable finish for the AMR-1: eleventh in only its second-ever race.

place and, as a Mazda 767 made a pit-stop, the Aston went up to eleventh. It held that position until the end of the race, to the absolute delight of everyone at Protech, as well as the British fans at the race on the day. This was only the AMR-1's second ever race.

Having returned from Le Mans with something to its credit, the team could now relax for a brief period, as a policy decision was made at the beginning of the season to miss the Spanish round of the World Sports Prototype Championship, preferring to have more time to prepare for the first British round at Brands Hatch in July. A lot of time was taken up with improving the suspension, then engine reliability and fuel consumption. The power output of 650bhp was thought plenty for the job in hand, but weight was another area of concern, and a lot of time was spent searching out even the smallest saving, with the view that grams add up to kilograms and with the knowledge that AMR-1/03 was already 40kg lighter than AMR-1/01.

The next AMR-1 to be built was AMR-1/04, and it weighed in at 920kg, a very creditable 60kg lighter than AMR-1/01. David Leslie was to drive this newest car, under Number 18, in the Brands Hatch race. He managed to reach fourteenth place on the grid, with a very useful qualifying lap time of just under 1 minute and 18 seconds. Brian Redman partnered Leslie for this race, and between them they gave Jaguar a fair run for its money, harrying an XJR-9 and a Spice on the way. At the front of the race, the leading turbocharged Jaguar XJR-11 was having serious problems keeping both Sauber-Mercedes at bay, as it battled with excessive fuel consumption.

Fewer than 20 laps from the end of the race, Mauro Baldi and Kenny Acheson's Sauber-Mercedes was in the lead, followed by Jo Schlesser and Jochen Mass's sister car. Following was Bob Wollek's Porsche and

Johnnie Dumfries's Toyota, then Jan Lammers' XJR-11, Bellini's Spice, Nielsen's Jaguar XJR-9, with the Aston Martin bringing up eighth place. As the pace and pressure increased, so cars began to drop out. Just 6 laps from the end, David Leslie couldn't believe his luck – he was in fourth place, behind the Baldi/Acheson Sauber-Mercedes, the Wollek/Jelinski Porsche and the Schlesser/Mass Sauber-Mercedes. Just imagine the reactions at Newport Pagnell, to say nothing of the atmosphere in the pits at the end of the race. Aston Martin had finished fourth in its third race, vanquishing all the Jaguars on the way. What a victory – and what a celebration afterwards.

THE SECOND HALF OF THE SEASON

Next on the racing calendar was Nürburgring, on 20 August, and again a single car was entered, to be driven by David Leslie and Brian Redman. By now, carbon-fibre brakes and revised rear suspension uprights had been fitted, though it was feared that the car wasn't ideally suited to this circuit. From a twenty-first position on the starting grid, David Leslie soon had the car up to fifteenth place, but the top-end speed and handling just weren't quite there, with the result that the Aston Martin would not win this race. Fuel consumption, on the other hand, was not a problem, whereas several other cars, especially the Jaguars, were running into trouble. At the end of that day, Aston Martin finished in a creditable, if not glorious, eighth place.

Early September saw another round of the Championship on home soil. This was at Donington Park, where much of the AMR-1's testing had been done. It should therefore have been no surprise to see an Aston Martin higher on the grid than it had been all season, with David Leslie putting

A beautiful surviving example of the 11.1hp Lagonda, this 1913 car was found alongside a Towns Lagonda V–8 at a recent classic car show.

The mightiest Aston Martin of them all. Winner of the 1959 Le Mans 24 Hours Race, this is DBR1/2, the car driven to victory by Roy Salvadori and Carroll Shelby, pictured at the Museum of British Road Transport in 1994.

The DBS–V8 'in the metal'.

The long, low lines of the Lagonda V8.

Tail end of the DBS-V8, this picture shows the clean, crisp line of the original design.

The vented cast road wheels of the DBS–V8 instantly identified it from the wires of the six-cylinder engined DBS. Reminiscent of Porsche's 'cookie cutters', this is actually a more functional and robust wheel.

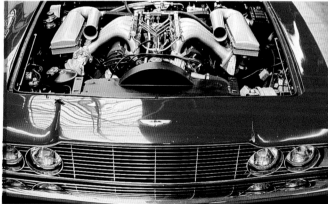

Two under-bonnet views of the DBS–V8s, that on the left being a US-specification car (with 'pancake' style air cleaners). The car on the right is a domestic-specification model.

The V–8 Volante. This is actually a 'PoW' (Prince of Wales) specification car.

Two V–8 Volante dashboards – one early, one late – showing that the differences over the years are very little. The steering wheel and column have changed, as has the radio installation, but very little else.

The second variant of the V8 Volante, with no bonnet bulge to intrude on the line of this truly elegant roadster.

The Nimrod Aston Martin, in Bovis colours, stands in the pits at Le Mans in 1983 (identified by the race number 39). Sadly, this car retired after eighteen hours.

Front and rear quarter views of the Bovis Nimrod, showing the neatness of line and finish.

When the team, the cars and the transporters were ready for a season's racing, this shot was taken of Ray Mallock, Michael Bowler and Richard Williams with one of the cars and the transporters . The Protech Aston Martins meant business.

No 18 on the circuit at Donington, driven by Brian Redman .

One of the fastest, and certainly the most exquisite, high-performance dropheads is the Virage Volante. This is the two-seat prototype . . .

. . . and this is the 2–4 seat Volante.

Practice over, AMR-1/05 is rolled into the pit garage at Donington Park, ready for the following day's race. David Leslie and Michael Roe took this car to sixth place in the race.

AMR-1/05 (numbered 19) into tenth position. A new car, AMR-1/05, was now complete, weighing in at 906kg, some 74kg lighter than /01. The driver line-up for Donington was Brian Redman and David Sears in AMR-1/04 (18) and David Leslie and Michael Roe in AMR-1/05.

The race was run in brilliant sunshine. Early on, Brian Redman managed to put Number 18 into fourth place, behind a Nissan, a Sauber-Mercedes and a Porsche. Michael Roe was just behind him, in fifth. However, a number of the others had been driving a 'tactical' race, in addition to which

Brian Redman on a charge, coming through into Goddards in the Donington Park Round of the 1989 World Sports Car Championship Series.

AMR-1/05 with David Leslie at the wheel.

David Sears began to suffer clutch-slip, and as if that was not enough, the front anti-roll bar broke and began to hack large lumps out of the front right-hand tyre. Even so, the two cars kept running, and by the end of the race were in sixth and seventh places, Number 19 being the lead car of the two. Donington Park had given the Protech team a good result and put another smile on Victor Gauntlett's face, especially as once again an Aston Martin was the first British car across the line.

Spa-Francorchamps was the penultimate round of the 1989 Championship. It was a bitterly fought race, with some less-than-gentlemanly practices employed by one of the Jaguar drivers at the start. Protech took two cars out again: AMR-1/04 as Number 18, piloted by Brian Redman/Stanley Dickens, and AMR-1/05 as Number 19 to be driven by David Leslie/David Sears. Dickens had driven in the Le Mans-winning Sauber-Mercedes, so when he became available was considered eminently suitable to partner Redman.

After a wet practice day, in which the Aston Martin ignition systems suffered, and handling needed some minor attention, the two cars went into the race from thirteenth and thirty-second places on the grid. Having 'tweaked' the suspensions on both cars to fit the conditions and the circuit, both unfortunately suffered from understeer. Nevertheless, cars and drivers went out and gave their best. Sadly, as Michael Roe rose to eighth place in Car 19, a connecting rod in the engine broke loose, and the engine blew up, so ending Roe's race.

Despite the first engine failure in a race with the AMR-1, Richard Williams was not downhearted, as he saw Brian Redman bring car Number 18 up to ninth place by lap 60. The Jaguars were out again, and by the end of the race – another Sauber-Mercedes benefit – the Aston Martin followed the Baldi/Acheson Sauber, a Porsche

962, a Nissan, another Porsche 962, a Spice-Cosworth and a third 962 to finish in a very well-earned sixth place.

The last race of the year was in Mexico, where only one AMR-1 was entered. Immediately, it was at a disadvantage because of the effects of altitude on its naturally aspirated engine. However, that engine was a much-modified 6.3-litre variant of the Aston Martin V-8, with cross-bolted big ends and improved power/torque characteristics. The single car was AMR-1/05 and the drivers were Brian Redman and David Leslie. With something over a 17 per cent power loss from the effects of altitude, they never went into this race expecting any spectacular result, so they drove just to stay in the race, which they certainly achieved.

Mexico was a crowded affair, with the whole field driving a very closed-up race. As a result, David Leslie had a hard time finding his way past his slower adversaries, especially the Porsche of Reuter and Konrad, though he did finally make it. However, he just could not get past the Spaniard, Pareja, in Walter Brun's Porsche 962, partly because the Porsche was quicker on the straights and partly because Pareja managed to make his car very wide when he needed it! At one point, it seems Leslie's foot slipped off the brake pedal into a corner, with the result that he shunted the Spaniard's car rather hard. There was some heated discussion after the race, but that had not deterred Leslie from finishing a very useful eighth place (again), just one second behind the Pareja Porsche.

That was the end of the 1989 season. It was not surprising that Aston Martin did not win a race in its first season out with the AMR-1. It had taken Jaguar more than a year to become competitive when it first went out to race with the XJR series of cars, and in this season just passed Aston Martin had out-stayed Jaguar more than once. To have finished fourth in one race, with two

Sauber-Mercedes (and the budget connected with that racing programme) ahead was highly creditable. One thing had been proved – Aston Martins were to be taken seriously. Now, it was back to Milton Keynes to review the past year and to plan for the next.

A new car was planned for the 1990 season – the AMR-2 – and whilst the exciting drama of 1989's racing was being played out, work behind the scenes proceeded at Milton Keynes on this new car. The shape was resolved out of the construction of two quarter-scale wind-tunnel models, and a full-sized body buck was made. Then came the blow everyone had dreaded, but hoped against hope would not happen. Ford Motor Company cried 'Enough'. Clearly, Jaguar had been working on its Group C cars longer than Aston Martin. Ford was concerned that the Aston Martin racing team was detracting from the manufacture of cars, and it did not want two competitors in the same family doing battle with each other, so Jaguar was to win the day and Aston Martin to cease racing in 1990. FISA's indecision over regulations didn't help, and in the end Protech was to be wound up and the cars sold off.

Ironically, the cars were to be sold on condition that they were not to be raced for at least two years. Somebody, somewhere, feared the possibility of an Aston Martin's comeback and the embarrassment of it winning. Whilst Ford had not paid the bills for the development of this race team, it was clear that its members had been heavily reliant on factory support in terms of component supply and the goodwill essential to running such a project. Now that the cars were raceable and had come quite close to the prospect of winning, Ford clearly did not want to be exposed to the risk of someone coming in, throwing a 'pot of gold' at the AMR-1s and taking the potential laurels of victory away from Jaguar. Early in 1990, the remaining car in the programme

Next stage in the development of the Aston Martin sports-racing programme was to be the AMR-2. This was the body buck, with a wind tunnel scale model posed next to it. With the abandonment of the AMR programme and the closure of Protech, the body buck was presented to the AMOC.

(AMR1-/06) was built up, the six cars were sold and Protech was wound up. The prospect of another Aston Martin Lagonda win at Le Mans – or anywhere else now – was gone, seemingly for ever.

In the light of the achievements from almost three years' work, that seems to have been a tragedy, for there are many (including the author) who believe that, with the right engine for the 3.5-litre limit and the right support, Aston Martin Lagonda could have done it again.

10 Odds and Ends – Development and Racing Specials

The first of the development vehicles in this chapter must be a six-cylinder engined car, which will appear out of sequence from the Development Project ('DP') numbers allocated by the factory, but it is because it was this car which conferred its model designation upon the car we all came to know as the DBS. That car was a two-seater built by Carrozzeria Touring in Milan, named 'DBS' (in the idiom of the 'DB3S'), to convey the image of a truly sporting, though thoroughly road-going, two-seater.

Carrozzeria Touring had a significant association with Aston Martin already, through the 'Superleggera' (Super Lightweight) coachwork concept already adopted by Aston Martin Lagonda Limited, and so the two companies knew each other well. Touring was therefore a natural choice to build this new project for Aston Martin and the Project Number allocated to it was MP/226. Two cars were built, Chassis Number 266/1/R (right-hand drive) and 266/2/L (left-hand drive). The first car was exhibited at

The original 'DBS' Aston Martin by Carrozzeria Touring.

165

the 1966 Turin Motor Show, followed by the second being shown in London, Paris and New York. They received rave receptions for this new car, designated 'DBS' (David Brown Special).

Because AML clearly wanted to capitalize on the publicity, it became difficult to think of renaming the production model 'DB7' which would have been logical as the next model number in line, so the appendage 'DBS' stuck. However, these Touring prototypes did not make it into production, for two main reasons. The first of those reasons was that the cash position of Touring was becoming more precarious by the day, and by 1967 the company was no more. The other reason was Aston Martin Lagonda Limited's inability to complete the detail design work essential to converting such a prototype into a production model. This was for no other reason than that AML did not have the people available to do that job. It is just possible that had Newport Pagnell had the people available to complete that detail design work, Carrozzeria Touring might have survived.

MP219, MP220, 001/D/P AND MP227/1

MP219 and MP220 were both experimental/development cars designed before the Touring DBS, though of these two, only MP219 was built. Their purpose was to provide development chassis for the prototype V-8 engine and independent rear suspension. MP220 was on the drawing board in 1963, presumably as board work was taking place on Tadek Marek's V-8 engine MP213. MP219, on the other hand, was an adaptation of an earlier prototype (DP200/1), a DB4 which was modified to accept a de Dion rear suspension unit and a 5-speed ZF gearbox. DP200 goes back to 1960 and was basically a production DB4 which was converted from

left-hand drive to right-hand and then fitted with the de Dion rear end. This was just a part of the natural development process of improving Aston Martin suspension and handling qualities. Once that task was complete, combined with the trial of the ZF gearbox, the car was adapted for use as a 'mule' for the V-8 power unit.

001/D/P started life in January 1965 as MP222. Its purpose was to provide a further test-bed for the Marek V-8 engine. Registered as NPP7D, it originated as a DB6, again fitted with a de Dion rear suspension. Imagine, if you will, a DB6 based on a DB5 chassis and fitted with a DB5 body and you have this prototype, according to the records. The original V-8 engine fitted to this chassis would certainly have guaranteed a hairy ride, as it was 480/001/P, a unit produced mainly from the components of one of the racing Lola-Aston engines (the fourth, to be precise). This car remained in factory experimental use until 1969, an unusually long time for such a car.

Then, the first prototype DBS itself came along, in the guise of MP227. Again, produced as a six-cylinder car, this was the prototype upon which the Towns-designed DBS body was first built. Unlike the production variants, this one car had a split front bumper and multiple louvres behind the front wheel arches (in the spirit of the 'DB' models, but brought 'up to date'). The first view the public had of this new car and its bodyline was in the *Autocar* magazine of 28 September 1967. Registered as WKX2E, it is believed the car was almost certainly scrapped after development work was completed with it.

FROM DBS TO DBS-V8

Three separate cars were used in the development of the DBS into the DBS-V8, the particular distinction between them

The first 'built from the ground up' DBS-V8 was MBH8H. This car carried the chassis number DBSV8/10001/R.

being the chassis numbers. DBS cars were numbered in a series beginning 5001, whereas the DBS-V8 was numbered in a series beginning with 10001. The second development DBS was registered BPP6F and was selected to be a development vehicle for the V-8 engine, so was retro-fitted with one to replace the original six-cylinder Vantage unit installed (400/3269/SVC). Described in *Autocar* on 2 October 1969, the car was viewed as being a welcome addition to the Aston Martin range and a worthy bearer of the name.

DBS/5072/RAC is credited with being *the* DBS-V8 prototype. It, too, was built originally as a DBS and fitted with a Vantage six-cylinder engine (Number 400/3748/SVC), but was, again, retro-fitted with a V-8. It's interesting to note that this car was originally destined for export to Cyprus, and one might conclude that the frustration of the order resulted in a spare car being available at just the time when a new development prototype was required, so it found itself handed over to the research and development team for adaptation into a V-8.

The next car in this development trio is a very interesting challenge to the historians, since it is listed in some quarters as DBSV8/5173/R. In the factory records, there is a DBS/5173/R, but not listed as DBS-V8 – the first definitive DBS-V8 entry is 10001, retained by the company and registered as MBH8H. DBS/5173/RAC was finished in 'Lagoon' blue with black trim and was originally fitted with Vantage engine Number 400/3626/SVC, but later acquired the V-8 engine Number V/535/013/P. This was a prototype Lola-Aston engine, which was fitted with downdraught Weber carburettors, so called for a 'power-bulge' to be introduced into the bonnet to cover them. The car is recorded as having been originally built for domestic sale and left production in October 1968. It must be presumed that this was another case of a frustrated sale which resulted in the car being diverted to development work.

The first truly definitive DBS-V8 was, in fact, DBSV8/10001/R. This car was built from the ground up as a V8 and so can fairly be described as the first completely purpose-built V-8 version of the DBS. Used as a factory demonstrator and development car,

Taking the Sir David Brown Aston Martin Lagonda into the post-DB era, this rear quarter view shows how the line was totally unspoiled by the 'stretch'. This particular car is the one displayed at the 1975 London Motor Show as a production car. Of course, the name 'Lagonda' was applied as a model name at this point, not as a make of car.

10001 was originally fitted with engine Number V/535/005/P and was used for a 50,000 mile (80,450km) exhaust emission test. It left the factory in September 1969 and so the DBS-V8 was now truly a production car, available at last for sale to an eager public.

MP230 AND THE 'SOTHEBY SPECIAL'

With apologies to Mrs Beeton, 'Take one DBS-V8 and stretch to add 12in (30cm) to the wheelbase. Then add, blending carefully, two doors, air-conditioning, electric door locking to (now) all four doors and fuel filler cap/boot lid and stereo radio cassette player with record facility. Reduce the fuel capacity to 23g (104.42l) (20g [90.8l] main tank and 3g [13.62l] reserve), then finish

with a coating of 'Cosmic Fire' paintwork and decorate with a Lagonda badge'. The result? MP230, the prototype Aston Martin Lagonda.

This project arose from Sir David Brown having a requirement for a four-door car of near-limousine quality. Clearly, he could hardly go out and buy a Bentley or a Rolls-Royce and since the 'limousine' bit was not entirely in keeping with the Aston Martin image anyway, it was perhaps less important than the four doors. It has long been thought in business circles that a company car should have four doors, so as to accommodate business passengers in the back seats with the minimum of inconvenience of entry and exit.

Without wishing to be sexist, the problem of entry and exit has been an issue in the retention of a lady's dignity in many cars – two- or four-door design – for years. When

The Sotheby Special was a little bit of nonsense created by Ogle Design for the Wills tobacco company and never really 'owned' by Aston Martin Lagonda Limited. 'Sotheby' was to be a new brand of cigarette.

wearing a dress or a skirt, it is always a fight between entering or leaving a car in safety and entering or leaving it with modesty intact, especially in cars of low build.

To all intents and purposes, MP230 was simply a stretched DBS-V8, but to give it 'that little extra', the nose of the car was decorated with a Lagonda badge, though the grille remained unaltered, unlike the later 'production' cars (if seven cars can be considered 'production'). Registered as JPP5G, MP230/1 continues to survive, though now with a production engine, and was the true prototype of the seven Aston Martin Lagondas built in the Company Developments era of Aston Martin Lagonda Limited.

DBSV8/10381/RC sounds like a perfectly normal DBS chassis number, as indeed it was, but the factory record shows an entry 'This Indent not used' and 10380 as being built up to chassis form for Ogle Design. However, DBSV8/10381 certainly was sold to Ogle and a hand-written entry records it

as 'Embassy Ogle'. This is the car upon which a very odd-looking body was fitted – for an Aston Martin at least. Indeed, AML was anxious that the finished car should not be described as an Aston Martin, for it was not being bodied as a factory project or in consultation with Newport Pagnell.

Designed by Tom Karen of Ogle, the odd combination of razor-edge treatment and long flowing curves made this vehicle look more like something out of the children's television series *Thunderbirds* than a practical design exercise. Ogle had previously made its name with a special-bodied sporting Austin Mini and later produced the basis for the modern Leyland truck cab design – neither of which was noted for its good looks. Hardly surprisingly, only one example was sold from this design, and that was in 1973, on Chassis Number V8/10581/RCA.

This odd design was sponsored by the Wills Tobacco arm of Imperial Tobacco Corporation and was to be known as the

'Sotheby Special', not because it had an involvement with that famous auction house, but because Wills were producing a new brand of cigarettes called 'Sotheby'. The original car was finished in that product's livery of dark-blue and gold and was exhibited at the 1972 Montreal Motor Show at the beginning of that year, the Geneva Motor Show in March then London in October.

There were, however, some very creditable features of this car, once you'd overcome the conviction that it looked as though it had been shunted up the rear. For example, it was glazed with Triplex 'Sundym', a glass that was heat-resistant; it had Kangol seat-belts which were wired into the ignition system so that you couldn't drive the car away without 'buckling up'; and it was a three-seater, which added a little to its eccentricity. Another very useful feature which was only considered again twenty years later was the 'head-up display' of warning lights from the instrument panel. Fighter pilots have had this facility for fifty years, so perhaps it was time to think about an application of it for cars. It hasn't happened universally yet, but Ogle did try to blaze that trail.

FROM HAMILTON AND PREECE TO BOND AND BULLDOG

Robin Hamilton's much-modified racing V-8 comes next in our schedule of odd Aston Martins. In fact, this car might better be described as an Aston Martin V-8 built by Robin Hamilton, for he did effectively build this car up from scratch around a set of Aston Martin components – hence its odd chassis number RHAM/001, with engine number RHV8/1. Robin Hamilton was a dedicated Aston Martin enthusiast who was determined to build up a car and go out there to do something the factory had

aspired to do again: win the Le Mans 24 Hours Race.

The first thing that can be said of the Hamilton Aston Martin is that it only vaguely resembled an Aston Martin when it was finished, for it had much-lowered suspension, widened wheel arches, very wide wheels and tyres, a huge tail-spoiler, an equally large front air dam and, of course, a highly tweaked engine and a rather racy paint job. The car had started life as DBSV8/10038/RC, but had been so modified, stripped and rebuilt, that it was decided to allocate it the new chassis number in 1976. This was some time after Hamilton had begun using it in competitions, however.

Robin Hamilton's first business contact with Aston Martin Lagonda Limited was as an appointed service agent for the company in 1973, after which he finally became a full dealer for part of the Midlands. Development of RHAM/001 progressed with the support of AML and his initial sponsor, the SAS Group. By 1977, he was ready for the ultimate race. His engine was pushing out 520bhp and producing 400lb/ft of torque, having been developed specifically for endurance racing.

The usual 'shake-down' race, the Silverstone 6 Hours, was chosen to sort out the bugs and have the car fully ready for Le Mans. Many lessons were learned at that event, including the need for a differential oil cooler because the inboard rear brakes were generating so much heat that the differential was boiling its contents and the oil seals failed. Nonetheless, the car was proven to have the road speed essential to the Sarthe Circuit, and the 1977 Le Mans saw Robin Hamilton, with Dave Preece and Mike Salmon (who had driven the last Aston Martin officially entered at Le Mans in 1964), driving RHAM/001.

Hamilton's car only managed to get into the race by the skin of its drivers' teeth. Its lap times originally were not quick enough

Whilst the car certainly had a family resemblance to Aston Martin, Robin Hamilton's RHAM/001 was built up from Aston Martin components purely as a racing car, which is why it didn't have a factory chassis number.

to earn it a qualifying place, but another car was found to be illegal, so the Aston was allowed to start after all. After an episode of cracked brake discs through overheating, and a very long pit-stop to replace them, the car finally managed to plough its way through to finish a very creditable seventeenth overall and third in its class. The car came back to Le Mans in 1979, this time turbocharged, and was going extremely quickly until a connecting rod broke after two and three-quarter hours, putting the team out of the race.

Dave Preece, in the meantime, after driving with Hamilton in the '77 Le Mans, had taken the bit between his teeth and decided he wanted to build his own car for a personal attack on the race. His idea was to take an Aston Martin V-8 engine and plant it into a mid-engined chassis. Work began in 1979, in company with a man named Ken Heywood, and financial support came from Gipfast, the principal sponsor, as well as Pace Petroleum, Duckhams Oil and others. The car was to be entered in the GT Prototype class, using a very lightweight car powered by a naturally aspirated engine.

The Gipfast Special first saw the light of day at the beginning of 1980. It was very low and had something of the look of Chevron about it. After a lot of technical hitches, it followed the pattern of such racing machines and was entered for the Silverstone 6 Hours as a preliminary to Le Mans. The car ran into trouble in practice for the 6 Hours, the crankshaft beginning to seize as the consequence of a spacer between the engine and transmission being too long, so causing excessive pressure on the crankshaft thrust washers. That sorted, with Aston Martin Lagonda Limited's help, the car went to the line and started the race, but when a suspension ball joint sheared, it was out. With insufficient sponsorship to support Le Mans, Preece had the car dismantled and abandoned the project.

Next comes a little bit of nonsense, in the form of another James Bond Aston Martin, prepared for the film *The Living Daylights*. The best-known Aston Martin 'Bond-Mobile' was, of course, the much-modified DB5 which had been used in the film *Goldfinger*, though a DBS Vantage was used in *On Her Majesty's Secret Service*. Of course, Aston

Once James Bond had used an Aston Martin (a DB5 in the film Goldfinger*), what else could come up to that standard? So, for the film* You Only Live Twice, *a V-8 was adopted. It was Victor Gauntlett's car, seen here with extended skis and (right) the rocket booster.*

Martin Lagonda would benefit from the publicity, and for *The Living Daylights* Victor Gauntlett's own V-8 Vantage and a V-8 Volante were the cars featured in the film. It was fitted with all kinds of 'Bond' gadgets. Missiles were mounted in firing tubes behind the fog lamps, a computerized 'head-up display' (remember Ogle?) was used for missile firing and out-rigged skis were fitted to the Vantage Saloon, the two cars being used so that a roof could mysteriously appear on 'the' car to protect against winter snows. It is said that Victor Gauntlett was even offered a part in the film (could hardly see 'M.V.G.' as a Russian agent though, could you?).

Whilst Alan Curtis was Chairman of AML, he decided to send Mike Loasby, his Engineering Director, off to Cranfield to set up a new company called Aston Martin Engineering Limited. Loasby and a small team then proceeded to lock themselves away for months to work on a project called, simply, DP K901. They were to produce a revolutionary development prototype Aston Martin which would be mid-engined, a departure for Aston Martins, aerodynamically clean, have all sorts of electronic gadgetry and look like a super-high-speed wedge that was intended to be just that.

It doesn't take too vivid an imagination to figure out what the 'K9' part of this Development Project number was intended to convey – the ultimate name of the car being 'Bulldog'. Something else linking an Aston Martin with Alan Curtis's consuming passion for aircraft was the Scottish Aviation 'Bulldog', which of course was the Royal Air Force's principal primary trainer before 'Tucano'. However, the name 'Bulldog' was forgivable in this context, since it was also explained that the bulldog is Britain's national dog and demonstrates the nature of the British people – the 'Bulldog Breed'. It was going to take quite a bit of Bulldog breed to see this project to conclusion.

DP K901 – THE 'BULLDOG'

The Aston Martin 'Bulldog' was a concept car, originally commissioned by Alan Curtis in 1976, in the wake of the then-new razor-edged Lagonda V-8 Saloon. It had originally been intended to develop it for the production of a limited edition of twenty-five examples for sale, but events overtook it, and it became a one-off with a different mission – publicity and 'making a statement' about the engineering prowess of Aston Martin Lagonda. It was also intended to show that the company was not blinkered to the view that Aston Martins had to be only front-engined, rear-wheel-drive cars.

Mike Loasby started this project off, as the Lagonda was being prepared for production and as a new V-8 Volante was in preparation, too. However, Mr Loasby didn't see it to conclusion because he was lured to the De Lorean Motor Company in Belfast. Mike Loasby's successor, Steve Coughlin (who was in the process of reorganizing his new job) established a Special Projects Department which was to be headed by Keith Martin, assisted by Steve Hallam. The project was theoretically well advanced by the time these two took it on, in 1979, but there was still a lot of work to be done.

The Special Projects Department had been set up with the objective of providing specific services to AML and selling its abilities and services to other motor manufacturers. It was at this point that 'Bulldog' changed from being a special limited edition for sale to a concept car and ambassador of its maker. Keith Martin inherited a tubular chassis minus suspension, an engine, a ZF gearbox, a collection of part-finished body panels and a huge box of bits. This was 'Bulldog'! He also had sixty-odd incomplete drawings, a total lack of development data and a collection of photographs which Roger Stowers had taken of the original clay model

Like something out of a space-age movie, DP-K901, the Bulldog – seen here with Keith Martin, the man responsible for its completion – was a development project aimed at promoting Aston Martin Lagonda's Special Projects Department, though originally intended for production in limited numbers. It might well have been an alternative for James Bond!

made by body designer William Towns. From this, Martin's team had to complete a car, which has been said to have been completed in twelve months from the drawing board, yet it was already almost three years since Alan Curtis had sown the seeds of the idea – and it still wasn't finished!

Because the decision was taken not to manufacture 'Bulldog' for sale, Keith Martin was instructed to take all necessary short cuts to complete the project as soon as possible, consistent with making it work properly. Once he had a rolling chassis, the William Towns body would be finished and then assembled onto the tubular framework, to bring the car to life. The body could hardly have been said to be pretty, but it was an aerodynamically super-clean concept, equipped with hydraulically operated gull-wing doors which would have put the Mercedes 300SL to shame. The glassware was bonded into place to keep it as flush and 'clean' as possible. The fuel tanks were four

in number, all interconnected and filled with 'explosafe' material, totalling 24g (108.96l) capacity. Instrumentation was by liquid crystal displays, Lagonda-like, though the 'Bulldog' did not use the full Lagonda system, just its pickups and sensors.

As Keith Martin and Steve Hallam advanced with the development, they decided to retain the Loasby-modified de Dion rear suspension, except they decided to change the originally intended transverse torsion bars for coil springs. The whole front suspension was redesigned along the lines of the Lagonda V-8 front end, to replace the de Dion intended by Mike Loasby. A DB6 type of steering rack was used and connected to Lagonda steering arms to finish off the directional control aspect of the 'Bulldog'. Stopping power was provided by 11½in (29.2cm) disc brakes. The twin-turbo engine, by the time it was fully ready for the car, produced 700bhp, which provided for a theoretical 237mph (381kph) maximum

Bulldog with the alternative to 'pop-up' headlamps, a lowering panel. Much more sensible, as there was less to fail.

speed! In tests at MIRA's Nuneaton test ground, it was actually propelled at 172mph (277kph) round the banked circuit – and it was only just into top gear at that pace.

Finally came press day. It had been intended to hold this event at MIRA, but the problems of security limited the number of passes, and the use of cameras there is very strictly controlled. Therefore, the general press viewing was switched to Mallory Park

Two kinds of Bulldogs here – the car and the aeroplane, the latter being used as a primary trainer in the Royal Air Force.

175

Aston Martin V8 'Bulldog' Project DP K901 – 1976–1980

Vehicle construction

Steel box-section chassis with roll-over bar and GRP composite body panels

Engine

Crankcase/cylinder block material	Aluminium alloy
Cylinder head material	Aluminium alloy, twin-plug
Number of cylinders	8 in 90° V-formation, wet liners
Cooling system	Water – pump and twin electric fans
Bore and stroke	100mm × 85mm
Engine capacity	5,340cc
Number of main bearings	Five
Valve gear and operation	Two chain-driven overhead camshafts per cylinder bank; two valves per cylinder
Fuel supply method and type	High-pressure pumps from tanks to Bosch Fuel injection, boosted by twin Garrett TO4B turbochargers
Quoted maximum power output	700bhp @ 6,000rpm (estimated)
Quoted maximum torque output	550lb/ft @ 5,500rpm (estimated)

Transmission

Clutch type and operation	Single 10½in plate, hydraulically actuated, coupled to ZF 5-speed gearbox
Gearbox ratios	8.256, 4.864, 3.264, 2.688, 2.24:1
Final drive ratio	3.20:1

Suspension and steering

Front suspension	Unequal length double wishbones, anti-roll bar and adjustable Koni shock absorbers
Rear suspension	De Dion, twin radius rods, Watts linkage and coil springs, with solid bushed lateral links connecting ZF transaxle to hub carriers via 'L'-shaped link bars
Steering type	DB6-type rack and pinion
Wheel type and size	Compomotive split rim alloy 8.5J × 15in front and 11J × 15in rear
Tyre size and rating	Pirelli P7 225/50VR × 15in front and 345/35VR × 15in rear
Brakes: type and actuation	Vented 296mm × 32mm discs all round with four-pot calliper actuation

Vehicle Dimensions

Overall Length	4,724mm
Overall Width	1,918mm
Wheelbase	2,769mm
Track (front and rear)	1,562mm/1,587mm
Overall height	1,092mm

racing circuit at the last minute, prior to which there had been a television session at Woburn Abbey. The 'Bulldog' had been completed only days before, so the Aston Martin team was crossing fingers very tightly, hoping that nothing would go wrong, for its toughest test was to come at the hands of Paul Frère and Mel Nicholls, who shared the car round Mallory for an hour.

The next hurdle was a test drive with *Autocar* and *Motor* magazines, led by John Miles, who was a former Lotus Grand Prix driver and an accomplished tester. The car's public announcement day was 14 April 1980, four years after the idea first came to Alan Curtis, and the car got rave notices. Its distinctive five-headlamp lighting, with a fold-down covering panel rather than 'pop-up' configuration, combined with its gull-wing doors, guaranteed that it would attract attention, quite apart from the fact that it was such a revolutionary car.

After press day, the car returned to a less vigorous testing programme, as most of the development team had been assigned by now to other experimental work. Keith Martin did most of the continuous testing himself, driving 'Bulldog' to and from MIRA in the process. A public day at the Aston Martin Owners' Club St John Horsfall Trophy Meeting at Silverstone saw Stirling Moss drive the car on a demonstration run, then back to testing. There were problems with turbocharger cooling, and as these were solved other engine developments went on until the car was finally sold to the United States.

FINALLY TO THE VIRAGE

Since the other important 'specials' are covered elsewhere in this book, such as Nimrod, AMR-1 and the Lagonda 'mule' for the Virage, there really is only the Virage development itself to consider here. Virage, of course, was DP2034 and DP2034/2 was used as the MIRA crash test car, whilst /3 and /5 were display cars. DP2054 was the development project number allocated to the Virage Volante, and the Shooting Brake was DP2099. The first Shooting Brake was exhibited at the 1992 Geneva Show, adorned by lots of co-ordinated accessories from Asprey's of London.

Clearly, as this book comes to its close, there are Development Projects continuing at Newport Pagnell which will remain shrouded in mystery for some time to come, and others which have been released to tease the market and gauge reaction, as well as potential sales – one being the magnificent new Lagonda V-12. There will always be the purists, who will say that what Aston Martin Lagonda is doing today detracts from the purity of the breed, but they and we should always remember that Lionel Martin started with a car built up from bits, as did A.C. Bertelli and even David Brown. What

This profile view of the Vignale Lagonda gives some idea of its size, but still doesn't finally bring it home that this car is actually bigger than a Rolls-Royce Silver Spur.

The Lagonda Shooting Brake conversion from a Virage Coupé makes a lot of sense if you want a five-door car in this class of motoring. To acquire either this or the four-door Saloon version, you already have to have a Virage available to convert.

the Ford-parented company does today, as long as it is in the spirit of what those founders of this magnificent dynasty did, must surely be in the interests of the names 'Aston Martin' and 'Lagonda'.

It does seem clear that Ford intends to retain and develop both the Aston Martin and Lagonda names in their future programmes. It will be interesting to see what these twin 'jewels in the crown' of the Ford empire are to become.

11 Aston Martin Lagonda Limited

ASTON MARTIN AND LAGONDA REBORN

David Brown Jr was a motor sporting enthusiast, having won a number of trophies as a driver in the late 1920s, before the pressures of business steered him away from that leisure pursuit. It had to be a combination of this enthusiasm and his sharp sense of business that persuaded him to the merits of buying Aston Martin Limited from the Sutherlands in 1947. He could clearly see an opportunity for development, especially as he bought the business for less than the written down value of the tools and equipment. Gordon Sutherland and Claude Hill were to stay as directors and the company would remain at Feltham. The acquisition of the assets and name of Lagonda in 1948 was a prudent afterthought, from which David Brown (Huddersfield) Limited formed the new subsidiary, Aston Martin Lagonda Limited.

The story goes that David Brown bought Aston Martin personally 'for a bit of fun' but that he was invited to go to see Lagonda by an old associate who had been appointed liquidator of the Lagonda business. Being interested in sporty cars, 'D.B.' went to Staines, met W.O. Bentley and went for a drive in one of the Lagonda prototypes. His immediate impression was that the Lagonda 2.6 engine would be ideal for the Aston Martin Atom! However, there were already three bidders offering far more than he thought the business was worth, so he

offered £50,000 and promptly forgot about it.

A few months later, after the other bidders had withdrawn, the liquidator came back to 'D.B.' and asked if he was still interested, to which the response came 'It depends on the price'. The price of £55,000 was finally settled upon, and David Brown (Huddersfield) Limited became the new owner of the Lagonda name, the design rights, drawings, prototypes and all the other assets of the business, except the buildings at Staines, which went to Petters. Aston Martin being so close, he rented the old hangars on Hanworth airfield and stored the Lagonda stocks and equipment there.

Despite Mr Brown's strong business qualities, it would be wrong to say that it was he alone who brought Aston Martin Lagonda 'from the abyss' to the pinnacle of success that it achieved. His cautious financial management certainly had a strong bearing on what the company could or could not do, and he was certainly in close consultation over the business decisions of AML, but John Wyer did more for the day-to-day development and management of this company than anyone else at the time.

It is true to say, though, that without David Brown, Aston Martin Lagonda Limited could, and almost certainly would, have sunk without trace years ago. It is also true that it was David Brown who conferred a stability on AML that neither Aston Martin nor Lagonda had ever experienced in its history. In certain quarters, it has been said that it was a standing joke that Aston

This superb drawing is the personification of David Brown. A similar image of the man who did so much to preserve the best of Britain hangs in the boardroom at Newport Pagnell.

were better endowed with imagination than money, so both businesses were established on a hand-to-mouth financial existence. Nonetheless, both built an enviable reputation. Without the reputations of both, combined with the economic prospect, David Brown would have given neither a second look.

CREATION OF A NEW LEGEND

John Wyer came into Aston Martin Lagonda Limited in 1950, with the intention of staying for only one year and with the task of creating a works racing team that could win races. His intention after that was to go and do some 'serious work', whatever that was. Perhaps he lost track of that in the process of becoming totally absorbed in the challenge that Aston Martin Lagonda Limited offered him, for he stayed rather more than that one year, finally leaving in 1963!

There is no doubt that Wyer was an extremely efficient pit organizer and race manager, but he also understood motor cars and was a thoroughly competent engineer. He had served an apprenticeship with Sunbeam at Wolverhampton, after which he worked in the drawing office for a year before joining Solex Carburettors as a sales and service engineer. His job with that company took him to India and Egypt, then during the Second World War he was appointed to take charge of production and materials control.

With a burning, and so far unsatisfied, ambition to make a name for himself in motor racing, John Wyer decided after the war that he ought to make a move in that direction before he was too old. Therefore, after hearing of the opportunity, he joined Monaco Motors as Managing Director. That company was engaged in preparing sports and racing cars for private entrants. The

Martin had been near to liquidation more times than the rest of the British motor industry, which is an unkind exaggeration, but a pointer as to how tight a shoestring it was being run upon.

The realities of the situation were that Aston Martin was created out of the ambitions of one man, Lionel Martin, and Lagonda out of the ambitions of another, Wilbur Gunn. These two men had one thing in common, the desire to build a quality automobile, each in his own time. Both were also keen to build vehicles which could win in competition and both were active competitors. Both were also men of vision who

Roy Salvadori is seen here piloting DB3S/7 in the 1955 Le Mans. The car retired after 106 laps with a crankcase failure.

other two directors of the company were Dudley Folland, an Aston Martin owner of some note, and Ian Connell, who had made something of a name for himself before the war with an ERA. It was whilst working on Folland's Aston Martin in the 1949 Spa 1,000 Kilometres Race that David Brown first saw him and was clearly impressed. In early 1950, 'D.B.' decided to recruit him into the works fold as team manager.

Among the drivers who worked with John Wyer were Roy Salvadori, Reg Parnell, Peter Collins, Lance Macklin, Eric Thompson, Geoff Duke, Dennis Poore, Pat Griffith, Tony Brooks, Stirling Moss, Paul Frère, Carroll Shelby, Innes Ireland and Graham Whitehead: a veritable *Who's Who* of motor sport from the 1950s. The three longest-serving drivers were Roy Salvadori, Reg Parnell and Peter Collins, who between them gave over twenty years to Aston Martin Lagonda Limited. The stability of David Brown's

backing was a major factor in that level of commitment from the team.

John Wyer brought the Feltham company, on a shoestring budget, from the position of being a joke with Ferrari and Jaguar in sports car racing to the position of being a serious force with which to be reckoned. Through the early entries of the DB2s, on to racing and rallying with DB2/4s and DB3s, he took the team, via the DB3S, the Lagonda V-12 and the DBR1, to final victory at Le Mans in 1959, so finally achieving David Brown's personal ambition. Just to endorse that victory, he then went on to hand to 'D.B.' the World Sports Car Championship for that year, too.

All this came from the man who was only intent on staying with the company for one year. That's not the whole story either, for in 1957 David Brown had asked Wyer to take on the general management of the whole company, Aston Martin Lagonda Limited.

181

The 1959 Le Mans 24 Hours was Aston Martin's pinnacle of achievement. Seen here is the DB4GT prototype (DP199/1 – race no. 21), driven by Patthey and Calderari, being passed by the much quicker DBR1/3 (4) driven by Stirling Moss, who was partnered by Jack Fairman. The DB4GT retired on lap 21 with a bearing failure and the Moss/Fairman car went out when an inlet valve broke.

Now, he had the pressures of production car manufacture, design, service and the financial burdens of the whole company.

Wyer applied himself to all his duties at AML with a vigour and commitment that was contagious, demonstrated by the loyalty he elicited from everyone who worked with him. He accepted the burden of product development, production management and all the things that were attached to the basic business of Aston Martin Lagonda Limited simply because he could still be involved in racing. Even when the company officially withdrew from racing at the end of the 1959 season, he knew it wouldn't completely disconnect itself from motor sport. The support of private entrants continued, and so the company was still involved. Therefore, so was John Wyer, despite the public face being that Aston Martin no longer raced.

As pressures began to be brought on 'D.B.' to return to racing, John Wyer was very careful not to be seen as associating with the instigators, though he was clearly continually hopeful that they would succeed. Of course, they did, with the result that DP212, a Grand Touring racer based on the DB4GT,

came about to be campaigned at the 1962 Le Mans, in the hope that AML could secure another victory there. After that came DP214 and DP215, both further aimed at the next year's Le Mans, but by the end of 1963, it was decided that the company's total effort and commitment should be concentrated on the manufacture of motor cars for sale, not racing.

It was the decision to withdraw irrevocably from racing that triggered John Wyer's decision to move on. Having heard the news of Aston Martin's withdrawal, Ford Motor Company approached Wyer with an offer that he felt he could not refuse. The deal was to organize and run a team of sports racing cars with the objective of winning at Le Mans, a target and experience very familiar to John Wyer. The car was to be the Ford GT40, the budget was huge and the objective was to break Ferrari's stranglehold on Le Mans.

In a meeting with David Brown, John Wyer put his position very plainly. The response was one of great regret that he had found it time to go, but that he went with D.B.'s blessing and best wishes for the success he expected would come. David Brown saw no point in trying to dissuade Wyer from leaving, for he knew that John Wyer was a racing man, not really a production man. True to expectations, the Ford team did win at Le Mans, and that 'procession' across the line in 1967 will probably never be forgotten by enthusiasts for the Sarthe Race.

RELOCATION AND DISPOSAL OF AML

The Tickford Motor Body Company was bought by the David Brown Corporation in 1953 and had been making bodies for Aston Martin cars since 1955. By 1957, complete cars were being built there, and ultimately, a few years later, it was decided that the Feltham site was neither big enough to accommodate the company nor in the most economic state of repair. As a consequence of that realization, it was decided to move Aston Martin Lagonda Limited, lock stock and barrel, to Tickford Street, Newport Pagnell, where the company has been based ever since.

The final move to Newport Pagnell took place in 1964, though complete cars were already being built up there. The platform chassis for the DB4, for example, had been built at the David Brown factory at Farsley, in Yorkshire, for some time, with Superleggera bodywork being formed and fitted at Tickford Street. Now, everything was to be under one roof, so to speak, though in actual fact it would be more correct to say that it was under several roofs on one site.

It was here, at Newport Pagnell, that Tadek Marek began work, in 1965, on the new V-8 engine which was to power the next generation of Aston Martins, and it was here that the whole new family of cars was to be born. Those cars came into being, beginning with the six-cylinder DBS in 1967, followed

by the DBS-V8 in 1970. David Brown was knighted for his services to industry in 1968, and at the time things were looking good on the surface, but there were problems on the horizon.

Firstly, the David Brown Tractor Division was suffering a downturn in business. Then, the Gears Division went through a bad patch, brought about especially by the reduction in demand for truck gearboxes (for which the David Brown name was and is renowned) with the decline in goods-vehicle sales in the early years of Harold Wilson's Labour government. Another downturn in business in 1970–71 bit harder into capital equipment sales, and truckmakers were feeling a severe pinch. Finally, as oil prices soared, so the demand for such thirsty cars as Aston Martins began to fall off.

The consequence of all this was the need for a tightening of belts in the David Brown Corporation, so that Aston Martin Lagonda Limited finally became an expensive luxury which the parent corporation could no longer afford to support. Today, it is called 'reverting to core business activity', but then there was no such cliché to cover the situation. All that Sir David Brown could do now was examine closely the businesses which made up the corporation and cut back where he could. Whilst the announcement came as a surprise when it was made public, it was really not surprising that Aston Martin Lagonda Limited should be offered for sale in the market place, for the company was in a deep financial predicament. It was first made known in business circles that the company was open to bids, then the press got hold of the story and, of course, gave rise to all kinds of alarm and despondency. Even so, a bid was finally received from an organization calling itself Company Developments Limited, headed by a man named S.W. Willson.

THE TRANSFER OF POWER

William Willson was a Birmingham-based businessman who was chairman of a business called Company Developments. Company Developments' object in life was to invest in or acquire ailing businesses and either turn them round so as to sell them on at a profit or, if they were equipped with assets worth selling, to asset-strip them as far as was practical whilst allowing the core business to continue its activities. Then, at an appropriate time, the core business itself would be sold on to make a double profit. There's a certain logic to that business attitude, in that many long-established companies often don't know the value of assets they own. Of course it also means they often don't realize that they could probably have done an asset-strip for their very survival. That's why the morality of asset-strippers is often brought into question.

Whatever the case with Aston Martin Lagonda, it could not have been said that Sir David Brown was likely not to have known there were assets he could have stripped. It is far more likely that he simply wanted a quick and straightforward sale, so was willing to let someone else have the benefits if he was willing to take up the responsibility. Hence the acceptance of a deal with William Willson. The unconfirmed story is that Willson paid just £100 for Aston Martin Lagonda, accepting all its liabilities as part of the deal, such was the parlous condition of AML's finances at that time.

Company Developments acquired the total shareholding of Aston Martin Lagonda Limited, together with its 23-acre site at Newport Pagnell, and William Willson became Chairman. To the surprise of many, whilst 'slimming down' took place, production at Newport Pagnell did not cease. All production effort was concentrated on the V-8 Saloon with the resultant withdrawal of the six-cylinder models from 1973, after the dropping of the DBS Vantage. Even so, over £1 million cash injection was needed to keep things going during 1972 and 1973.

William Willson was well known to local Birmingham M.P. Dennis Howell, who was then Britain's first Minister for Sports, a parliamentary post much maligned but one in which, it must be said, he excelled. Mr Howell was also well thought of in certain circles in the Labour government of the day, so it is eminently possible that his support for William Willson's next move would have been invaluable. However it happened, William Willson made an approach, cloaked in great secrecy, to the British government, through the recently created and much-heralded Department of Industry, to provide the kind of financial support he had been unable to raise through normal commercial sources. The task was to achieve working capital (cash flow) to fund the modification of the V-8 so that it could meet United States Federal Motor Vehicle Safety Standards and emission standards. Since that market was crucial to sales of the V-8, it was thought that, with sympathizers on the inside, there would be no serious problems. Alas, Mr Willson was wrong.

Despite the belief that the government would favour this approach because of its stated attitude to manufacturing industry (this was the government that introduced the infamous Selective Employment Tax in an attempt to steer investment towards manufacturing), the application failed. The rejection was even despite the government's stance on the need to export British goods. However, it can be seen in the light of logic that it would have been a politically hard decision for that government to make, since Labour was the party of the worker, and Aston Martins or Lagondas were hardly cars for the worker, despite the fact that jobs could depend on their sales.

The situation at Newport Pagnell became

Fred Hartley was sales manager when AML went into receivership in December 1974 and was left in charge of the business prior to the arrival on the scene of Peter Sprague and George Minden. He's seen here in happier times, with the first Japanese specification V-8.

worse as the year advanced, with costs escalating (inflation was now well into two figures), sales declining and national unemployment rising. By September, it was decided to make another application to the Department of Industry. A month later, a reply was received from the government, approving the application for funding, but with the rather curious condition that the North American distributor be changed to a company called Alco Corporation, instead of the existing Royston Distributors, whose performance to date was perfectly satisfactory.

Royston, it seems, had orders on its books for cars worth over £2 million, but it would not now conclude the order on AML until it had assurance that the British government would support the rescue package. The deal was a £600,000 loan from the government, against an injection of £400,000 from Company Developments, to be backed by the order for £2 million from Royston. However, the government would not support it, and Royston was now suspicious that AML

would not come up with the cars. The London Motor Show came and went, introducing the four-door Aston Martin Lagonda on the way, and the money was not forthcoming, so the position reached impasse. The company could not progress without financial support; the government would not give an answer, and the orders were at risk of slipping away. As a consequence, Aston Martin Lagonda Limited was put into receivership in December 1974.

Fred Hartley, Aston Martin Lagonda's Sales Manager, was left in charge of the business under the receivers, as 450 workers at Newport Pagnell were made redundant. All seemed bleak, as the prospects of AML resuming production appeared remote. Finally, two enthusiasts from North American shores came to the rescue, and Aston Martin Lagonda Limited would soon be back on the road. Such was, and is, the great loyalty felt among Aston Martin and Lagonda enthusiasts, that this move did not come as any great surprise.

ASTON MARTIN LAGONDA (1975) LIMITED

Peter Sprague was an American entrepreneur who loved Aston Martins, whilst George Minden was a Canadian sports car dealer, who also loved Aston Martins. These two saw the plight that AML was in and saw the opportunity of a business gain. Both were members of the Aston Martin Owners' Club, and both were keen to see the Aston Martin Lagonda name perpetuated. They, therefore, put up £1.05 million to secure the assets and plant of the company. Their offer was accepted by the receiver on 27 June 1975, and so AML was saved again.

Naturally, reorganization of the company was essential, and a new board of directors was appointed. The new chairman was Alan Curtis, supported by Fred Hartley as Managing Director and Denis Flather. Mike Loasby came back to the company, and Harold Beach was retained as a consultant. It is a great credit to this management team and to the workers they restored to employment that production of the V-8 was up to

George Minden (left) and Peter Sprague were the saviours of Aston Martin Lagonda Limited in 1975.

Alan Curtis was a man who believed in talking to his work force, as he saw this to be the best way of gaining their confidence. Here, he is seen in one of his many shop-floor conferences.

six cars a week by the middle of 1976, which was where production levels had stood three years earlier. Alan Curtis, it has to be said, probably did more to drive the company on to greater successes than anyone else since John Wyer's departure in 1963.

By 1980, the chairman of Pace Petroleum, Victor Gauntlett, was on the scene, becoming a shareholder in that year. Also, a company named CH Industrials, represented by Tim Hearley bought a share in Aston Martin Lagonda Limited, as had Peter Cadbury of the chocolate firm, so the inflow of cash met the needs of the company to develop its product range and promote sales in important markets, the most significant of which was the United States. However, disagreement was about to disrupt the boardroom.

Sales were in decline, and Alan Curtis was proposing to cut production to one car a week, in order to keep the company afloat. Messrs Cadbury, Gauntlett and Hearley positively did not agree. There was no resolution to the argument, so Pace

Petroleum and CH Industrials put up the money to secure 96 per cent of the shareholding, the other 4 per cent remaining with Peter Cadbury. The result was that Alan Curtis left the company and it was renamed Aston Martin Lagonda Limited, the '(1975)' being dropped.

NEW OWNERS – NEW DIRECTIONS

Now there had to be some hard selling done, especially in the North American and Middle East markets. The Towns Lagonda was responsible for much of the recovery in the Middle East, the Saudis in particular falling in love with it and increasing 1980 sales by twenty-five in the following year of that model alone. Also, Tickford, which specialized in modifying production cars, was doing well with the Tickford Ford Capri and the Tickford MG Metro. The Capri was in fact offered by Ford as a special vehicle option, so

Victor Gauntlett

The town of Ripley, in Surrey, was the birthplace of Malcolm Victor Gauntlett and his year of birth was 1942. Upon leaving Marylebone Grammar School, he was accepted into a short service commission with the Royal Air Force. His return to civilian life brought a job, through the good offices of his uncle (who was a partner in the law firm which represented BP), with British Petroleum.

By 1967, Victor had outgrown BP and moved to Total, working with its Middle East operation from the London and Paris offices. Soon, he was able to take over a Total marketing agency in Britain, but that didn't satisfy his ambitions for long. After meeting up with a man called Digby Blakiston, Victor Gauntlett joined up in partnership with him in 1972 to form Pace Petroleum. They did well, and by 1979 there were 500 Pace stations in Great Britain. The Gauntlett love of high-performance quality cars comes in here, for in 1980, he made his first move into Aston Martin Lagonda Limited. Another year later, Pace Petroleum owned 48 per cent of AML, and Victor Gauntlett was to become a familiar figure at Newport Pagnell.

Taking full-time management control of AML in 1983, Gauntlett worked hard to keep the Aston Martin Lagonda profile high and to steer the company into profit. It was Victor Gauntlett who revived the Zagato connection, and he who finally took Aston Martin back to the World Sports Car Championship and to the Le Mans 24 Hours Race in 1989. Had the team been allowed to continue in 1990, who can say whether or not they might have won both, had it not been for the constantly changing rules of FISA and the intervention of Ford Motor Company. In 1991, Victor Gauntlett left AML, handing over to Walter Hayes, but not before leaving a permanent impression on the company.

sales there were pushed through that company's dealer network.

Victor Gauntlett was, at this time, splitting his time between AML and his other interests at Pace Petroleum, but pressure began to build up at Pace, as oil stocks built up in the world, and prices fell. Thus, for a time, his efforts were concentrated entirely on Pace, during which period problems began to brew at Newport Pagnell. The managing director of the time was Bill Archer, and he ran into a dispute with shop floor workers about bonuses. As a consequence of the difference of opinion, there were some dismissals and this caused disruption in the boardroom. Shortly afterwards, Bill Archer resigned, and Victor Gauntlett then returned to AML on a full-time basis.

At the same time, Aston Martin Lagonda Incorporated, the American distributor for Aston Martin Lagonda Limited, found itself a new major shareholder. This was Peter Livanos, son of a Greek shipping magnate, who had been into the New York showroom to buy a used Aston Martin and, as the saying goes 'liked the product so much, he bought the company' – well almost. He certainly liked the product, and did become a dedicated Aston Martin enthusiast. In fact, he became a strong moving force in the company's fortunes over the next few years.

Having bought into AML Incorporated, Peter Livanos brought another shipping family into the picture – the Papanicolaou brothers. Between them, they formed a new company called Automotive Investments Incorporated. Now, they took a majority shareholding in the American business, then they acquired the total shareholding of Pace Petroleum. This gave Automotive Investments a 55 per cent majority holding in Aston Martin Lagonda Limited, though a condition of the acquisition was that Victor Gauntlett remain in post as Chairman.

Next, Automotive Investments bought out CH Industrials' share in AML as well, also

Victor Gauntlett is a man who loves sports cars. When the opportunity to invest in AML came, he seized it and ultimately came to lead the company into greater stability and prosperity. It was he, also, who led AML into the Ford acquisition, with the intention of safeguarding the company's long-term future.

buying into Aston Martin Tickford. Its investment extended to a new engineering facility and Michael Bowler (later to become operations director at Proteus Technology Limited when Aston Martins returned to racing). At the end of 1984, the Automotive Investments 100 per cent stake was split up to allow the Papanicolaou family to meet other commitments, so a 75 per cent shareholding in Aston Martin Lagonda went to Peter Livanos and a 25 per cent stake to Victor Gauntlett.

This is how the shareholding of the company remained for three years. Then, with a view to the future of the company and the ever-changing and ever more complicated legislation controlling such things as type approval and exhaust emission standards throughout the world, Victor Gauntlett and Peter Livanos began to take stock. They concluded that a new owner was needed to take Aston Martin Lagonda into safer financial waters, to provide the technological support essential to new research and development and to provide buying 'muscle' in an ever-tougher supplies situation. Eventually, Ford Motor Company took up the challenge.

FORD AND ASTON MARTIN LAGONDA

The announcement came in 1987. Ford Motor Company had bought a majority shareholding in Aston Martin Lagonda Limited, with the commitment that Victor Gauntlett would remain as Chairman and Chief Executive. Peter Livanos and Victor Gauntlett both retained a 12½ per cent share each in the company, Ford taking up the other 75 per cent. Now it was firmly felt that AML would have a secure future, especially since Ford had said that it had no intention of interfering with the day-to-day management of its new subsidiary. The credibility of that statement was lent weight when Ford said it would not interfere with the new AMR-1 racing car project, as long as it did not have to pay the bills or suffer any interruption to the activities of the basic business of Aston Martin Lagonda Limited, which was making cars to sell.

The Virage was the first new project which came about under Ford ownership, and it seemed to suffer little interference in its development. Indeed, it was a model which seems to have benefited from the new owners' presence. As this book closes for press the Vantage, the Virage Volante, the

Walter Hayes, CBE

For Walter Hayes this was effectively his third career. His first was as a journalist, rising to become associate editor of the *Daily Mail* and editor-in-chief of the now-defunct *Sunday Dispatch*; his second was with Ford, where he became Vice-Chairman of Ford of Europe, then Vice-President of the Ford Motor Company. His third career began after formal retirement when he took over the reins as Chairman of Aston Martin Lagonda Limited upon the departure from that office of Victor Gauntlett.

Joining Ford in 1962, Walter Hayes was involved in its return to the international motor sport arena and the GT40 Le Mans project which led to a Ford victory there. He was also in the negotiations which led to the Ford-Cosworth Grand Prix engine, arguably the most successful Formula One engine in history. A C.B.E. rewarded his service to industry in 1980.

This chairman of Aston Martin Lagonda Limited was very different from his predecessor. He did not have the physical stature, nor the ebullience, of Victor Gauntlett. A hint of the nature of the man is that it was he who negotiated the acquisition by Ford of AML, so his approach and the assurances he gave had to be acceptable to his predecessor in order to complete the deal

Walter Hayes cared with a quiet, unassuming passion about the future of

Just weeks before he retired, Walter Hayes was involved in the opening of a magnificent display of Aston Martins at the Museum of British Road Transport in Coventry, in January 1994. He is seen here about to introduce Stirling Moss, who officially opened the exhibition.

Aston Martin Lagonda. He has a strong sense of history (it was he who brought back the 'DB' prefix to Aston Martin nomenclature and he who hung the picture of Sir David Brown in the boardroom), yet he has a clear view of what the company should be doing to survive. He became an AML board member upon Ford's acquisition of the company. It was he who gave Aston Martin Lagonda Limited a 'road-map' for its future and he who returned from a comfortable retirement at 67 years of age to take over this flagship of the British motor industry. He finally retired again in February, 1994.

Virage Shooting Brake and the Virage Coupé are all continuous products of the range, and there is strong hope of a new Lagonda coming into the product list. In addition to that, there is also a car which is not the subject of these pages for no other reason than it has a six-cylinder engine – the exquisitely styled Aston Martin DB7.

One significant change has taken place at Newport Pagnell, however. Victor Gauntlett is no longer at the helm of Aston Martin Lagonda. In what was said to be a difference of opinion over the future of the DB7, he departed to pastures new. Now, the company was headed by Walter Hayes, a Ford man who was brought out of retirement for the job. Certainly, he was right in many ways, not least for his deep sense of history.

It was Walter Hayes who brought a picture of Sir David Brown to the boardroom at Newport Pagnell and initiated the naming of the new six-cylinder car as the 'DB7'. It was Walter Hayes who 'got things done' today, through the establishment of Aston Martin (Oxford) Limited for the construction of the DB7.

In reviving the Lagonda name, it may well be that the car will be built onto a Ford chassis pan, but there also seems promise that it could well have its own V-12 engine, albeit a derivative of a Ford unit. That may seem sacrilege to some, but as long as Lagonda stays in the super-luxury class of car, as it seems destined to do, and bearing in mind that the Cosworth V-8 Grand Prix engine is a Ford unit (demonstrating that not all Ford engines are mass-produced or below standard), that may not be as bad as it seems. The Vignale Lagonda shown at Geneva in 1993 lights a way ahead.

Where does the future lie for Aston Martin Lagonda Limited? Well, it is certain that the company will need to repay its new masters their investment when the good times return (if they do). It is also certain that the new masters (now not-so-new, since they've owned the company since 1987) are putting in a great deal of effort to keep Aston Martin Lagonda in the true supercar class, where it rightfully belongs.

As this book closes for press, a new chairman sits in the boardroom of Aston Martin Lagonda Limited.

John Oldfield

John Oldfield became the Executive Chairman of Aston Martin Lagonda on February 1, 1994. Previously he was the Vice President responsible for Ford product development in Europe.

Born in London on January 13, 1937, John Oldfield holds a Master of Science Degree from the Cranfield Institute of Technology. He joined Ford of Britain's Engineering staff in 1958 and specialized in suspension, steering, transmission and chassis design before he was appointed Manager, Light and Large Car Development for Ford in Europe in 1973. The following year Mr Oldfield became the Chief Engineer of Ford in Brazil and on his return to Great Britain in 1976 was appointed the Chief Engineer responsible for Ford Chassis Engineering in Europe and then Chief Vehicle Engineer for the Escort programme.

From 1980 to 1983 he was Ford Vice President Product Planning in Europe and then Director of Vehicle Engineering before accepting a special one year assignment with Ford in North America as Executive Director of the Engineering and Manufacturing staff. In this role he was commissioned to investigate and advise on the feasibility for the design and development of a single range of medium size cars which would be manufactured and marketed in both Europe and North America. As a result of this study John Oldfield was assigned overall responsibility for the design and development of the Ford Mondeo and its North American counterparts the Mercury Mystique and the Ford Contour.

He was elected to the position of European Vice President for product development in 1989 and became corporate Vice President of Ford Motor Company in January, 1991.

Mr Oldfield is married to Iris, has three sons and one daughter and is a keen golfer. His other hobbies and leisure activities include tennis and fast cars.

12 Owning and Caring for your V-8

Aston Martin Lagonda Limited is the first motor manufacturer in the world to be brave enough to stand up and describe its product as 'A Car For Life'. If you ever stuck your nose into the Service Department at Tickford Street, you would see why. Most of the body bucks for the previous model Aston Martins have survived and are today able to be used in the recreation of panels for damaged or tired cars – or whole bodies if the need were to arise. This is all at a price, of course, but we are talking about one of the finest vehicles built anywhere in the world.

You can also have every kind of major – or minor – mechanical work carried out at the factory's Service Department. From the earliest LB6 engines to the latest twin-supercharged Vantage V-8, you can go from a plug change to a major overhaul at Newport Pagnell. The fact is, it's a very good place to go to bring your Aston Martin or Lagonda up to the best of mechanical and cosmetic health. If the factory has the parts and can do the job, it can make a lot of sense to give it the job and enjoy the benefit of having the people who built the car bring it back to its former glory.

THE SPECIALISTS

In addition to the factory Service Department, there are also several Aston Martin Lagonda specialists up and down the country, who mostly perform an outstanding job of work. They are, to be fair, a mixture of companies, in terms of size, facilities and levels of skills and public image, but in the main they share one very special quality – a boundless enthusiasm for Aston Martins and Lagondas.

A large number of these specialists are, of course, either Aston Martin or Lagonda dealers or Sevice Agents, but many more are fairly described as specialists because they have developed a specialized knowledge and experience of Aston Martins and either deal only in used cars or perhaps don't even sell cars at all, preferring to only maintain, repair, overhaul or restore the cars they deal with. Equally, there are those who will tell you they are Aston Martin Lagonda specialists, who are of a less reputable calibre, and it is these of whom the loving Aston or Lagonda owner needs beware. Happily, such characters are few in these circles, for most have been weeded out by a network of enthusiasts talking to each other.

Specialists of one kind or another are people with whom the Aston Martin and Lagonda owner must be acquainted, for even if he or she intends to carry out the day-to-day maintenance of a car, when it comes to major repairs or overhauls, the private individual rarely has the resources or equipment to do them satisfactorily. A friendly specialist (and most of them are) is an important asset. It is not the task of this book to attempt to name any of the specialists out there in the big wide world, but contact with Aston Martin Lagonda Limited will bring information on the approved dealers,

Aston Martins in the workshops of Richard Stewart Williams Limited at Cobham. Yes, it really is a workshop, not a display area!

whilst membership of the Aston Martin Owners' Club will almost certainly bring information on the others.

It is impossible, of course, to give any indication of what it really costs to maintain an Aston Martin or Lagonda V-engined car (other than a new or recent one, for which there are scheduled service and repair charges available), save to say it will not be cheap, especially if its history is not known, and it has been bought from either a private owner with whom the prospective purchaser is not familiar or a back-street garage, who may have 'bodged' it to sell it. Be wary, and seek the help of a specialist if you can. Specialists, incidentally, are not just people who work full-time with these cars. They can be people who know the cars inside-out from the experience of ownership. Whatever you do, as you are introduced to these beautiful beasts for the first time, use those skills to help you select the car you finally buy because the chances are that you will want to keep it for a very long time.

BUYING YOUR ASTON MARTIN OR LAGONDA V-8

This almost sounds trite, but you must first ensure before you buy your used car that it is genuine. What is meant by 'genuine'? Make sure that the car has not been in a major accident and even that it is one car, rather than the bits of a pair bodged together after being written off. Make sure you check the chassis number and cross-check it to the vehicle registration document (the V5 in Great Britain) to be sure that those numbers match. Check the engine number, too, and make sure you are satisfied with the explanation you are given if it isn't the original one.

After this first step, you need to go round the car and examine it very closely for deterioration, dents and repairs. Remember that a DBS-V8 can now be almost twenty-five years old and a lot of deterioration can have taken place in that time, no matter how well built it was in the first place. It is important to check the chassis carefully for repairs, distortions or rust damage, for it can be a serious problem with early cars. Particularly don't take somebody's word for it if he tells you that the sills need replacing, because that usually means that a large chunk of the chassis, floorpan or wheel arches are also in an advanced state of decay. Also, recognizing that AML does the best it can to protect against the effects of electrolytic action between steel and aluminium connecting faces, decay can occur around the areas where the body joins the chassis. Wherever water can be trapped is an area for close inspection.

Aluminium bodywork also simply cracks with age and many alloy-bodied cars tend to generate cracks around the base of the windscreen pillars. Then there's the boot lid area, where constant raising and lowering (and slamming) of the boot lid over a period of years will crack the corners of the boot aperture. A bit of body filler and a touch of paint might cover this up so that you can't see it. If you notice an area of paint touched up such as that, then beware again, for it could be covering up a disaster. Door-shuts are another area where stress and corrosion can occur. If the door hinges are worn slack (usually through lack of lubrication), then the door drops, and the bottom edge rubs on the inner face of the sill. As you won't know how long that's been going on, you won't know how much metal is left beneath the scuffing.

Corrosion can also occur around the screen apertures, where the trim clips sit. The problem is that water collects around the trim clips and corrosion begins from the inside. When the observer looks at mild corrosion signs on the outside, it may not look serious enough to merit a second glance, but if it's there at all, check into it more carefully, because you could very easily find that there's deep corrosion on the inside, calling for removal of the screen, then drilling out of the clips, cleaning up the metal and treating it with an anti-corrosive.

CHECKING OUT THE ENGINE

If the bodywork hasn't frightened you off your first Aston Martin or Lagonda, then take the car for a drive. Whilst driving, make sure you can go where you can push the engine up to 4,000rpm or more, just to see whether the head gaskets are still intact or not. The Aston Martin V-8 doesn't often deposit oil in the coolant when a gasket has failed, nor give that familiar nauseating smell of exhaust in the header tank between the cylinders, but you can find out from the overflow tank on the side of the radiator cowling, which should be half-full when you start your test drive and should still be half-full when you've finished it, even after pushing the engine hard. If it's filled up, or worse, if it's pressuring out of the tank, then you have a gasket problem which needs prompt attention.

Oil pressure is the next question. Is the oil pressure, when the engine is at operating temperature, between five and twenty psi at idling speeds? Does it go up to seventy or eighty at just over 3,000rpm? If the answer to these two questions is 'Yes' then you're on your way to a sound engine, provided it doesn't rumble, and they usually don't at those pressures. However, if the pressure on idle is zero, or thereabouts, and runs up to only fifty-ish, then you could have a problem, but don't panic yet, because it could be just a crankshaft core plug that has dropped out, which is curable.

Crankshaft core plugs are fitted on the last big-end journal, and sometimes they do drop out. When this happens, the oil has a larger space to slosh about in before building up pressure under pumping – and, of course, the pressure is down on normal. In this case, you can heave a sigh of relief as the prospect of a bill for a whole new set of big-end and main-bearing shells recedes, to say nothing of the crank regrind which you'd need.

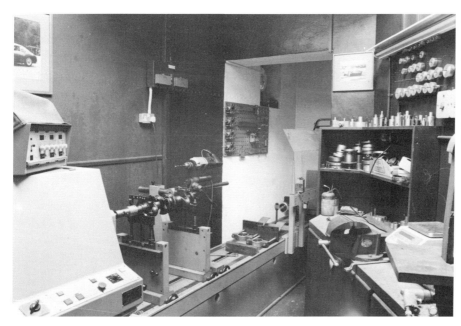

Engine work in progress at Richard Williams', demonstrating very well the kind of environment in which Aston Martin and Lagonda engines should be worked upon.

As you will already have read, Aston Martin Lagonda used fuel injection and carburettors at various times on the V-8 engine. Carburettors are easier for the amateur to set up, but if the engine is fuel injected, by either the Bosch or Weber-Marelli systems, and it's running rough, then the best advice you can possibly have is to leave it alone.

This kind of test equipment is not available in a back-street workshop, which is why it pays to take your beloved charge to those who can test what they've done, as it really costs less in the long run.

Call in a fuel-injection expert, despite the fact that it can cost you, it doesn't have to be overexpensive when you consider the number of fuel-injection specialists there are about, quite apart from people who work on Astons for a living.

Fuel lines need to be checked, too, as do fuel pumps, all in the interests of making sure the system as a whole is working efficiently. There's no way in fact that you can make a fuel-injection system work properly if fuel lines and fuel pumps are clogged up. Check fuel filters regularly. When you're examining a car prior to deciding to buy it, check to see if the fuel filters look as though they might have been replaced reasonably recently. If not, you may be confronting a sloppy owner whose car isn't worth buying, for fear of all the other things which could be wrong with it.

Engine noises are always a problem, especially if it's an engine you're not familiar with, because you can be fobbed off with all kinds of excuses as to what the noises are. You know the kind of thing: 'Well, all Astons do that', or 'It's a common fault, you know, but nothing to worry about', or worse, 'It only does it cold'. If you hear a noise that you don't like, then check it out or get someone who can to check it out for you. Don't take your seller at his word, just because he wants to stuff you up with a car he doesn't want to spend a fortune on, because you'll end up spending the fortune on it instead!

Bearing rumble is an all-too-familiar sound and usually goes with low oil pressure – so a thoroughly worn engine. Camshaft wear is something else. Valve-gear rattle is usually caused by one (or all) of three things: badly adjusted valve gear, worn cam profiles and/or worn valve guides. If the valve guides are worn, then there's usually an oily exhaust to tell you so. Either way, cylinder head overhauls are not cheap, so again, get an Aston Martin specialist to have a listen and take a look. Even if it's just a matter of adjustment, somebody who knows what he's doing can give good advice and save a lot of money later on.

THE V-8 DRIVELINE

A surprisingly large number of Aston Martin DBSs and V-8s, as well as all the Lagondas, are equipped with the Chrysler Torqueflite automatic transmission. After a few years in service, it's an oily beast, given to leaving large embarrassing patches on the drive-way. It doesn't seem to suffer too badly from operational failures as a consequence, but who wants to walk through oil patches when the car isn't covering them over?

Among the most common places for leak-age on the Torqueflite are the input and output shaft oil seals, but also, the selector shaft oil seal, where the main control shaft passes through the transmission casing. One of the problems with oil leaks on an auto-matic transmission is that they leave the unit low on oil, resulting in dragged changes. This brings with it wear on the torque converter plates, which in turn can cause a faint clicking sound in drive, or when changing from forward drive to reverse. If the oil is blackened, or has a burnt smell to it, then something's not quite right in there, and it could cost the price of a strip-down and rebuild.

The Aston Martin differential is not prone to a great deal of trouble, but if you hear a chattering when moving off from a stand-still, you could have worn clutch plates or the first signs of a differential breaking up. It will rarely be a crown-wheel or pinion fault. If it clunks, it could be pinion bearings or, more likely, a universal joint. If you hear a low groaning sound from the back end, it could either be a worn differential, or even worn hub bearings. Either way, you're on your way back to your Aston specialist.

BRAKES, STEERING AND SUSPENSION

When you've bought this magic machine that is going to propel you along the high-ways and byways at startling speeds, spare a thought for what's going to stop you when you need it – because when you need it, you usually need it urgently. The stopping power of all V-8 cars should be little short of astounding. However, it isn't always, because again we can be talking of cars well over twenty years old and the rear brakes, especially, are prone to collecting water (because they're inboard) and to cracking up.

The rear inboard brakes are built up in three pieces, and corrosion can cause the retaining ring to split away, so bringing in its wake a potentially large problem. The rear discs and disc hubs need to be regularly and carefully checked because if the retain-ing ring is broken away, then a replacement of the disc assembly is essential. Front discs are outboard, so are, in theory at least, less exposed and so less prone to the problems of the rears. However, if you find brake judder occurring at mid-range road speeds, then your discs could be distorted through over-heating (they may or may not be able to be skimmed to cure the problem), or they may be cracked radially from the hub, or simply worn, in which case replace them – and do it quickly while you're still around to tell the tale.

Steering of all the cars considered in this book is by rack and pinion, and it is nor-mally a relatively trouble-free component of any Aston or Lagonda. As for the power-steering pump, these very rarely give any trouble, even when the oil tank is allowed to run low, though it should be regularly checked and often isn't. Nevertheless, there sometimes are little problems, like a leaking pinion oil seal, which can be replaced *in situ*. Perished or damaged gaiters on the ends of the rack need to be replaced, but if they're full of fluid, you have an internal oil seal replacement job on your hands, which effec-tively means a rack removal and overhaul.

The front and rear suspension of these cars is generally relatively trouble-free, except for the shock absorbers. If you are about to buy a low-mileage car that has been either stored, jacked up or used only occasionally, it is highly likely that the Konis have seized up. There's not much you can do with seized shock absorbers, though if they're just binding slightly, you can try spraying a little WD-40 on the spindles to see if that'll work. Otherwise it's another replacement. This is potentially expensive, isn't it?

BUYING REPLACEMENT PARTS

One of the most familiar complaints about any supercar is that its spare parts are expensive. Often, this is because they are expensive to make, but sometimes it can be because they're bought in and, entirely reasonably, there is a cost for handling, packing and storing them, so you pay more than you would if you knew the proprietary source from which they came. This is relevant when you think of parts sourced for Aston Martins from such makes as Vauxhall, Ford or Audi, to name just a few.

Before you 'go off the handle' and accuse AML of profiteering at your expense, remember it is in the business of making money from making super motor cars and there is a cost to buying parts in, packaging them, listing them and stocking them, so you're not being ripped off; it's just part of the cost of the business, and you can go off and source many of these parts from the original manufacturer without causing any problems. For example, you can buy headlamp units, tail light clusters, indicator lights and control stalks all from their original product sources without putting your Aston at risk at all. On the other hand, don't go silly and buy spurious parts of doubtful origin when it

comes to major mechanical components because that's the road to disaster.

If you own or are about to buy a DBS-V8, and it needs replacement front side and indicator lights (all-in-one units), then go looking through your local Ford dealer's parts bins for Mark II Cortina ones – they're the same, except for the box. The same component for the V-8, post-DBS, comes from the MGB, whereas the tail-light assembly for both DBS-V8 and V-8 is from the Hillman Hunter (in Iran, the Peykan). You probably won't save any money from knowing that the front brake calipers for all V-8 models are from the Lamborghini Miura, but you might from knowing that the starter motor is a Chrysler part. Electrical switchgear comes from a wide range of alternatives in the Bosch catalogue, some clearly identifiable as Mercedes-Benz bits, with all sorts of switches from other cars, down to the indicator stalk from the Vauxhall Astra (or Opel Kadett in Europe). On the Lagonda, you can certainly save a few pounds from finding out which Jaguar model the front uprights came from, whilst your DBS-V8 will benefit just as much from the use of a Jaguar XJ6 air filter as from one with the AML logo on the box. There are, of course, many Ford bits used on the Virage models, and this is clearly a trend that will increase as time goes on, though the headlamps are Audi, except for the Vantage, which has these tiny torch-sized headlamps.

One area where you will certainly need a specialist's help is in untangling the electronic gadgetry of the Series 2 to 4 Lagonda. There is no way anyone would sensibly advise an owner/driver to become involved in trying to trace a fault in that system. You definitely need the expertise of someone who has diagnostic equipment to unveil the mysteries of that – and don't let anybody tell you differently, or it will almost certainly become very expensive.

ENJOYING YOUR V-8 OR LAGONDA

Enjoying your Aston Martin or Lagonda V-8 is something you would hardly be expected not to do. After all, why would you own such a car if it were not for the enjoyment of it? And the most important key to that enjoyment is to bring your car to, and to keep it in, the best possible condition. That may be limited to keeping it in the best possible condition you can afford, but that should then be your target. Keep the car regularly maintained and even if you do routine maintenance yourself, as many enthusiasts will, do take the precaution of having it checked over every six months or so by your chosen Aston Martin Lagonda specialist. It may cost a bit, but it has to be worth that investment in the longer term.

Having bought your new pride and joy, if you've never driven an Aston Martin or a V-8 Lagonda before, the first thing you need to remember is that these are heavy cars – powerful but heavy. It may sound a bit like preaching to the converted, but with that power and weight in mind, you need to take your time to get used to the car and to find its balance. Be prepared for quite a bit of wheel reaction to rough road surfaces at low speeds, though if you hold the steering wheel quite lightly, it's surprising how well the car will stay on line, and the driving will be a better experience.

At high road speeds, a DBS-V8 or V-8 seems to lose some of its road noise, as the tyres smooth out the road surface (Avons were never noted for their quiet running), and the steering becomes more precise as the speed rises. This, of course, is also due to the suspension frequency settling down too, so that there are less 'highs' and 'lows' in the stroke of the shock absorbers and suspension links, though potholes are still recognized fairly abruptly by Aston Martin suspension at any speed. The message out of all this is

that these cars are not designed to be driven at mediocre speeds in a mediocre fashion. For pure driving pleasure, there's no doubt that the manual gearbox is far preferable to the Chrysler Torqueflite, not least because the driver has a greater sense of control – and control is one thing you absolutely must have with such a large car.

Given that you have achieved the full enjoyment value of driving your V-8, there are other ways to enjoy it, too. For example, you can achieve the pleasure and camaraderie of joining the appropriate club for your car and driving with, or competing against, other like-minded owners. There are two such one-make car clubs: the Aston Martin Owners' Club and the Lagonda Club. They both cater in considerable detail for enthusiasts just like you, people who have a love of their car and perhaps want to know more about them, meet other owners of the same model, drive in events (social or competitive) and generally derive the best pleasure from ownership of these fine vehicles.

The Aston Martin Owners' Club has twenty-one centres up and down the length and breadth of Britain, together with many overseas sections, too. Club membership provides anything from a chat at the bar to out-and-out racing with other cars of similar types, though not necessarily of the same make, for the annual St John Horsfall Meeting at Silverstone accepts entries of a wide range of makes of cars. You could find yourself pitting your Aston against Ferraris, Lamborghinis and all sorts – if you're willing to chance your car, that is.

The Lagonda Club is perhaps a little less ambitious in its competitive programmes, but that in part is due perhaps to the fact that Lagondas were, from the David Brown years onwards anyway, less openly competitive (with the exception of the 1954/55 V-12). The club devotes a great deal of time to ensuring that the maximum number of Lagondas stays on the road in good running order. In the light of the modern aura of Lagondas, it is almost certain that this club can perfectly satisfy the aspirations of the owner. Either way, these two clubs do an outstanding job of promoting their cars' reputations and preserving the interests of their members.

There is one other club open to entry from those enthusiastic enough to want to race their cars regularly. This is the Historic Sports Car Club, a fairly small but dedicated band of folk who promote the interests of sports car racing. Their scope embraces cars from Formula 3 500cc racers, through Formula Junior to Grand Prix Formula 1 and sports racing cars of all kinds. If you want to race above all else, then here's another club for you.

In any event, whichever car you own and whatever you want to do with it, there is one single final message – enjoy your car, but do it with safety. Your car deserves it.

Further Reading

Whilst much of the material listed here has been used for reference in the preparation of this book, much of it has not, but it is relevant as reading material for the enthusiast of the V-engined Aston Martins and Lagondas and so is listed. Some of the books mentioned are no longer in print; others are on remainder bookshop shelves. Wherever they may be, they can be found if an enthusiast in search of material on this subject is tenacious enough in his or her quest. The odd one out is the *Aston Martin Register*, which is only available to members of the AMOC, but the reference value, along with all the other services of the Club, is well worth the cost of the membership subscription.

The reading list, then, looks like this:

Aston Martin, the Post
   War Road Cars   Henry Rassmussen
Lola T70 V-8 Coupés   Ian Bamsey
Lagonda – A History of
   the Marque   Arnold Davey/Anthony May
Aston Martin Gold Portfolio
   1972 to 1985   Brooklands Books

Lagonda Gold Portfolio
   1919 to 1964   Brooklands Books
Road and Track on Aston Martin
   1962 to 1990   Brooklands Books
The Aston Martin Register Aston Martin OC
Aston Martin Lagonda –
   The Best of British   David G. Styles
Racing with the David Brown
   Aston Martins (2 vols)   Chris Nixon
The Aston Martin Virage   Chris Nixon
Aston Martin V-8 Race Cars Paul Chudecki
The Power Behind
   Aston Martin   Geoff Courtney
Lionel Martin – A Biography A.B. Demaus
The Aston Martin Shire Album Alan Archer
Aston Martin
   Heritage   Chris Nixon/Roger Newton

In addition to this list, the reader is recommended to refer to various motoring magazines from which reference material can be obtained, such as: *Motor Sport, Autocar, Motor, Fast Lane, Performance Car, Road and Track* (U.S.), *Car and Driver* (U.S.), *The Automobile* (U.S.) and many others around the world.

Appendix

ASTON MARTIN AND LAGONDA CLUBS

Wherever there are Aston Martins or Lagondas, there are gatherings of enthusiasts around the world. Below are the names and addresses of some of those clubs and international sections. There may be others which have been missed, but these are the significant ones.

P.H.J. Whyman, Secretary
Aston Martin Owners' Club
1a High Street
Sutton
Near Ely
Cambridge CB6 2RB

The Lagonda Club
68 Savill Road
Lindfield
Haywards Heath
Sussex RH16 2NN

Australia and New Zealand

G. Venn
AMOC (ACT)
P.O. Box 607
Manuka
ACT 2603

Peter Hammond
AMOC (NSW)
90a Tarrants Avenue
Eastwood
New South Wales 2122

Bob Rusk
AMOC (Queensland)
28 Bulolo Avenue
Runaway Bay
Queensland 4216

Terry Holt
AMOC (SA)
4/680 Goodwood Road
Daw Park
South Australia 5041

Bill Griffiths
AMOC (Tasmania)
45 Elphin Road
Launceston
Tasmania 7250

Allan Lowe
AMOC (Victoria)
1a Stornoway Road
Burwood
Victoria 3125

Jim Tweddle
AMOC (WA)
10a Edgar Way
Mount Pleasant
Western Australia 6153

Peter Lowe
11a Corunna Avenue
Parnell
Auckland 1
New Zealand

Europe

Marc van der Stricht
AMOC (Belgium)
65 Avenue Beau Sejour
1180 Brussels
Belgium

Jean-Philippe Gouraud
131 Avenue du Roule
F-92200 Neuilly-sur-Seine
France

Robert Leyba
AMOC (Germany)
Esplanade 37
D-2000 Hamburg 36
Germany

Peter Swager
Postbus 7448
4800 G.K. Breda
Holland

Joachin Folch
R.-Corachan
Avda Pearson 44
08034 Barcelona
Spain

Per Fahlstadius
Riddervagan 1
18142 Lidingo
Sweden

Jürg Furter
Humbelrain 2
8824 Schönenberg
Switzerland

North America

Peter Schurmann
299 Roehampton Avenue
Suite 1135
Toronto
Ontario M4P 1S2
Canada

Dr Robert Follows
4125 Marine Drive
West Vancouver
British Colombia V7V 1N8
Canada

Morris Evans
606 South William Street
New York
NY 12095
U.S.A.

Larry and Lori Davis
6578 Crystalaire Drive
San Diego
California 92120
U.S.A.

Rest of World

Yasuhiko Shimazaki
4-20 Minami Aoyama
7-Chome
Minato-Ku
Tokyo 107
Japan

Nick Pryke
50 Lyndhurst Road
Lyndhurst
Johannesburg
South Africa

Index